FAIRY TALES and FEMINISM

DATE DUE

~~MAY 0 1 2007~~	
~~NOV 2 6 2007~~	

DEMCO, INC. 38-2931

SERIES IN FAIRY-TALE STUDIES

General Editor

DONALD HAASE
Wayne State University

Advisory Editors

FAIRY TALES and FEMINISM

New Approaches

Edited by

Donald Haase

WAYNE STATE UNIVERSITY PRESS   DETROIT

Copyright © 2004 by Wayne State University Press,
Detroit, Michigan 48201. All rights are reserved.
No part of this book may be reproduced without formal permission.
Manufactured in the United States of America.
08 07 06 05 04   5 4 3 2 1

Library of Congress Cataloging-in-Publication Data

Fairy tales and feminism : new approaches / edited by Donald Haase.
     p. cm. — (Fairy-tale studies)
  Includes bibliographical references.
  ISBN 0-8143-3030-4 (pbk. : alk. paper)
  1. Fairy tales — History and criticism.   2. Feminist literary criticism   3. Feminism
and literature.   I. Haase, Donald   II. Series.
  GR550.F24 2004
  398.2'082—dc22

                                                                    2004006485

∞ The paper used in this publication meets the minimum requirements of the American
National Standard for Information Sciences—Permanence of Paper for Printed Library
Materials, ANSI Z39.48-1984.

Contents

Preface

This volume of essays originated in a special issue of *Marvels & Tales* devoted to feminist fairy-tale studies. The title of that special issue, *Fairy Tale Liberation—Thirty Years Later,* referred to the fact that it had been three decades since Alison Lurie published "Fairy Tale Liberation," her controversial article of 1970 that sparked a serious and, it turns out, lasting debate about the relationship of women to fairy tales. The purpose of that special issue was to take stock of feminist fairy-tale scholarship, offer new contributions that advance the discussion of women in fairy tales, and encourage new directions in fairy-tale research. This book shares that purpose. To that end it brings together six critical essays from the special issue with five new studies that expand the field of inquiry.

The critical history and contemporary context of feminist fairy-tale studies is described at length in the first essay, "Feminist Fairy-Tale Scholarship." The scope of that survey relies on the fact that scholarly research explicitly devoted to feminist issues in fairy-tale studies began in earnest in 1970 and was propelled by the feminist movement's second wave. The onset of this critical activity in the 1970s, however, does not mean that the fairy tale's role in the sociocultural discourse about gender had not been recognized earlier. As Christine Shojaei Kawan has pointed out, Simone de Beauvoir, in *Le deuxième sexe* (1949; *The Second Sex*), anticipated the feminist critique of the fairy tale's socializing power by several decades.

But even Beauvoir's critique must be seen as part of a larger tradition. Awareness of the fairy tale as a primary site for asserting and subverting ideologies of gender is evident throughout the genre's history. This is especially evident and most readily documented in the development of the literary fairy tale. Already in the seventeenth and eighteenth centuries, women writers in France—the *conteuses*—had identified the fairy tale as a genre with something to say about gender and sexuality. In their own fairy tales they experimented with constructions and reconstructions of the male and female, and thus gave voice to a complex fairy-tale language that was distinct from that of Charles Perrault (Harries, *Twice*; Seifert, *Fairy Tales*; Warner, *From the Beast*). In eighteenth- and nineteenth-century Germany, women writers such as Benedikte Naubert, Bettina von Arnim, and Gisela von Arnim recognized the predominantly male point of view that characterized influential fairy-tale publications, especially those by Johann Karl August Musäus and the Brothers Grimm, and they consciously challenged these collections by creating a female perspective and by pointedly deconstructing the models of gender offered by their more widely read male counterparts (L. Martin; Jarvis, "Trivial Pursuit" and "Feminism" 156). In nineteenth-century England, women writers such as Emily and Charlotte Brontë and Jane Austen responded to the constructions of gender in classical fairy tales by playing off of these widely known stories in their novels (Gilbert and Gubar; Knoepflmacher, "Introduction" 22–32). As the literary fairy tale emerged in the course of the nineteenth century, both male and female Victorian writers developed entirely new tales that showed just how well they understood the fairy tale's complicity in the ideology of gender. Women writers like Jean Ingelow, Christina Rossetti, and Juliana Horatia Ewing entered into intertextual dialogue with the fairy tales of male contemporaries by publishing their own "countertexts" (Knoepflmacher, *Ventures* 427), in which they would deliberately "rewrite, unwrite, and replace" the "male-authored constructions of 'femininity'" (426). In the United States, Louisa May Alcott drew upon tales like "Beauty and the Beast" and "Cinderella" in *Little Women* to offer revisions of conventional ideas about men, women, courtship, and marriage (Knoepflmacher, "Introduction" 26–29); and Emma Wolf alluded to the fairy tale when she explored middle-class women and marriage at the turn of the century in her story "One-Eye, Two-Eye, Three-Eye," which takes its title from a Cinderella-type tale in the Grimms' collection. More than fifty years earlier, Margaret Fuller had briefly invoked Cinderella in her feminist treatise of 1845, *Woman in the Nineteenth Century,* a move that may have been the first to introduce the fairy tale into the public discussion of women's rights.

Clearly, there has long been a tacit awareness of the fairy tale's role in the cultural discourse on gender, and many fairy-tale texts constitute implicit critical commentaries on that discourse. As the introductory survey of scholarship documents, one of the achievements of feminist fairy-tale scholarship has been to reveal how women have—for three hundred years at least—quite intentionally used the fairy tale to engage questions of gender and to create tales spoken or written differently from those told or penned by men. Demonstrating what Shawn Jarvis has described as "the continuity of feminist concerns in literary history" ("Feminism" 156), these early commentaries in the form of literary fairy tales not only prefigure the work in twentieth-century literature and film by women such as Anne Sexton, Angela Carter, Margaret Atwood, Emma Donaghue, Jane Yolen, Terri Windling, Jane Campion, Victoria Ocampo, María Luisa Bombal, Luisa Valenzuela, Suniti Namjoshi, and many others; they also foreshadow the feminist critique articulated so vigorously in fairy-tale scholarship since the 1970s.

For all the vitality, diversity, and—it must be noted—uneven quality of this woman-centered fairy-tale scholarship, there has been no visible effort to assess these three decades of research. Jack Zipes's anthology of 1986, *Don't Bet on the Prince: Contemporary Feminist Fairy Tales of North America and England,* which reprinted representative stories along with several important critical essays, documented the early years of feminist fairy-tale research. Kay Stone's essay of the same year, "Feminist Approaches to the Interpretation of Fairy Tales," also provided a useful assessment for its time. But since 1986, fairy-tale scholarship focused on women has significantly expanded, not only in terms of the quantity produced but also in terms of its scope, variety, and complexity. The time has come again to draw a new map of the field.

A critical survey of previous work and a presentation of contemporary research seem all the more necessary in a field like fairy-tale studies, which is conducted across a range of disciplines and national literatures. All too many studies suffer (and this applies to fairy-tale studies generally) from a disciplinary myopia—from having overlooked relevant scholarship, often because it lies beyond the limits of a given discipline or linguistic ability.[1] Scholars sometimes needlessly and unwittingly rehash topics that have been previously treated, or they produce work that is not intelligently informed by important, more sophisticated analyses. In answering the question "What Ails Feminist Criticism?" Susan Gubar has described in another context the propensity to treat every text as "grist for a mill that proves the same intellectually vapid—though politically appalling—point that racism, classism, sexism, and homophobia reign supreme" (891). Some feminist fairy-tale analyses remain stuck in a mode of interpretation able to do no more than reconfirm stereotypical generalizations about the fairy tale's sexist stereotypes. Such studies are oblivious to the complexities of fairy-tale production and reception, sociohistorical contexts, cultural traditions, the historical development of the genre, and the challenges of fairy-tale textuality. The essays in this volume demonstrate the possibilities of feminist-inspired fairy-tale studies and their potential to advance our understanding of the fairy tale. They eschew a monolithic view of the woman-centered fairy tale; allow for ambiguity within female-authored tales and for ambivalence in their reception; explore new texts and contexts; and reconsider the national, cultural, and generic boundaries that have shaped the fairy tale and often limited our understanding of it.

From the beginning, the feminist critique of fairy tales has centered on depictions of the fairy-tale heroine. Perhaps it was inevitable that the fictional stereotype identified in classic fairy tales would also become a critical stereotype. Ruth B. Bottigheimer's essay in the present text reexamines conventional wisdom about the modern fairy-tale heroine in collections of European tales by considering the heroine's precursors in medieval and early modern tales—not in the abstract but in light of crucial sociohistorical information regarding the sexual, reproductive, and economic lives of women. Bottigheimer revises our historical understanding of the fairy-tale heroine by identifying major shifts in the way women are depicted at important historical moments, and then by linking these shifts to what is known about the historical changes affecting women's ability to control their own fertility.

The need to find approaches that lead, like Bottigheimer's, to a more nuanced and multidimensional appreciation of the complex relationships between women and fairy tales is evident throughout the essays. In considering the literary tales of seventeenth-century Frenchwomen, Lewis C. Seifert argues that it is not enough to focus on the subversive thrust of these texts and determine the degree to which they successfully subvert social ideologies. Such an approach underestimates the tales' central ambiguities, which Seifert illustrates by examining their problematic representations of personal autonomy, nostalgia, and marriage. Seifert urges feminist critics to develop interpretive approaches that can come to grips with these rich ambiguities and account for the historical and textual complexity of female-authored tales.

The critical commitment to the subversive element in women's fairy tales may not only forestall appreciation of textual complexity and ambiguity, but it may also obscure the diverse motivations that drive women's production and reception of the genre. To provide insight into the difficult question of what fairy tales meant to women in the eighteenth and nineteenth centuries, Jeannine Blackwell offers translations and commentary on a variety of texts produced by German women writers of that era. In addition to documenting a neglected tradition of female-penned literary tales, Blackwell foregrounds the diverse, even contradictory purposes to which women put the fairy tale, thereby giving us a fuller and more multifaceted picture of female responses. Elizabeth Wanning Harries also resists a one-dimensional view of woman's productive reception of the fairy tale. In her examination of postwar autobiographies by English writer Carolyn Kay Steedman and German author Christa Wolf, Harries reveals the complexity of their responses to the classical fairy tale, especially in relation to problematic questions of female identity. The autobiographical essay by Kay Stone—whose work figures significantly in the history of feminist fairy-tale scholarship and storytelling—also illuminates women's responses by challenging prevalent views of the fairy-tale heroine. Stone relates how she has come to question the simplistic dichotomy of passive and active heroines and the conventional judgment that active heroines have more to offer women than their victimized counterparts. Drawing on her earlier study of women's responses to fairy tales and her own experience as a storyteller, Stone lays bare the heroic potential of the persecuted heroine, who has an unexpectedly empowering appeal for female readers and storytellers.

Progress in feminist fairy-tale studies requires not only a determination to rethink the complexity of fairy-tale texts and responses to them but also a willingness to expand the field of inquiry across national and cultural boundaries. In general, the most influential works of feminist fairy-tale scholarship—those that have had a significant impact across disciplines—have focused on European and Anglo-American texts and writers. In particular they have concentrated on German, French, and English-language tales.[2] Several essays in this volume seek to foreground creative work that has been considerably less visible—and in one case less audible. Of course, this volume does not pretend to be geographcally or culturally comprehensive, and these essays are not intended to close all the gaps. Instead, they act in an exemplary way by pointing up the richness of cultural traditions that feminist fairy-tale studies have yet to embrace and by describing texts, contexts, and perspectives that suggest possibilities for new research.

Patricia Anne Odber de Baubeta's essay draws attention to a long tradition of productive fairy-tale reception by women writers in Portugal, Spain, and Latin America. In addition to introducing fairy-tale scholars to the ways in which Iberian and Latin American writers have used the fairy tale as an intertext in their prose fiction over the course of seventy years, Odber also provides a bibliography of primary texts and identifies

categories that can be used in future analyses. Fiona Mackintosh follows
Odber's comprehensive survey with an in-depth examination of the fairy
tale in twentieth-century Argentine women's writing. Mackintosh considers the diverse strategies these women have for engaging the fairy tale
to deal with a variety of topics, including sexual politics. She particularly
highlights how these authors appropriate the European fairy-tale tradition
with humor primarily in order to explore the irony and ambiguities of cultural identity—that is, to express their eccentricity as Latin American
women who are located both inside and outside the European tradition.

The expression of gender by women confronted with a multiplicity
of cultural identities is also taken up by Lee Haring, who shifts our focus
from the literary fairy tale to the oral folktale and the hybrid cultures of the
Indian Ocean. Haring views women as central figures in the process of tran-
sculturation because they act as the principal agents of creolization in those
places where cultures intersect. Drawing attention to woman-centered folktales in Madagascar, Mauritius, Seychelles, Réunion, and the Comoros,
Haring argues that female storytellers mediate cultural identities through
the performance of their tales and that they consequently have a pivotal
role in constructing the social identities and behaviors that define gender.
Feminist theorists and critics who fix their sights on European or American
literature, Haring concludes, fail to recognize that the oral narratives of
women in vernacular cultures are indispensable for the empirical and sub-
stantive study of gender.

Representations of gender and local culture in transnational contexts stand at the center of Cristina Bacchilega's essay, which analyzes three
Indo-Anglian and South Asian diasporic texts that contest the Western
idea of India as a wonder tale. As Bacchilega shows, the Orientalist notion
of India as a land of wonder and birthplace of the fairy tale corresponds
to the idealization of woman as the mysterious Other and seductive teller
of tales (à la Sheherazade). The analysis of the intercultural novels by
Salman Rushdie, Chitra Banerjee Divakaruni, and Arundhati Roy reveals
how each of these texts invokes the fairy tale and the discourse of wonder
to challenge the fantasy image of India. Yet, as Bacchilega emphasizes,
the efforts in these novels to contest the stereotype of exotic India do not
necessarily correspond to the authors' sexual politics and use of gender
stereotypes, which in some cases are interrogated far less critically.

Cathy Lynn Preston's essay pursues the inconsistent relation between
gender and genre. Preston is specifically interested in media texts that have
emerged in the era following the second-wave feminist critique of the fairy
tale—a "Frog King" joke posted on an Internet Listserv, the feature film

Ever After, a magazine advertisement for the Web site women.com, and the television special *Who Wants to Marry a Millionaire?* By blurring the boundaries of the fairy-tale genre—particularly by confusing the line between fiction and reality and thus blurring the distinction between fairy tale and legend—each of these disruptive texts complicates and competes with the older fairy-tale tradition. However, as Preston demonstrates, these multivocal and generically transgressive texts do not consistently embrace a new sexual politics or progressive constructions of gender. Instead, they work in different ways not simply to contest but sometimes to reconfirm—and sometimes simultaneously to resist *and* reaffirm—the boundaries of gender and the masculine authority associated with older fairy tales.

When Preston reads these disruptive texts as a competitive fairy-tale tradition that has occurred in response to new media and to the critique staged by the second wave of feminism, she reminds us that the fairy tale is still emerging. But the continuously emergent nature of the fairy tale and its powerful, if unpredictable, relation to gender are the common threads of all of these essays. To understand the fairy tale's historical development and to keep pace with its movement beyond the revisionist texts of feminist writers and beyond the feminist scholarship of the last thirty years—which new versions of the genre have already incorporated and contested—the scholarship on fairy tales must also continue expanding its scope and developing new approaches. These must be approaches that can situate the fairy tale's treatment of gender in relation to the dynamics of history and the shifting boundaries of society, culture, and nation. And they must be approaches that can discern the ideological ambiguities and textual complexities inherent in texts that paradoxically both reject and rely on the fairy tale's power to define gender.

The main title of this book—*Fairy Tales and Feminism*—creates a mirror image of the title Karen E. Rowe gave to her important article "Feminism and Fairy Tales," which she published in the journal *Women's Studies* in 1979. That pivotal article illustrated how feminists could use fairy tales to illuminate the concerns of contemporary women. At the same time, it demonstrated how scholars of fairy tales could use feminism to understand the genre's sociocultural meaning. Since then, both feminism and the study of fairy tales have emerged as growth industries and have become institutionalized. In fact, fairy-tale studies has developed into a coherent discipline that has been profoundly influenced by feminism. The juxtaposition of *fairy tales* and *feminism* in this book's title reflects this interdisciplinary relationship. In writing about the problems of institutionalization and the current state of women's studies, Biddy Martin has cautioned that "our modes of interacting with one another across disciplines have become so entrenched as to be stultifying" and that these entrenched modes of interaction "are often protected from challenge and change by the piety with which they are repeatedly invoked and the familiarity they have come to enjoy" (354). To keep the collaboration of fairy-tale studies with feminism robust, we need to reappraise the successes and failures of the last thirty-odd years, question what has become too familiar, and become more curious about things not yet familiar enough. This book is offered as a contribution to that project.

As noted at the outset, the first six essays appeared initially in *Marvels & Tales: Journal of Fairy-Tale Studies* 14.1 (2000). They have been modified and updated where necessary for publication in this volume. The contribution by Lee Haring has been revised from an article entitled "The Multilingual Subaltern: Creolization as Agency," which first appeared in *Estudos literatura oral* 5 (1999): 109–19. I am grateful to Isabel Cardigos, the editor of *Estudos literatura oral,* for permission to publish that article here in its revised and retitled form. Thanks are also due to Barbara Henninger for permission to reprint her cartoon of a subversive Sleeping Beauty, which originally appeared in *Putz! Frauen* (Berlin: Elefanten Press Verlag GmbH, 1983).

Arthur Evans, former director of Wayne State University Press, encouraged this project from its beginning. Jane Hoehner, the current director, also believed in it and saw it through to this happy end. I thank both of them, along with Alice Nigoghosian, Kathryn Wildfong, Kristin Harpster Lawrence, and Renée Tambeau, for their advice, encouragement, and strong support of fairy-tale studies at Wayne State University Press.

NOTES

1. Jack Zipes describes this problem as it relates to research on the Grimms' tales in the preface to the new edition of *Brothers Grimm* (2002) xii–xv.

2. The focus on Western European and North American fairy tales has not been exclusive, of course. See, for example, the studies referenced in my survey of feminist scholarship in this volume (36n44). However, the most influential and widely known studies of women and fairy tales are arguably those that deal with canonical literary fairy tales or fairy-tale collections from these regions. I have in mind such frequently cited works as those by Bacchilega, *Postmodern Fairy Tales;* Bottigheimer, *Grimms' Bad Girls;* Gilbert and Gubar; Tatar, *Hard Facts;* Seifert, *Fairy Tales;* Stone, "Things"; Warner, *From the Beast;* and Zipes, *Don't Bet on the Prince.*

1

Feminist Fairy-Tale Scholarship

Donald Haase

*I*n 1970 Alison Lurie fueled feminist scholarship on fairy tales by publishing "Fairy Tale Liberation" in the *New York Review of Books*. That article and its 1971 sequel, "Witches and Fairies," argued that folktales and fairy tales can advance the cause of women's liberation, because they depict strong females. Together, Lurie's two articles took the position that strong female characters could be found not only among the classic fairy tales but also among the much larger and more representative corpus of lesser-known tales. The presence of these competent, resourceful, and powerful female characters, Lurie concluded, ought to make fairy tales "one of the few sorts of classic children's literature of which a radical feminist would approve."[1]

Lurie's position provoked Marcia R. Lieberman, who in 1972 published a forceful rebuttal titled "'Some Day My Prince Will Come': Female Acculturation through the Fairy Tale." Lieberman was neither sympathetic to Lurie's main argument that fairy tales portrayed strong female characters nor receptive to her important qualification that liberating stories had been obscured by males who dominated the selection, editing, and publication of fairy tales. According to Lieberman, this latter argument was "beside the point" because as a feminist scholar she was specifically concerned with the contemporary process of female acculturation: "Only the best-known stories, those that everyone has read or heard, indeed, those that Disney has popularized, have affected masses of children in our culture. Cinderella, the Sleeping Beauty, and Snow White are mythic figures who have replaced the old Greek and Norse gods, goddesses, and heroes for most children. The 'folk tales recorded in the field by scholars,' to which Ms. Lurie refers, or even Andrew Lang's later collections, are so relatively unknown that they cannot seriously be considered in a study of the meaning of fairy tales to women" (383–84).

1

In the catalytic exchange between Lurie and Lieberman during the early 1970s, we witness simultaneously the inchoate discourse of early feminist fairy-tale research and the advent of modern fairy-tale studies, with its emphases on the genre's sociopolitical and sociohistorical contexts. Already anticipated in their terms of debate are nascent questions and critical problems that over the next thirty years would constitute the agenda of much fairy-tale research. To come to grips with the arguments and evidence advanced by Lurie and Lieberman, gender-based scholarship would have to explore not simply the fairy tale's content but also the process of canonization and the institutional control of the classical fairy-tale collections. Questions about canonization and the male-dominated fairy-tale tradition would lead to the discovery and recovery of alternative fairy-tale narratives and to the identification of the woman's voice in fairy-tale production, from the earliest documented references to the present. The initial and rather simplistic debate over the effects of fairy tales on "the masses of children in our culture" and "the meaning of fairy tales to women" would require more detailed study of the relation between the process of socialization and the development of the classical fairy tale, as well as more convincingly documented studies of the fairy tale's reception by children and adults. Ultimately, there would be the development of an increasingly nuanced view of the relation between gender and fairy tale, a view that avoids insupportable generalizations about the genre as a whole and does justice to the complexity and diversity of the fairy-tale corpus and the responses it elicits.

So what began essentially as a debate over the value of fairy tales based on their representation of females would become a more multifaceted discussion of the genre's history and a more nuanced analysis of its production and reception, as this collection of essays demonstrates. In this introductory essay, I want to identify significant developments in feminist fairy-tale scholarship in order to chart the progress that has been made, provide a context for the research presented in the essays that follow, and suggest some directions for further research.[2]

GENDER AND SOCIALIZATION

Rooted in sociocultural critique and in the controversy "about what is biologically determined and what is learned" (Lieberman 394), early feminist criticism of fairy tales, as seen in the Lurie-Lieberman debate, was principally concerned with the genre's representation of females and the effects of these representations on the gender identity and behavior of children in particular. As Lieberman concluded, "We must consider the possibility that the classical attributes of 'femininity' found in these stories are in fact imprinted in children and reinforced by the stories themselves. Analyses of the influence of the most popular children's literature may give us an insight into some of the origins of psycho-sexual identity" (395). There was—and still is—widespread agreement with Lieberman's argument that fairy tales "have been made the repositories of the dreams, hopes, and fantasies of generations of girls" and that "millions of women must surely have formed their psycho-sexual self-concepts, and their ideas of what they could or could not accomplish, what sort of behavior would be rewarded, and of the nature of reward itself, in part from their favorite fairy tales" (385).

Throughout the 1970s these ideas were repeated in writings by American feminists, which did not always analyze fairy tales in depth but more frequently utilized them simply as evidence to demonstrate the sociocultural myths and mechanisms that oppress women.[3] In 1974, for example, Andrea Dworkin's *Woman Hating* echoed Lieberman's thesis by asserting that fairy tales shape our cultural values and understanding of gender roles by invariably depicting women as wicked, beautiful, and passive, while portraying men, in absolute contrast, as good, active, and heroic. Similarly, Susan Brownmiller, in the course of her book *Against Our Will: Men, Women and Rape* (1975), offered the tale of "Little Red Riding Hood" as a parable of rape and argued that fairy tales—particularly classic tales like "Cinderella," "Sleeping Beauty," and "Snow White"—train women to be rape victims (309–10). And in 1978 Mary Daly began the first chapter of *Gyn/Ecology: The Metaethics of Radical Feminism* by pointing to the fairy tale as a carrier of the toxic patriarchal myths that are used to deceive women: "The child who is fed tales such as *Snow White* is not told that the tale itself is a poisonous apple, and the Wicked Queen (her mother/teacher), having herself been drugged by the same deadly diet throughout her lifetime . . . , is unaware of her venomous part in the patriarchal plot" (44).

By the end of the decade, both in scholarship and in books intended for mass-market distribution, these oversimplifications of the fairy tale's problematic relation to social values and the construction of gender identity gave way to somewhat more complex, or at least more ambivalent, approaches. In 1979 Karen E. Rowe reaffirmed the "significance of romantic tales in forming female attitudes toward the self, men, marriage and society." Moreover, Rowe emphasized in particular that the idealized

Illustration by Barbara Henniger from *Putz! Frauen,* by Claire Bretecher et al. (Berlin: Elefanten Press, 1983) n. pag. Illustration © Barbara Henniger. Reproduced with permission.

romantic patterns in fairy tales were also evident in mass-market reading materials intended for adult women, including erotic, ladies', and gothic fictions. The fairy tale's romantic paradigms could therefore be viewed as influential not simply in childhood but also in the lives of adult women, who "internalize romantic patterns from ancient tales" and "continue to tailor their aspirations and capabilities to conform with romantic paradigms" ("Feminism and Fairy Tales" 222).

However, Rowe also observed that ever since modern feminists had begun to expose and challenge society's "previous mores and those fairy tales which inculcate romantic ideals" (211), modern women had become increasingly conscious of the gap between romantic ideals and the reality that "all men are not princes" (222). Consequently, Rowe's work asserted that fairy tales "no longer provide[d] mythic validations of desirable female behavior . . . [and had] lost their potency because of the widening gap between social practice and romantic idealization" (211). According to Rowe, the result for women was an ambiguity that left them in an unresolved tension between enacting cultural change and adhering to the deceptive ideals of the fairy tale, which still exerted an "awesome imaginative power over the female psyche" (218):

> Today women are caught in a dialectic between the cultural *status quo* and the evolving feminist movement, between a need to preserve values and yet to accommodate changing mores, between romantic fantasies and contemporary realities. The capacity of women to achieve equality and of culture to rejuvenate itself depends, I would suggest, upon the metamorphosis of these tensions into balances, of antagonisms into viable cooperations. But one question remains unresolved: do we have the courageous vision and energy to cultivate a newly fertile ground of psychic and cultural experience from which will grow fairy tales for human beings in the future? (223)

In Rowe's view, the fairy tale—perhaps precisely because of its "awesome imaginative power"—had a role to play in cultivating equality among men and women, but it would have to be a rejuvenated fairy tale fully divested of its idealized romantic fantasies.

Other feminists of the same era had specific ideas about how the fairy tale could be employed "to cultivate a newly fertile ground of psychic and cultural experience." In 1979 feminist literary scholar Carolyn G. Heilbrun proposed that "myth, tale, and tragedy must be transformed by bold acts of reinterpretation in order to enter the experience of the emerging female self" (150). Citing Rowe's essay, which she knew then as a 1978 working paper from the Radcliffe Institute, Heilbrun offered the Grimms' fairy tales as an example of cultural texts whose models of male selfhood could be adopted and reinterpreted by women in light of their own search for identity:

> One feels particularly the importance of not limiting the female imagination to female models. Bettelheim has shown how small boys can use the female model of helplessness in fairy tales to reduce their anxieties and unmentionable fears; similarly, young girls should be able to use male models to enhance their feelings of daring and adventure. To choose only the most obvious example, consider the many Grimm fairy tales employing the theme of the "three brothers." What if the girl could conceive of herself as the youngest of the three? Powerless, scorned, the one from whom least is expected, even by himself, this third brother, because of virtues clearly "feminine"—animal-loving, kind, generous, affectionate, warm to the possibilities of affiliation—this third brother, again and again rejected, nonetheless persists to success with the help of his unlikely friends, and despite the enmity of what, in the person of the two older brothers, might be called the "male" establishment. (147)

Drawing on "The Golden Bird," "The Queen Bee," "The Three Feathers," "The Golden Goose," and "The Water of Life," Heilbrun suggested how the youngest brother's situation is actually "a paradigm of female experience in the male power structure that no woman with aspirations above that of sleeping princess will fail to recognize" (148). Identification with the male hero is possible, Heilbrun argued, once women recognize "that the structures [of the fairy tale] are human, not sexually dictated": "What woman must learn to assume is that she is not confined to the role of the princess; that the hero, who wakens Sleeping Beauty with a kiss, is that part of herself that awakens conventional girlhood to the possibility of life and action" (150).

As if on cue and in the same year, Madonna Kolbenschlag published *Kiss Sleeping Beauty Good-Bye: Breaking the Spell of Feminine Myths and Models.* In an eclectic approach that combined social concerns with psychology and religion, Kolbenschlag discussed fairy tales to expose the feminine myths of Western culture while reasserting the potential such stories have to awaken and liberate women. In other words, she took an approach that reconciled the cultural specificity of fairy tales as "parables of feminine socialization" (3) with the view that the same stories can call "women forth to an 'awakening' and to spiritual maturity" (4). As she notes in her introduction, "Much of what we live by and attribute to nature or destiny is, in reality, a pervasive cultural mythology. Because myths are no less powerful than nature and because they mirror as well as model our existence, I have introduced six familiar fairy tales as heuristic devices for interpreting the experience of women. These tales are parables of what women have become; and at the same time, prophecies of the spiritual metamorphosis to which they are called" (x).

Similarly, Colette Dowling's popular volume of 1981, *The Cinderella Complex: Women's Hidden Fear of Independence,* did not simply indict the fairy tale but instead suggested how women's psychological and social attitudes are mirrored in the stories. From this perspective, a critical understanding of the classical fairy tale as a mirror of the forces limiting women makes it possible to project alternative ways of constructing lives. This had been the goal, too, of Linda Chervin and Mary Neill's *The Woman's Tale: A Journal of Inner Exploration* (1980). By sharing the authors' personal reflections on fairy tales—such as "Rapunzel," "Hansel and Gretel," "Cinderella," "Little Red Riding Hood," "Sleeping Beauty," and "Snow White and Rose Red"—Chervin and Neill hoped to encourage women to reflect on their own responses to the stories and on their inner, or spiritual, journeys. In *Leaving My Father's House: A Journey to Conscious Femininity* (1992), feminist psychoanalyst Marion Woodman offered a Jungian interpretation of the Grimms' "All Fur" and the commentaries of her female patients to demonstrate how women could regain autonomy in a society dominated by men. Despite the diverse orientations of these works—which ranged from the literary to the psychological and sociological, to the philosophical and spiritual—they all encouraged a self-conscious, critical engagement with the classical tales as a means to liberate women to imagine and construct new identities.[4]

Folktale and Fairy-Tale Anthologies

Lurie, of course, had already advanced the idea that fairy tales could "prepare children for women's liberation" ("Fairy Tale Liberation" 42), and in 1978 Heather Lyons cautioned that critical feminist interpretations should be reconsidered, since one could identify extant tales that included strong heroines, stupid men, and the ambiguous treatment of otherwise stereotypical traits such as beauty.[5] These ideas lay behind new collections featuring lesser-known stories with unconventional heroines or better-known tales anthologized in such a way so as to foreground the strength of their female characters. These included Lurie's own collection, *Clever Gretchen and Other Forgotten Folktales* (1980), Rosemary Minard's *Womenfolk and Fairy Tales* (1975), and Ethel Johnston Phelps's two anthologies, *Tatterhood and Other Tales* (1978) and *The Maid of the North: Feminist Folk Tales from Around the World* (1981).

These early collections were followed over the next two decades by a second wave of fairy-tale collections emphasizing the breadth and diversity of women in fairy tales. As their titles and subtitles indicate, many of these foregrounded the cultural diversity of women's tales, including Sigrid Früh's *Europäische Frauenmärchen* (*European Fairy Tales about Women*, 2nd ed. 1996; 1st ed. 1985), Ines Köhler-Zülch and Christine Shojaei Kawan's *Schneewittchen hat viele Schwestern: Frauengestalten in europäischen Märchen* (*Snow White Has Many Sisters: Female Characters in European Fairy Tales*, 1988), Suzanne Barchers's *Wise Women: Folk and Fairy Tales from Around the World* (1990), Virginia Hamilton's *Her Stories: African American Folktales, Fairy Tales, and True Tales* (1995), A. B. Chinen's *Waking the World: Classic Tales of Women and the Heroic Feminine* (1996), and Kathleen Ragan's *Fearless Girls, Wise Women, and Beloved Sisters: Heroines in Folktales from Around the World* (1998). Despite the common attempt to revive and promote women-centered tales, the editors who collected (and in some cases retold) these tales do not present a uniform image or definition of the fairy-tale heroine. Interested in presenting a variety of European tale variants, folklorists Ines Köhler-Zülch and Christine Shojaei Kawan noted that folk narratives "offer a multicolored spectrum of female characters," who have every chance of being "sly," "lazy," "old," or "strong" (7).[6] Far more mythically inclined, Sigrid Früh, on the other hand, hoped to present "as broad as possible a spectrum of strong, active, and loving women" (195), so she privileged tales whose female characters could be classified under distinctly edifying rubrics: "saviors," "the helpful and faithful," "the clever and cunning," "warriors and rulers," and "the fates, the Great Mother, and goddesses." Kathleen Ragan, who gave priority to tales in which "main characters are female and . . . worthy of emulation" (xxvi), differentiated her idea of the exemplary heroine from Angela Carter's, whose first collection Ragan described as being based on a "view of women in folktales that includes sexual exploits and victims as well as heroines" (437).

Angela Carter, of course, had no interest in presenting a one-dimensional view of women—let alone heroines without sexuality. Her first folktale collection, published in the United States as *The Old Wives' Fairy Tale Book* (1990), took pleasure in highlighting the heroine's multiple identities. "These stories have only one thing in common," wrote Carter in her introduction, "they all centre around a female protagonist; be she clever, or brave, or good, or silly, or cruel, or sinister, or awesomely unfortunate, she is centre stage, as large as life" (xiii). Moreover, Carter's two folktale collections aimed at reasserting precisely those dimensions of a woman's life—including sexuality—that male editors had suppressed. As Marina Warner explained in the introduction to Carter's second, posthumously published collection, *Strange Things Sometimes Still Happen: Fairy Tales from Around the World* (1992): "Angela Carter's partisan feeling for women, which burns in all her work, never led her to any conventional form of feminism; but she continues [in this collection] one of her original and effective strategies, snatching out of the jaws of misogyny itself, 'useful stories' for women. . . . [H]ere she turns topsy-turvy some cautionary folk tales and shakes out the fear and dislike of women they once expressed to create a new set of values, about strong, outspoken, zestful, sexual women who can't be kept down" (x).

Anthologies of literary fairy tales by and about women complemented these collections of folktales from the 1980s and 1990s. Some of these drew attention to historically neglected fairy tales penned by women.[7] Others assembled contemporary fairy tales authored by men and women engaged in the cultural debate over gender and sexual politics.[8] The most critically provocative of all these anthologies was *The Trials and Tribulations of Little Red Riding Hood,* published by Jack Zipes in 1983 (2nd ed. 1993). This anthology presented over thirty literary adaptations of "Little Red Riding Hood" in chronological order, thus encouraging an illuminating comparison of variants and a historical analysis of the tale's development. *Trials and Tribulations* contributed significantly to feminist fairy-tale scholarship not only in terms of the conclusions Zipes reached in his critical commentary but also in terms of the work's organization and methodology, which revealed just how vital the comparison of both oral and literary variants in sociohistorical contexts could be in understanding the fairy tale's relation to gender and socialization.[9] Zipes's introductory study of the story's history confirmed that "Little Red Riding Hood" not only reflects the civilizing process in Western societies but also has played a central role in that process by reinforcing the cultural ideology of the middle class. More specifically, he showed that the tale's many adaptations embody a cultural struggle over attitudes toward sexuality and sex roles and toward male and female power. Furthermore, by showing how Charles Perrault and the Brothers Grimm produced versions of the story that dramatically altered the oral folktale, erasing its positive references to sexuality and female power, Zipes exposed how the classical tale came to be "a male creation and projection" that "reflects men's fear of women's sexuality—and of their own as well" (80, 81).

EDITING AND THE FEMALE IMAGE: GRIMMS' FAIRY TALES

Demystifying the classical fairy tales as tools of socialization by exposing their male bias took a leap forward with research on the Grimms' *Kinder- und Hausmärchen*. The impetus originated in Germany in the 1970s, where ideological critics and left-wing pedagogues challenged sentimental views of the Grimms' stories by historicizing the tales and criticizing them for their role in promulgating repressive nineteenth-century bourgeois values.[10] At the same time, Heinz Rölleke began publishing his important philological-textual studies and fairy-tale editions that brilliantly illuminated the collecting and editing practices of the Brothers Grimm. In particular, his 1975 edition of the Grimms' tales in manuscript form—the so-called Ölenberg manuscript of 1810—permitted comparison of the brothers' original transcriptions with their published texts; and in a groundbreaking essay, also from 1975, he set the record straight on the nature of the Grimms' oral informants.[11] Specifically, Rölleke helped debunk the persistent myth that the brothers' tales were authentic transcriptions of the German folk tradition by demonstrating in convincing detail not only that the Grimms had relied heavily on literary sources and literate middle-class informants but also that they had undertaken significant editorial interventions in the texts they selected to publish.

It was not long before feminist-oriented Grimm scholars—especially in the United States—recognized the importance of these findings and built on them to show how the two brothers had revised tales so that they reflected or shaped the sociocultural values of their time. Jack Zipes led the way in 1979–1980 with his essay "Who's Afraid of the Brothers Grimm? Socialization and Politi[ci]zation through Fairy Tales." Zipes compared passages from different versions collected and edited by the Grimms to illustrate how they had altered tales to promote patriarchal bourgeois values as part of the socialization process. This research was integrated into Zipes's *Fairy Tales and the Art of Subversion,* which appeared in 1983 and discussed the Grimms' editing and appropriation of the oral tradition as part of a much larger social history of the fairy tale. In specific sociohistorical contexts Zipes demonstrated how the folktale had been appropriated and reappropriated by European and American writers as a special discourse on sociocultural values and how that fairy-tale discourse was intended to function in the socialization of children—especially in its modeling of gender-specific identity and behavior.

The pedagogical agenda and editorial history of the *Kinder- und Hausmärchen* were also the starting point for Maria Tatar's studies of male and female characters in the Grimms' tales. Published in the mid-1980s, these studies came together in *The Hard Facts of the Grimms' Fairy Tales*, which reexamined the perennial topics of sex and violence in fairy tales.[12] Stressing that the examination of "hard facts" like these "calls first for a long, hard look at the genesis and publishing history of *The Nursery and Household Tales*" (xxi), Tatar clarified how the ebb and flow of sex and violence in the collection relate to the Grimms' sociocultural attitudes and textual editing. But for Tatar, editorial history served only as a threshold to a broader study of sex and violence, one drawing productively on folklore, structuralism, and judiciously chosen concepts from psychoanalysis. Moreover, although Tatar illuminated the differences between male and female characters by organizing her interpretations of heroes and villains according to their gender, in the final analysis gender functioned primarily as a lens to view sex and violence. To be sure, Tatar certainly considered the construction of gender through the editorial process to be an indicator of how the classic fairy tale was appropriated to serve the purpose of socializing children. However, *The Hard Facts* and Tatar's later book *Off with Their Heads! Fairy Tales and the Culture of Childhood* remain ultimately concerned with what that process tells us not simply about male constructions of the female but about adult constructions of childhood as well.

The most detailed study of the effects of the editorial process on gender in the Grimms' fairy tales came in the pioneering research of Ruth B. Bottigheimer. In a series of articles from 1980 to 1985, Bottigheimer demonstrated how the Grimms' editorial interventions—including their apparently simple lexical revisions—weakened once-strong female characters, demonized female power, imposed a male perspective on stories voicing women's discontents, and rendered heroines powerless by depriving them of speech, all in accord with the social values of their time ("The Transformed Queen"; "Tale Spinners"; "Silenced Women"). Bottigheimer's research on the relation among gender, social values, and the Grimms' editing led to her important book of 1987, *Grimms' Bad Girls and Bold Boys: The Moral and Social Vision of the Tales*. Here she elucidated the Grimms' treatment of gender by closely analyzing the entire corpus of their tales in light of nineteenth-century social trends and the collection's editorial history.

It is important to note, however, that Bottigheimer did not simply replicate Zipes's conclusions or the widespread understanding that the Brothers Grimm had imposed bourgeois values on the folktale. To be sure, there were instances where she found that to be true. However, her attention to the Grimms' sources themselves convinced her that it was not their editorial revisions alone, or even primarily, that shaped the representations of women in their collection. She found among the brothers' stories, in fact, competing views of gender that were inherent in their sources, as well as "kindred values [that the collection] revived and incorporated from preceding centuries" (168). She made this case even more explicitly in her essay "From Gold to Guilt: The Forces Which Reshaped *Grimms' Tales*," where she took pains to distinguish her view from that of Marxist critics who claim that the Grimms transformed folktales by imposing bourgeois attitudes on the stories (she cites only Zipes). Instead, Bottigheimer argued that the image of women in the tales resulted in part from Wilhelm's increasing reliance on misogynistic folktales from the sixteenth and seventeenth centuries—not the magic tales of the Grimms' bourgeois informants. In other words, she claimed that it was the adopted voice of the folk, not the voice of the bourgeoisie, that spoke in such tales: "If . . . isolation and silence for heroines creeps inexorably into *Grimms' Tales* . . . , it is not from bourgeois experience, but is, instead, part and parcel of the restrictive values that emerge from the 'folk' versions of the tales. . . . It is the dictates of hard peasant and artisan life that produce domestic tyranny, female silence, and isolation in *Grimms' Tales*" ("From Gold to Guilt" 198).[13]

If the idealization of the folk and folk sources introduced "restrictive values" and negative images of women into the Grimms' collection, then the Romantic idealization of women and nature—effected through the Grimms' editing—introduced an opposite but equally restrictive stereotype. This is evident in what Renate Steinchen has referred to as the Grimms' "representation and polarization of two images of women" (293). Drawing on both sociocultural history and the publishing history of the Grimms' collection, Steinchen illustrated how repressive female models were idealized and elevated to mythic images for middle-class readers. Steinchen not only critiqued the myth of the idealized female storyteller that the brothers had presented in the preface to their collection, but she also compared their versions of "Snow White" from four different editions to analyze how Wilhelm Grimm had intervened in the story to shape idealized representations of men, women, nature, and romantic love, which were meant to serve as models for middle-class readers.

In emphasizing the Grimms' bipolar view of women, Steinchen's analysis of the brothers' "Snow White" parallels the influential interpretation offered by Sandra M. Gilbert and Susan Gubar in their book *The Madwoman in the Attic* (3–44). Without recourse to the tale's editorial history, Gilbert and Gubar stressed the conflict between the egotistically assertive stepmother and the angelically passive Snow White, and they interpreted this bipolar image of woman as a reflection of the self-destructive roles imposed by patriarchy, which reifies females as powerless aesthetic objects and subverts their creative powers.[14] Gilbert and Gubar's stimulating reading stands on its own, but that is precisely its weakness. Their interpretation lacks the contexts, both sociocultural and textual, that would justify their assertion that the voice of patriarchy is not only present in the story of "Snow White" but is also its controlling voice—the voice of the mirror that dominates each woman's sense of self. Steinchen's analysis, informed by both the textual and sociocultural history at work in the Grimms' tale, clearly demonstrates the shaping hand of patriarchy behind the representations of both the demonized queen and the idealized daughter, thereby providing a compelling sociohistorical basis for the speculative psychosocial interpretation presented by Gilbert and Gubar.

As in the early feminist treatises cited above, fairy tales are frequently considered out of context as exemplary texts that can be used to construct generalizations and theories. The studies by Zipes, Tatar, Bottigheimer, and Steinchen underline the need for feminist scholars to take both the textual and sociocultural contexts into account when generalizing or theorizing on the basis of fairy tales. Take, for example, Sandra Gilbert's article "Life's Empty Pack: Notes Towards a Literary Daughteronomy," in which she argues that the model of female maturation and duty in patriarchal society is based on father-daughter incest. She focuses principally on George Eliot, Edith Wharton, and Sigmund Freud, but she also introduces the Grimms' "All Fur" as a fairy tale that presents the paradigm of father-daughter incest in "its most essential psychic outline" (376).[15] However, Gilbert's close reading relies on a crucial line from the fairy tale that actually depends on a grammatical distinction that is significantly more ambiguous in German than it is in the English translation she uses, and this ambiguity bears directly on the question of incest that she is discussing.[16] Furthermore, a complete understanding of the incest theme in "All Fur" depends on knowledge of the tale's textual history and the alterations made by Wilhelm Grimm to render it more appropriate for his middle-class and juvenile audience.[17] Read in these contexts, "All Fur" becomes an even more credible and authoritative illustration of Gilbert's theory, which is otherwise founded on an essentializing psychological understanding of the story.

In his own essay on women in the Grimms' fairy tales, Heinz Rölleke advised feminist readers of these tales to avoid making generalized claims that were not based on rigorous studies of a tale's textual history ("Die Frau"). Rölleke's approach to the question of gender in the *Kinder- und Hausmärchen* takes into account the brothers' attitude toward women,[18] the sources of their tales, and the general representation of women in the collection, all of which tend to mitigate, according to Rölleke, the feminist critique of the stories. Like his other research on the textual provenance and sources of the Grimms' collection, Rölleke's essay on women helps to focus attention on the fact that females were among the most important of the brothers' informants and were the source for many of their important tales. Moreover, in identifying these female informants as largely young, educated women of the bourgeoisie, Rölleke helped to further demythologize the stereotype of the *Märchenfrau*.

Much later, in 1993, Maureen Thum followed Rölleke's lead by arguing that a discriminating analysis of the Grimms' stories in light of their informants gives us a much more complex view of female stereotypes in their collection. Thum argued that although tales contributed by Marie Hassenpflug, Dorothea Wild, and Friedrich Krause depict women with considerable differentiation, stories contributed by Dorothea Viehmann (the Grimms' ideal storyteller) portray positive female characters that resist the expected stereotype. Applying Mikhail Bakhtin's concept of "heteroglossia," Thum consequently confirmed the multiplicity of voices—including female voices—in the *Kinder- und Hausmärchen* and underlined, as had Bottigheimer earlier, the relative complexity of the Grimms' women.[19]

In terms of feminist fairy-tale scholarship, then, research based on the textual and editorial history of the Grimm brothers' tales has had far-reaching consequences. First, it laid bare the inscription of patriarchal values in the classic fairy tale, documented the appropriation of the genre by male editors and collectors, and sharpened our understanding of the complex editorial and cultural processes involved in the representation of women. Second, it confirmed the role of fairy tales in the process of socialization by showing how Wilhelm Grimm's representation of women helped construct a culturally specific model of gender identity. Finally, by renewing attention to the Grimms' female informants, it also identified the presence of female voices in the brothers' collection, revealed the diversity of those voices, and stimulated the search for narratives and characters that resisted the Grimm stereotype.[20]

Woman's Voice in Fairy Tales

The female voice in the fairy tale had initially been conceived as a historical voice—not that of an individual informant—and recognition of that collective female voice was an opportunity to reassert women's ownership of the genre. In the 1980s feminists such as Heide Göttner-Abendroth, Sonja Rüttner-Cova, and Gertrud Jungblut reappropriated the genre from its male collectors and editors by looking to the fairy tale for evidence of prehistoric matriarchal myths. Göttner-Abendroth's influential study *Die Göttin und ihr Heros* (1980) argued that fairy tales reflect the practices and customs of prehistorical societies, which were in her view "primarily matriarchal societies" (134).[21] Accordingly, she analyzed selected tales from the Grimms' collection to prove that fairy tales contained remnants of a prehistoric matriarchal mythology (thereby using the brothers' theory that myth antedates the märchen to reclaim the stories from them) and to show that changes in the matriarchal structure of the fairy tale reflected society's movement toward patriarchy. That the fundamental matriarchal content and narratives of the fairy tale could still be discerned, she argued, was due to the fact that the original myths had not been deformed beyond recognition by patriarchy but had been protectively camouflaged in order to ensure their transmission during the course of increasing patriarchalization: "In those places where it lived on without disruption—in the lower strata of society and in geographical fringe groups—the old matriarchal world view was therefore passed on in disguised form [*verschleiert*]" (134).

This historical view of the fairy tale's origins and development has influenced the way some feminist readers have interpreted specific fairy tales. Bottigheimer's essay on "The Transformed Queen," for example, maintained that Wilhelm Grimm's editorial emendations suppressed female power in tales that originally gave voice to matriarchal myths, including "The Twelve Brothers," "The Seven Ravens," "The Six Swans," "All Fur," and "The Goose Girl." Utilizing the work of Göttner-Abendroth and August Nitschke, who also had found evidence of a matriarchal social order in fairy tales,[22] Jack Zipes analyzed French versions of "Beauty and the Beast" and European variants of "Cinderella" to show how these literary tales, in the service of the civilizing process, had reformulated themes involving gender and sexuality, thereby deviating from the oral folktales that had originated in matriarchal societies (*Fairy Tales and the Art of Subversion* 30–41; see also Zipes, *Brothers Grimm* [1988] 137–46).

However, Zipes's sociohistorical analysis did not intend to discredit the classical tale entirely. To the contrary, he suggested that the remnants of matriarchal themes from the folktale gave the literary version a positive potential: "The importance of the first three major literary *Cinderellas*—by Giambattista Basile, Charles Perrault, and the Brothers Grimm—consists in the manner in which they continue to transmit residues and traces of the matrilineal tradition (*perhaps enhancing this tradition by marking them down in script*), while also reformulating how oral symbolical motifs and topoi could be used to represent social experience" (*Brothers Grimm* [1988] 141; emphasis mine). Published tales like "Cinderella," in other words, could store and transmit matriarchal values that remained camouflaged or embedded in the tale type, despite the changes wrought by patriarchy and the written word. Indeed, in another feminist reading of Cinderella variants, Louise Bernikow argued that the Brothers Grimm version of the story had actually preserved its matriarchal thrust. Unlike the versions by Charles Perrault and Walt Disney, both of whom had severely minimized woman's power, the Grimms' "Cinderella," according to Bernikow, maintained the powerful connection between mother and daughter, who are pitted against a woman compromised by patriarchy.[23]

Still, feminist readings in general have relied less on the historical view of matriarchal social orders than on the argument that storytelling is "semiotically a female art." Karen E. Rowe articulated that point of view in 1986 by pointing not only to women's traditional role as storytellers but also to the ways they have been represented as the spinners of tales in folktale collections, frame stories, and literary tales. She showed that through their association with the fates, fairies, and spinning, women are identified with the art and power of spinning tales. The history of the male appropriation of folktales is the history of the male's attempt to control this female power, to co-opt the female art of storytelling:

> To have the antiquarian Grimm Brothers regarded as the fathers of modern folklore is perhaps to forget the maternal lineage, the "mothers" who in the French *veillées* and English nurseries, in court salons and the German *Spinnstube*, in Paris and on the Yorkshire moors, passed on their wisdom. The Grimm brothers, like Tereus, Ovid, King Shahryar, Basile, Perrault, and others reshaped what they could not precisely comprehend, because only for women does the thread, which spins out the lore of life itself, create a tapestry to be fully read and understood. Strand by strand weaving . . . is the true art of the fairy tale—and it is, I would submit, semiotically a female art. ("To Spin a Yarn" 68, 71)

Beyond this explanation for the male appropriation of the female voice,[24] Rowe suggested "that in the history of folktale and fairy tale, women as storytellers have woven or spun their yarns, speaking at one level to a total culture, but at another to a sisterhood of readers who will understand the hidden language, the secret revelations of the tale" (57). In this view the fairy tale becomes a coded text in which the female voice, despite the attempt by men to control it, not only continues to speak but also speaks a secret, subversive language.[25] Like the historical theory of disguised matriarchal myths, Rowe's arguments reclaimed the fairy tale for women and provided reasons for feminist scholars and readers to reassess the genre's significance for women.

Recovering the Female Fairy-Tale Tradition

Rowe's claim for the fairy tale as a female art initiated lines of feminist inquiry that would require significant rewriting of the genre's history. The best-known and most comprehensive work of scholarship on this topic is Marina Warner's book of 1994, *From the Beast to the Blonde: On Fairy Tales and Their Tellers,* which expanded Rowe's initial exploration of female storytellers and their representations into a panoramic history. While Warner's expansive, multidisciplinary study offered a macroscopic view of the female voice in storytelling, scholars of specific national literatures engaged in innovative research and recovery work that brought to light forgotten, neglected, or unknown examples of female fairy-tale production and reception.

In 1987 Jeannine Blackwell published an important article that documented female contributions to the fairy tale in nineteenth-century Germany ("Fractured Fairy Tales"). In her attention to the reception of fairy tales by women in the nineteenth-century home and to women's independent authorship of literary tales, Blackwell uncovered the efforts of women to restore a female narrative voice to the genre that in Germany had been largely appropriated and defined by the Grimms. Subsequent research began to flesh out those findings with specific studies, editions, and translations of individual German women writers who had engaged the fairy tale in various ways during the eighteenth and nineteenth centuries.[26] That work continues in this volume with the translations and commentaries by Blackwell. In addition, Blackwell and Shawn C. Jarvis have published a major translation project, *The Queen's Mirror: Fairy Tales by German Women, 1780–1900.* Building on the previous scholarship— which stressed the tales' social criticism, the attempts to construct new models of female behavior, and women's struggle to define the genre for themselves—the translations and commentary in the work of Jarvis and Blackwell underline the diversity and complexity that characterized the production of fairy tales by German Romantic women writers.

The recovery of the French female fairy-tale tradition has moved at a somewhat faster pace than the recovery and assessment of tales by German women writers; however, both strands of scholarship have

revealed the complexity involved in women's reappropriation of the genre.
The production of fairy tales by seventeenth- and eighteenth-century
Frenchwomen had not been completely unknown, of course, but their
works, which had not enjoyed the canonical status of Perrault's *Contes*,
were in need of rediscovery and reassessment, especially in light of feminist scholarship. Rowe, in fact, had suggested that it was time "to
reconceptualize Madame d'Aulnoy, Mlle. L'Héritier, and Madame de
Beaumont, not as pseudomasculine appropriators of a folkloric tradition,
but as reappropriators of a female art of tale-telling" ("To Spin a Yarn"
71). These authors—the *conteuses*—had been acknowledged in books by
Jacques Barchilon and Raymonde Robert, who sought to redirect attention to French fairy-tale production generally, but not necessarily in feminist terms. This general recovery, however, facilitated the feminist project
to reassess the fairy tales of the *conteuses*, which generated numerous articles, monographs, dissertations, editions, and anthologies.[27] As Rowe had
anticipated, much of this criticism grappled with the inscription of a subversive female voice onto the genre. However, as Lewis Seifert's expert
discussion of this scholarship shows later in this volume, the women's subversion of the fairy tale is accompanied by still unresolved ideological
ambiguities that expose the true complexity involved in the female production of literary fairy tales in the seventeenth century. Among these
writers there is no uniform female "voice" informing the subversive tendencies and no ideologically coherent treatment of those fairy-tale themes
and structures—such as the marriage motif—that bear on questions of
gender and female identity.

The diversity and ambiguities of fairy tales produced by women in
Germany and France during the seventeenth, eighteenth, and nineteenth
centuries must be seen in tandem with the emergence of the modern
European literary fairy tale during that same period. In her important
study *Twice upon a Time: Women Writers and the History of the Fairy Tale*,
Elizabeth Wanning Harries argues convincingly that the history of the
fairy tale involves the development of two models, which she labels "compact" and "complex":

> "Compact" fairy tales are usually presented as foundational or original, lit-
> erally as stories that tell us of origins, as stories that do not seem to depend
> on other stories but come to us as unmediated expressions of the folk and
> its desires. Their carefully constructed simplicity works as an implicit guar-
> antee of their traditional and authentic status. "Complex" tales, on the other
> hand, work to reveal the stories behind other stories, the unvoiced possi-
> bilities that tell a different tale. They are determinedly and openly "inter-

textual" and "stereophonic," Roland Barthes's terms for the ways all writing is intertwined with other writing. (17)

In her analysis of this dual tradition, Harries identifies the classic stories of Perrault and the Grimms as compact tales and the "long, intricate, digressive, playful, self-referential, and self-conscious" tales written by the *conteuses* between 1690–1715 as complex tales. This fresh classification provides a valuable tool for understanding the literary achievement of the *conteuses*. It also allows Harries to redraw the trajectory of the female fairy-tale tradition over the course of three hundred years. With their inter-textualities, sophisticated framing devices, and new models of femininity, the complex tales of the *conteuses* not only contributed in a significant way to the origin of the literary fairy tale (17) but also provided a model for twentieth-century women writers who (re)wrote fairy tales in order to interrogate gender.

The challenge for the women writers who participated in the creation of the literary fairy tales was not simply to engage the emerging genre but to do so under sociocultural and economic conditions that discouraged female authorship. The complex, ambiguous, ambivalent, experimental, and sometimes fragmented fairy tales penned by women reflect their struggle to find their voices in a literary form that was to become institutionalized and aligned very quickly with the values and perspectives of patriarchy. As Ruth B. Bottigheimer argues in her essay in this volume, the restrictive image of the modern European fairy-tale heroine came into being during precisely this period, confirming the parallel development of the literary fairy tale, male dominance of the genre, and women's loss of control over their own bodies. Accordingly, the corpus of literary fairy tales became one locus of struggle over questions and constructions of sexuality, gender, and power.

WOMEN WRITERS AND THE FAIRY TALE AS INTERTEXT

Because the birth and institutionalization of the modern literary fairy tale occurred initially in Italy, France, and Germany between 1500 and the early 1800s, feminist studies in Anglo-American contexts focused initially on the nineteenth- and twentieth-century reception by women authors who were reacting to a more or less established, canonical fairy-tale tradition, not an emerging one. These authors were responding to precisely the structures and images of female disempowerment inherent in narratives of the modern fairy-tale heroine. Accordingly, feminist scholarship has focused frequently on women novelists who rely on classic fairy tales as intertexts to inform their adult novels and critically engage the tradition. Gilbert and Gubar noted this already in 1979 in *The Madwoman in the Attic*, where they discussed how writers such as Emily Brontë and Charlotte Brontë used fairy-tale allusions, structures, and characters in their novels to repudiate the fairy tale's repressive fantasies and to foreground feminist themes. In the wake of Gilbert and Gubar, other feminist scholars continued to investigate the intertextual role of classic tales in the works of nineteenth-century English women novelists, including the Brontës, Jane Austen, Frances Hodgson Burnett, Frances Burney, and Charlotte Smith.[28] In general, such studies confirmed that these novelists used fairy-tale intertexts—in particular the well-known story of Cinderella—as subversive strategies to contest the idealized outcomes of fairy tales and their representations of gender and female identity.

It would not be accurate, however, to understand the relation of these women writers to the fairy-tale tradition simply as a unilateral rejection of it. As Huang Mei demonstrated in her study of four nineteenth-century female novelists, *Transforming the Cinderella Dream: From Frances Burney to Charlotte Brontë*, the intertextual relation between novel and fairy tale generates a complex dialogue that is "multidimensioned and multilayered" (28).[29] According to Huang, the complexity of female responses derives in part from the fact that "the Cinderella theme is itself essentially ambiguous and dialogic, with a constant tension built on the desire/self-denial, passion/reason dichotomy" (28). Moreover, Huang read the novels in her study not only as responses to Perrault's classic version of "Cinderella" but also as responses to the Cinderella theme embodied in Samuel Richardson's *Pamela*, which "grafts the central dialectics of Protestant individualism onto the structural ambiguity of the original tale" (23). "As a result," Huang maintained, "the Cinderella myth has functioned as a double-edged (or multiedged) ideological weapon. On the one hand, the code of propriety is carefully woven into a myth that romanticizes woman's subordinate and domesticated role within the patriarchy; on the other hand, the Protestant individualism that is simultaneously programmed into the plot inevitably arouses in women . . . a sense of individual dignity and an urge for self-realization" (25). Huang identified, then, "a natural ambivalence on the part of the women writers" (29) toward the Cinderella story and in their literary responses to it. Refusing to consider the story's oppositions as absolute, women novelists embrace the story's individualizing thrust while struggling to feminize the traditional patriarchal narrative: "Women novelists intuitively develop the paradox of the existing Cinderella theme, explore it from a feminine or feminist angle, and stretch it to create a larger imaginative, as well as existential, space. . . . Trying to tailor their female experience and sensibility to the inherited narrative paradigm, they end up by retailoring the paradigm itself and parading their Otherness. And it is this entangled verbal wrestling that gives the texts by women their special power and vitality" (29).

More recently, in *Ventures into Childland: Victorians, Fairy Tales, and Femininity,* U. C. Knoepflmacher has moved beyond the response of women novelists to classical tales. Instead, he considers the construction of gender in the emerging tradition of the English literary fairy tale—particularly in the interplay among the works of John Ruskin, William Makepeace Thackeray, George MacDonald, Lewis Carroll, Jean Ingelow, Christina Rossetti, and Juliana Horatia Ewing. Knoepflmacher's study is important because it embraces both male *and* female writers, includes literature written for children, and discerns a vital connection between constructions of gender and constructions of childhood. The treatment of gender and generation breaks down largely along gender lines. Whereas the tales of Victorian men present sentimental visions of the feminine within a nostalgic childhood that inhibits growth, the tales by Victorian women strive to "repossess" femininity and resurrect "maternal authority" (427) in a world that allows children to mature. Huang had characterized nineteenth-century women novelists as naturally ambivalent about the fairy tale—prizing its idea of self-realization while reclaiming it from men—and Knoepflmacher's argument about the female authors of Victorian literary tales has a similar thrust. However, Knoepflmacher exposes ambivalence in male constructions of femininity too. Whereas the men he discusses question their own formulations and produce experimental gender constructs characterized by "instability, variety, and tentativeness" (427), the women writers engage in an intertextual dialogue driven by ideological uniformity. While Huang claimed "verbal wrestling" with the inherited narratives gave women's texts special power and vitality, Knoepflmacher notes that "the intertextual squabbles" (428) among Victorian fairy-tale authors often nourished the perception, at least, that the women's works were "nothing but pale imitations" (427) of the male-authored texts they contested. Still, as Knoepflmacher shows, the intertextual debate among male and female writers produced tales and formulations of gender that were "inventive and radical" on both sides and contributed to the complexity, variety, and vitality of the literary fairy tale.

REVISIONIST MYTHMAKING AND THE FEMALE SUBJECT

The fairy-tale texts produced by twentieth-century women writers—particularly those published since the advent of feminist fairy-tale criticism in 1970—have received extensive critical attention by feminist scholars.[30] If seventeenth- and eighteenth-century European women authors of literary tales were reclaiming their roles as "spinners" of tales, as Rowe suggested, and if nineteenth-century English women novelists were, to use Huang's metaphor, "retailoring" the classic fairy-tale narratives they had inherited, then late-twentieth-century feminist writers have been viewed not simply as spinners and seamstresses but as "thieves of language"—"female Prometheuses"—involved in a conscious feminist project of mythic proportion.[31]

Alluding to the feminist theory of Claudine Herrmann, Alicia Ostriker used the Promethean imagery of theft in her 1982 essay "The Thieves of Language: Women Poets and Revisionist Mythmaking." Ostriker was interested specifically in recent poetry by American women "in which the project of defining a female self has been a major endeavor" (70). According to Ostriker, the distinguishing characteristic of these poets is not a shared female language "but a vigorous and various invasion of the sanctuaries of existing language, the treasuries where our meanings for 'male' and 'female' are themselves preserved." The fairy tale, of course, constitutes one of these sanctuaries of cultural myth—the space where gender identity is constructed. In advancing "the idea that revisionist mythmaking in women's poetry may offer us one significant means of redefining ourselves and consequently our culture" (71), Ostriker would build in part on Anne Sexton's fairy-tale poems from *Transformations* (1971). Significantly, the most important of Ostriker's conclusions about women's revisionist mythmaking pertains to her analysis of the text's construction of subjective identity. The revisionist myths of female poets like Sexton do not simply enact feminist antiauthoritarianism, reevaluate the patriarchal values of patriarchal mythologies, and consciously assert their theft and revision of tradition; most significantly, they reject the model of the integrated subject that texts such as fairy tales hold up as normative.[32] Women's revisionist myths, Ostriker concluded, are characterized not by a single subject or voice but by "multiple intertwined voices"—that is, a multivocality of "divided voices evok[ing] divided selves" and "challeng[ing] the validity of the 'I,' of any 'I'" (88).

Revisionist mythmaking and the nature of the female subject in contemporary fairy-tale adaptations have been the focus of much feminist criticism. However, despite the importance of Ostriker's paradigmatic essay—which focused solely on poetry[33]—her metaphor of the female Prometheus has not been widely adopted by fairy-tale scholarship. Nancy A. Walker utilized the concept and echoed the metaphor in *Disobedient Writers,* a study of nineteenth- and twentieth-century women whose "revisionary, 'disobedient' narratives . . . expose or upset the paradigms of authority inherent in the texts they appropriate" (7), including fairy tales. Nonetheless, the metaphor that has dominated feminist investigations of the female subject in fairy-tale texts has been the magic mirror, which Gilbert and Gubar had used in their influential work of 1979. For Gilbert and Gubar, the mirror was the patriarchal tale itself, which holds up before women the male's projection of female identity. In 1983 Ellen Cronan Rose drew on this metaphor when she published "Through the Looking Glass: When Women Tell Fairy Tales," an examination of Sexton's *Transformations,* Olga Broumas's *Beginning with O* (1977), and Angela Carter's *The Bloody Chamber* (1979). Like Ostriker, Rose was intent on examining "what happens when a woman writer turns to the male cultural myths embedded in fairy tales." In terms of the essay's controlling metaphor, Rose wanted to understand what occurs when women shatter the fairy-tale mirror held up to them by a patriarchal society and undertake an independent quest for identity. However, because Rose relies on Bruno Bettelheim's view of fairy tales as "embryonic tales of *Bildung*" (211), the essay remains focused on what a woman can "discover about her natural, innate pattern of development when she rewrites a fairy tale 'so as to make it a more accurate mirror of female experience'" (211–12)[34]—that is, when she sees through patriarchy's distorted paradigm of socialization and individual development and uses her own experience to envision a model of female development. Consequently, Rose does not move beyond the notion of a singular development—albeit female development—that can be discerned in fairy tales retold by women. To be sure, that development includes discovery and acceptance of female sexuality, but in its most optimistic form it remains nonetheless a linear development toward a coherent self, a "healthy adult identity" (222).[35]

In *Postmodern Fairy Tales: Gender and Narrative Strategies* (1997), Cristina Bacchilega undertook a much more sophisticated reading of revisionist fairy tales by both male and female authors and filmmakers, including Donald Barthelme, Robert Coover, Angela Carter, Neil Jordan, Margaret Atwood, and Jane Campion.[36] Rose's interpretations of contemporary fairy-tale revisions were based on the problematic concept of "natural development" and on a simplistic view of "rewriting," whereby patriarchal views are merely reevaluated and revised. In contrast, Bacchilega's study denaturalized the concepts of both gender and narrative and articulated a much more complex view of postmodern revisions, one that acknowledges the multivocality of both the traditional texts and the revisions that entered into dialogue with them:

> Rereading is the magic key to rewriting: re-viewing a narrative . . . raises questions that demand revising its naturalized artifice. . . . [T]his rewriting need not be simply a stylistic or ideological updating to make the tale more appealing to late twentieth-century adult audiences. . . . [I]t involves substantive though diverse questioning of both narrative construction and assumptions about gender. Nor is such a narrative and ideological critique necessarily one-sided or negative. Postmodern revision is often two-fold, seeking to expose, make visible, the fairy tale's complicity with "exhausted" narrative and gender ideologies, and, by working from the fairy tales' multiple versions, seeking to expose, bring out, what the institutionalization of such tales for children has forgotten or left unexploited. This kind of rereading does more than interpret anew or shake the genre's ground rules. It listens for the many "voices" of fairy tales as well. (50)

Such a perspective enabled Bacchilega to conclude, for example, that Carter's revisions of "Little Red Riding Hood" engage a fairy-tale image that itself "explodes into voices," and that "Carter's self-conscious exploration of this multi-valency complicates any either/or, inside/outside construction of gendered identity, or of gendered narrative forms" (70).

Moreover, Bacchilega conceptualized the magic mirror as something more subtle than a static image that could be simply shattered—or replaced with a truer mirror—to reveal women's "real" or "natural" identity. Unlike Rose, who subscribed to the idea that women might create "a more accurate mirror" to reflect "her natural pattern of development," Bacchilega understood that mirrors—even those created by women—are neither natural objects nor unmediated reflections of what is natural: "As with all mirrors, . . . refraction and the shaping presence of a frame mediate the fairy tale's reflection. As it images our potential for transformation, the fairy tale refracts what we wish or fear to become. Human—and thus changeable—ideas, desires, and practices frame the tale's images. Further, if we see more of the mirror rather than its images, questions rather than answers emerge. Who is holding the mirror and whose desires does it represent and contain? Or, more pointedly, how is the fairy tale's magic produced narratively?" (28). Recognizing the magic mirror as the "controlling metaphor" (10) of the magic tale—and of its revisions—

Bacchilega's study foregrounded the artifice at work in constructing *and* deconstructing patriarchal images and in reconstructing alternative visions. In other words, Bacchilega invoked the metaphor of the mirror to reveal how postmodern fairy tales lay bare *the shaping* of human desire by history, ideology, and material conditions. As she observed in concluding her book: "The wonder of fairy tales, indeed, relies on the magic mirror which artfully reflects and frames desire. Overtly re-producing the workings of desire, postmodern wonders perform multiple tricks with that mirror to re-envision its images of *story* and *woman*" (146).

The mirror continues to act as an illuminating metaphor for feminist scholars investigating questions of female identity in the context of fairy-tale reception and production. For the volume *Mirror, Mirror on the Wall*, Kate Bernheimer asked women writers to reflect on "how fairy tales affected their thinking about emotion, the self, gender and culture," with results that confirm the diversity of female perceptions as well as "the very multiplicity contained within fairy tale literature itself" ([1998] xviii).[37] And in the present volume, Elizabeth Wanning Harries argues on the basis of women's autobiographical writings that fairy tales act as broken mirrors for women who use them to construct incoherent and unknowable images of themselves, thereby confirming the complex and problematic relation between the classic tales and constructions of female subjectivity.

GENDER AND THE PASSIVE RECEPTION OF FAIRY TALES

The tendency of scholarship to problematize the fairy tale's relation to gender construction and female subjectivity leads back to the question at the root of early feminist interest in the genre—namely, to what extent does the classic fairy tale engender the sociocultural behavior and attitudes of its female readers and listeners? To reprise Lieberman's words, what do we really know about "the meaning of fairy tales to women"? In 1993 I asserted that in fact we knew relatively little, that theorizing about the psychosocial effects of fairy tales had outdistanced empirical studies of their reception ("Response" 239–43). Certainly, the study of creative writers and filmmakers who use fairy tales as intertexts and engage in revisionist mythmaking illuminates the productive reception of fairy tales by women. But the genre's passive reception—the experience of fairy tale by recipients who do not make their responses public (Link 99)—has received far less attention.[38] This remains in part a methodological problem.

Although scholars can demonstrate how fairy tales have been intentionally manipulated to serve in the processes of socialization and constructing gender, we have a much more difficult time documenting personal
responses of recipients and the genre's actual influence on their attitudes
and behaviors.

In this field of inquiry, the works of Kay Stone have provided some
of the most useful results and methodological models. Based on interviews with both males and females of varying ages, Stone's studies have
confirmed the ambiguity of fairy-tale reception and the ambivalence of
the recipients. Her dissertation on "Romantic Heroines in Anglo-
American Folk and Popular Literature" and her frequently cited article
"Things Walt Disney Never Told Us" both appeared in 1975 and came
to grips with the early debate over the nature and reception of the traditional fairy-tale heroine. These initial studies confirmed that in North
America a woman's experience of fairy tales relied on Grimm and Disney,
whose tales did evince a paucity of active heroines. So the fact that many
of Stone's respondents admitted to being influenced by the passive heroines they had encountered seemed to substantiate the role played by the
classical fairy tale in promulgating gender stereotypes.

But already in that early work Stone noted that some women whom
she had interviewed about their childhood experience of fairy tales "performed a fascinating feat of selective memory by transforming relatively
passive heroines into active ones" ("Things" 49). In subsequent work
Stone explored this ambiguity, which attested ultimately not only to the
variability of interpretation but also to a woman's ongoing and potentially liberating engagement with fairy tales over the course of her lifetime. In 1985 she analyzed her interviews to determine whether fairy
tales were, as psychoanalysts suggested, "problem-solving" or, as many
feminists argued, "problem-creating" ("Misuses"). She confirmed the
feminist view that fairy tales generate problems of identity by presenting readers with unrealizable romantic myths. However, she also noted
that men and women respond differently to the idealized gender roles
they encounter[39] and that women in particular do not stop "struggling
with the problem of female roles as they are presented in fairy tales"
("Misuses" 142). Then, in a turn that reclaimed the fairy tale in the struggle to define the self, Stone concluded that "many females find in fairy
tales an echo of their own struggles to become human beings" (144). In
other words, while the romantic myths idealized in fairy tales may negatively affect a woman's self-perception, Stone's evidence shows that the
dissonance that eventually emerges, the struggle that ensues, can pro-

voke a critical and creative engagement: "If women remember fairy tales, consciously or unconsciously, they can reinterpret them as well. It is the possibility of such reinterpretation that gives hope that women can eventually free themselves from the bonds of fairy tale magic, magic that transforms positively at one age and negatively at another" (143). Stone's data and her analysis of it—as well as her more recent accounts of her own transformation as a female storyteller and feminist scholar, including her essay in this volume[40]—seem to support the more speculative thinking of Kolbenschlag and others that the classic tales can be both "parables of feminine socialization" *and* stories that ultimately call "women forth to an 'awakening.'"[41]

Stymied, perhaps, by the interdisciplinary expertise and methods required, scholars of fairy tales have not eagerly pursued the study of women's passive reception, despite Stone's intriguing results. Only more recently, in 1995, did a dissertation in clinical psychology and women's studies by Rita J. Comtois pick up precisely where Stone had begun. Stimulated by the same controversy in fairy-tale scholarship as Stone had been—the conflict between those interpretations asserting the fairy tale's psychological value and those criticizing its negative effect on socialization and gender role development—Comtois interviewed Caucasian women of diverse backgrounds about their perceptions of the fairy tale. Her study concluded that women perceive fairy tales not as helpful but as problematic because of the discrepancies between their own life circumstances and those described for the fairy-tale heroine. Comtois noted in particular the negative responses among those women whose personal lives and social views contradicted the fairy tale's traditional depiction of women. These findings would seem to bear out Stone's idea that fairy tales remain a source of cognitive dissonance for adult women and thus a potential locus for critical engagement and ongoing self-reflection, perhaps even more so in the 1990s, given the increased level of awareness concerning women's issues. So the question arises: To what extent have women's—and for that matter men's—responses to fairy tales changed in light of social changes and the feminist project to subvert and feminize the fairy-tale canon?

DIRECTIONS FOR FUTURE RESEARCH

Having described the principal trends and developments in feminist fairy-tale scholarship, I would like to conclude by suggesting certain lines of inquiry that future research could profitably pursue. Some recommendations follow from the significant work that has been done, others from the relative lack of research in important areas.

Reception Studies

Because the fairy tale's role in constructing gender roles has been repeatedly foregrounded for the past three decades, it is time for scholars to assess the impact of feminism and feminist criticism itself on the way contemporary readers experience fairy tales. On the one hand, this kind of assessment could involve the analysis of anthologies, textbooks, course syllabi, library holdings, and publication and sales figures. On the other hand, in order to study the passive reception of the fairy tale, we need to develop credible methods for eliciting and analyzing reliable data from recipients—including questionnaires, interviews, and other forms of data gathering and experimentation. Here the work of Stone, Comtois, and Wardetzky can provide preliminary models.[42]

Interdisciplinary Research

Serious reception studies require serious interdisciplinary methods, knowledge, and collaboration. However, the fairy tale's psychosocial impact is only one topic requiring interdisciplinary investigation. The textual research that has been done on the editorial history of the Grimms' fairy tales, for example, has proven itself to be indispensable in reaching informed conclusions about the representation of gender in these classic tales. Consequently, critics who would offer feminist interpretations of the Grimms' stories or who would use these texts to illustrate feminist theories must become familiar with the tools available to Grimm scholars and take the tales' textual and editorial history into account in order to produce credible readings. The fairy tale has been similarly shaped by social, cultural, and historical conditions. The most illuminating feminist readings are those that can interpret the fairy-tale text concretely in these contexts—for example, Zipes's interpretation of "Rumpelstiltskin" in light of the socioeconomic history of spinning ("Rumpelstiltskin and the Decline of Female Productivity"). Furthermore, because questions of gender in the fairy tale are also linked to the complex relation between the folktale and the literary fairy tale—between oral and print cultures— further cooperation among folklorists, anthropologists, and literary scholars is essential. Much of the best fairy-tale scholarship discussed here has benefited from such inter- and multidisciplinary perspectives, which need to become even more common.

Comparative, Multicultural, and Transnational Research

The focus in this survey has been on scholarship devoted to Germany, France, the United Kingdom, the United States, and Canada. The paucity of references to gender-related research in other cultural contexts suggests how focused the debate has been on Western society. When Lieberman, for example, spoke of the fairy tale's influence in "our culture" and in the lives of "most children," she was speaking at best of North America. The necessity of interpretations solidly grounded in textual and sociocultural history, however, does not diminish the importance of comparing variants from across cultures. To test generalizations and to theorize the role of gender in folktales and fairy tales, scholars need to expand the focus of feminist fairy-tale research beyond the Western European and Anglo-American tradition, and even within those traditions to investigate the fairy-tale intertexts in the work of minority writers and performers.[43] It is time for fairy-tale scholars, particularly in North America, to expand the scope of their research and bibliography.[44] The essays in this volume by Patricia Anne Odber de Baubeta, Fiona Mackintosh, Lee Haring, and Cristina Bacchilega demonstrate the scope of materials still to be studied and the productive questions still to be asked. Of course, pursuing such research can be daunting. As Kathleen Ragan has noted, her attempts to make *Fearless Girls, Wise Women, and Beloved Sisters* "a truly multicultural anthology" were frustrated by the largely British and American sources available to her and the American libraries she used (xxv). Removing these constraints and enabling genuinely comparative studies and anthologies will require cross-disciplinary conversations, linguistic retooling, and translations of both scholarship and primary texts. Fairy-tale scholars who have no access to the important comparative perspectives provided by the *Enzyklopädie des Märchens,* for example, conduct comparative, multicultural, and transnational research under a severe handicap (see Uther).

Recovery Work

The comparative studies and anthologies described above presuppose that the recovery of neglected fairy-tale texts by women will continue and that these texts will be made available in new editions and translations. Scholars like Blackwell and Jarvis are doing exemplary work within the field of

German literary history, and the work of the French *conteuses* has certainly enjoyed a critical renaissance. Nonetheless, similar projects to resurrect women's fairy tales need to be undertaken in other cultural contexts and with the work of disregarded women writers and storytellers. While recovery work may reflect an earlier phase of feminist scholarship, in fairy-tale studies it remains an urgent desideratum.

Interpretation and Close Reading

Because of the social, political, and educational uses to which classic fairy tales have been put, the temptation is strong to identify a didactic purpose and to abstract a moral—whether repressive or emancipatory—from the overall plot of a story. Readings of revisionist texts do not have immunity from this tendency and can just as easily gloss over ideological complexities and contradictions, despite advances in feminist and gender theory. However, understood as a locus of struggle over cultural values and individual desires, the fairy tale actually invites thematic instability and contradictory impulses. Interpretations of classical and revisionist texts must be attentive to that struggle—that is, to the ambivalence with which women writers and other creative artists often approach the genre. Revisionist mythmaking, after all, enacts ambivalence by simultaneously rejecting and embracing the fairy tale. A number of essays in this volume make just that point. So sociohistorical and comparative study needs to be based on textual interpretation that is sensitive not only to didacticism on one hand and subversion on the other but also to ambiguity, irony, and paradox. Close reading is required to come to grips with the complex cultural conversations, coding, and personal voices embedded in the language and structures of the fairy tale.

Film and Other Media

Studies of fairy tales by and about women have concentrated largely, but not exclusively, on oral storytelling and literature. More research needs to be devoted to other significant media, such as film, video, and television as well as art and illustration. The gender-related work that has been done in these areas needs to be expanded—not only with more individual interpretations and with work on media creations by women but also with comprehensive studies contributing in a broader way to the history of the fairy tale.[45] Research on film, video, and animation needs especially to look beyond the works of Disney and to track fairy-tale motifs and intertexts in both mainstream and independent filmmaking. For instance, the new release of fairy-tale films produced by DEFA, the state-sponsored production company of the former East Germany, should be of special interest to feminist fairy-tale scholars interested in the construction of gender in socialist societies. In addition, the Internet has become a source of scholarly and popular fairy-tale materials, which now require description, analysis, and evaluation.[46] In fact, scholars have yet to explore in any comprehensive way the role played by the popular press and electronic media in shaping, disseminating, and challenging the popular perception of fairy tales, especially in terms of gender.[47] In the essay concluding this volume, Cathy Lynn Preston helps us move in this direction by considering how the fairy tale continues to emerge in contemporary media and to redefine in unpredictable ways its relation to both genre and gender. Given the role of electronic and visual media as primary sites for the performance and transmission of fairy tales, work of this kind is critical for understanding the fairy tale's unstable generic identity and multivocality concerning gender in the contemporary world.

As I have sketched it, the agenda for feminist fairy-tale scholarship parallels in large measure the agenda for fairy-tale studies itself. After all, feminist scholarship and modern fairy-tale studies emerged in tandem during the early 1970s, with both asking important questions about sociocultural institutions and the process of socialization. In retrospect, the debate framed by Lurie and Lieberman about "fairy tale liberation" might seem somewhat simplistic in light of the knowledge generated subsequently by scholars about the complexities of editorial history and canonization, the fairy tale's problematic ambiguities, the female fairy-tale tradition, and the vagaries of fairy-tale reception. Nonetheless, the clash between Lurie and Lieberman thirty years ago initiated serious thinking about the role of women in the fairy tale and about the role of the fairy tale in women's studies. This intersection of feminism and fairy-tale studies created a powerful synergy that has dramatically and permanently affected the way fairy tales are produced, received, studied, and taught.

NOTES

1. Lurie, "Fairy Tale Liberation" 42. Lurie revised and reprinted this essay as "Folktale Liberation" in her 1990 book, *Don't Tell the Grown-Ups*. I am using the original essay from 1970.

2. Earlier discussions of feminist fairy-tale scholarship through approximately 1985 can be found in Stone, "Feminist Approaches," and in Zipes, *Don't Bet on the Prince*

1–36. See also McGlathery's brief discussions of feminist research on the Grimms' tales (*Grimms' Fairy Tales* 25–27, 51–53). A well-annotated bibliography of fairy-tale research and collections from the perspective of women's studies can be found in Helms. A good, up-to-date summary of feminism and fairy tales is provided by Jarvis, "Feminism." For a discussion of research on women and oral narrative in general, see Moser-Rath. DeGraff's partially annotated bibliography, which includes only thirteen items, is very brief and selective. An incomplete and unsympathetic summary of feminist scholarship on the Grimms' tales is found in the generally unreliable and problematic study of the Brothers Grimm by Kamenetsky (279–87).

3. Early critiques from the 1970s sometimes invoked the even earlier observation of Simone de Beauvoir, who wrote in *The Second Sex:* "Woman is the Sleeping Beauty, Cinderella, Snow White, she who receives and submits. In song and story the young man is seen departing adventurously in search of a woman; he slays the dragon, he battles giants; she is locked in a tower, a palace, a garden, a cave, she is chained to a rock, a captive, sound asleep: she waits" (qtd. in Kolbenschlag 1). Kay Stone notes that early feminist works of the 1950s and 1960s—like those of de Beauvoir and Betty Friedan—viewed the fairy tale "uncritically . . . as one of the many socializing forces that discouraged females from realizing their full human potential. Few writers from this period focused exclusively on the Märchen since it was only one of many sources of stereotyping. Thus critical descriptions tended to be vague and generalized" ("Feminist Approaches" 229). Christine Shojaei Kawan defends de Beauvoir against this depiction of her work and makes a strong case for viewing the French writer not just as an incidental precursor of feminist fairy-tale criticism but as an influential model, whose analysis of the fairy tale shaped the arguments of Lurie and Lieberman (see Shojaei Kawan 37–42).

4. Similarly, the men's movement, especially in its quasi-religious and religious manifestations, has given the fairy tale a role in defining and redefining manhood (Haase, "German Fairy Tales"). The most obvious example is, of course, Robert Bly's *Iron John,* which is roundly debunked by Zipes, "Spreading Myths."

5. In 1975 Kay Stone verified that more active heroines could be found in Anglo-American collections of folktales but that these collections were not as well known to readers as those of the Grimms (see Stone, "Romantic Heroines" and "Things").

6. Unless otherwise noted, translations of quotations and titles are mine throughout.

7. See Zipes, *Beauties* and *Victorian Fairy Tales,* and Auerbach and Knoepflmacher. These anthologies are part of the research that has been carried out to recover and make accessible the fairy tales of women writers, as discussed below in the section "Recovering the Female Fairy-Tale Tradition."

8. See Zipes, *Don't Bet on the Prince* and *The Outspoken Princess and the Gentle Knight.* I am focusing this survey on feminist fairy-tale scholarship, not on fairy-tale revisions by feminist writers. For a bibliographic overview of primary literature up to 1986, see Zipes, *Don't Bet on the Prince* 11–33; see also Zipes, *Fairy Tale as Myth* 138–61, and "The Struggle." Feminist criticism on contemporary revisionist fairy tales is discussed below in the section on "Revisionist Mythmaking and the Female Subject."

9. Maria Tatar's 1999 anthology, *The Classic Fairy Tales,* also groups folktales and fairy tales together by type; and in her introductory essays to each tale type, Tatar undertakes comparisons that frequently draw attention to representations of women. Alan Dundes, of course, has argued persuasively that responsible interpretations of fairy tales must take into account not simply a single text but the extant variants of that tale type: "It is never appropriate to analyze a folktale (or any other exemplar of a folklore genre) on the

basis of a single text" ("Interpreting" 18). In his own study of "Little Red Riding Hood," Dundes reviews Zipes's analysis and notes: "The problem for the folklorist . . . is that Zipes is really interested only in the particular impact of the Perrault and Grimm versions of AT 333 upon European society from the seventeenth century to the present" (40). Zipes responds to Dundes in the prologue to the second edition of *The Trials and Tribulations of Little Red Riding Hood* (1–15), where he faults Dundes for dehistoricizing the tale.

10. See, for example, Bürger, "Das Märchen und die Entwicklung," "Märchen und Sage," and "Die soziale Funktion"; and Gmelin. For attitudes toward the Grimms' tales in postwar Germany, see Zipes, "The Struggle" 167–74. On the ideological and textual reevaluation of the Grimms' work, in the 1970s and 1980s, see Haase, "Re-Viewing the Grimm Corpus" 127–29. See also the overview of Grimm scholarship in McGlathery, *Grimms' Fairy Tales*, especially 43–58.

11. See Rölleke, *Die älteste Märchensammlung* and "The 'Utterly Hessian' Fairy Tales by 'Old Marie.'" Rölleke's early essays on the editorial history of the Grimms' tales are collected in "*Nebeninschriften*" and "*Wo das Wünschen noch geholfen hat*." His scholarly edition of the Grimms' seventh edition of 1857, *Kinder- und Hausmärchen: Ausgabe letzter Hand,* was also to become important upon its publication in 1980.

12. See Tatar, "Beauties vs. Beasts," "Born Yesterday," and "From Nags to Witches." All of these are revised and reprinted in Tatar's *Hard Facts.*

13. For an excellent discussion of the relative merits of the research published by Zipes, Tatar, and Bottigheimer, see Blackwell, "The Many Names of Rumpelstiltskin."

14. Employing an eclectic and rather confusing array of approaches, Ingrid Spörk's *Studien zu ausgewählten Märchen der Brüder Grimm* also singled out the relationship between mother and daughter as a significant structure, leading Spörk to identify the "mother-märchen" as a fundamental type among the Grimms' classic tales. On mother-daughter relationships in the Grimms' tales, see also Barzilai; Liebs; Lundell, *Fairy Tale Mothers.* Cristina Bacchilega offers an excellent reading of gender in the Snow White tale, especially in light of previous scholarship and literary adaptations by Angela Carter and Robert Coover ("The Framing of 'Snow White'").

15. See also Hirsch.

16. The line in question occurs after the daughter has fled from home to avoid her father's incestuous plan and arrives in a great forest: "Da trug es sich zu, daß der König, dem dieser Wald gehörte, darin jagte" (Rölleke, *Kinder- und Hausmärchen* 1: 352). A significant ambiguity arises from the fact that the German clause "dem dieser Wald gehörte" ("to whom this forest belonged") can be taken as either a restrictive or nonrestrictive clause, leaving a question as to whether the king mentioned here, who later marries All Fur, is another king or, in fact, her father. English translators must decide on one of the two mutually exclusive options: either the restrictive clause implying a different king, as in the translation Gilbert uses, "Then it so happened that the King to whom this forest belonged, was hunting in it" (Hunt 328); or the nonrestrictive clause implying her father the king, "Then it so happened that the King, to whom this forest belonged, was hunting in it" (my revision of Hunt's translation).

17. On the editorial history of "All Fur," see Dollerup, Reventlow, and Hansen.

18. A very interesting and worthwhile German master's thesis by Susanne Ude-Koeller in 1985 investigates the changing image of the female in the Grimms' collection against the background of the brothers' lives and their relationship to women.

19. Without specifically approaching the tales from a feminist point of view, Lutz Röhrich also pointed to the diversity of feminine characters and character traits in the Grimms' collection.

20. See, for example, Hayley S. Thomas, who makes the case for a subversive female perspective in "The Worn-Out Dancing Shoes."

21. Such arguments had been made decades earlier (see, for example, Pancritius). As Jungblut noted, Johann Jakob Bachofen had discovered matriarchal rule and set it "in opposition to the Greco-Roman principle of patriarchy" long before feminist scholarship (500). Jungian scholars, of course, have also dealt with mythic representations of the feminine, in particular the archetype of the Great Mother, as well as other issues related to the "feminine." See, for example, Birkhäuser-Oeri; Pinkola Estés; von Franz; Grabinska; and Graham. In developing her idea that "myth, tale, and tragedy must be transformed by bold acts of reinterpretation in order to enter the experience of the emerging female self" (150), Heilbrun pointed to Erich Neumann's Jungian-oriented interpretation of "Amor and Psyche."

22. Göttner-Abendroth's feminist analysis of the fairy tale's matriarchal roots has been linked several times to August Nitschke's sociohistorical study, *Soziale Ordnungen im Spiegel der Märchen* (see Zipes, *Fairy Tales and the Art of Subversion* 43n29, and *Brothers Grimm* [1988] 137). Göttner-Abendroth, however, faults Nitschke's anthropological expertise and questions his readings of fairy tales because he confuses the various stages of matriarchy and patriarchy (Göttner-Abendroth, *Die Göttin und ihr Heros* 232–33n6).

23. See, however, the discussion below of Huang's book *Transforming the Cinderella Dream.* Huang acknowledges that Christianity has come to replace "pantheist" elements in Perrault's version of "Cinderella" (2–3), but she also notes "its puzzling textual complexity and ambiguity, which stand out strikingly in spite of the authorial effort to integrate the text with Christian morality" (4). In Huang's view, "Perrault's Cinderella, though apparently more passive than other of her sister cinder girls, does express her will and take the initiative at the crucial points of her life." Accordingly, she attributes a measure of power to Perrault's Cinderella, who "is active, rather than passive, and forges her own lot" (4).

24. See also Leblans on the male appropriation of the female's role and her storytelling art.

25. See also Radner.

26. See Blackwell, "Laying the Rod to Rest" and "Die verlorene Lehre"; Jarvis, "Literary Legerdemain," "Spare the Rod," "Trivial Pursuit," and "The Vanished Woman"; Morris-Keitel, "The Audience"; Royer; Runge; and Vogele. Important translations and editions of works by Bettina von Arnim, Gisela von Arnim, and Caroline Stahl have been produced by Jarvis (*Märchenbriefe, Das Leben,* "The Rose Cloud," and "The Wicked Sisters") and by Morris-Keitel ("Tale of the Lucky Purse").

27. See all the works by Chartrand, Cooper, Defrance, Duggan, M. Farrell, Hannon, Harries, Hoffmann, Marin, Seifert, R. Simpson, Thirard, Trost, G. Verdier, Welch, and Zuerner. Warner's *From the Beast to the Blonde* treats the *conteuses* throughout. Warner also published *Wonder Tales,* an anthology of French tales in translation. Zipes's anthology of French tales in translation, *Beauties, Beasts, and Enchantment,* stimulated increased interest among English-speaking readers. Important editions of d'Aulnoy's tales were published in France (*Contes* and *Contes de Madame d'Aulnoy*). See also the reprint of *Nouveau cabinet des fées.*

28. See, for example, Connell; Huang; Lappas; Rowe, "Fairy-born"; Rowen; and J. Simpson.

29. Huang, whose study focuses on "Cinderella," questions Gilbert and Gubar's application of "Snow White" as the "universal pattern" in women's literary works: "My suggestion is that the thriving tribe of apparently docile and virtuous girls is to a larger

degree patterned on Cinderella, who is much more active and complex than our cursory first impression indicates. We do not have to read every wicked mother figure . . . into an antipatriarchal subverter to discover a fermenting female consciousness and dynamic textual intricacies" (7).

30. Revisionist writers of fairy tales from before 1970 have been discussed in dissertations by Green (Eudora Welty and Truman Capote) and by Theodosiadou (Eudora Welty). Verity Smith notes that revisionist fairy-tale writing occurs as early as the 1930s in the protofeminist Latin American fiction of María Luisa Bombal and Dulce María Loynaz, who subvert cultural myths inhibiting female development.

31. Critics often invoke the mythic dimension as a criterion to assess the value of feminists' revisionist tales. In the case of Margaret Atwood, for example, Sharon Rose Wilson notes approvingly that "fairy-tale intertext in Atwood's work reverberates with mythic significance, giving us courage to face themes of sexual politics—in literature, society, and our lives" (*Margaret Atwood's Fairy-Tale Sexual Politics* xv). Scholars of children's literature in particular have debated the aesthetic and literary value of feminist revisions in similar terms. Anna E. Altmann, for example, has argued in "Parody and Poesis in Feminist Fairy Tales" that parodic rewritings are useful because they "can bring us to an awareness of the need for change" but that feminist fairy tales engaged in poesis create "new images that deepen our understanding of what it is to be human and to live in the world" (30). Cornelia Hoogland, on the other hand, has criticized feminist fairy tales because they do not permit open-ended, imaginative readings. See also MacDonald.

32. Not all traditional tales, of course, lead to the integration of the subject. Incoherent subjects are more common in the *Schwank*, or humorous folktale, than in the magic tale. The Grimms' tale of "Freddy and Katy," for example, depicts a woman's psychological disintegration and loss of self. See Metzger.

33. See von Bechtolsheim for a treatment of American women poets who adapted tales from Grimm. For a good discussion of the complexity of fairy-tale heroines and their re-creation in the German American poetry of Geertje Suhr, see Kellenter. For excellent anthologies of fairy-tale poetry, including that of many women, see Mieder, *Disenchantments* and *Mädchen, pfeif auf den Prinzen!*

34. Rose is quoting Gilbert and Gubar (220).

35. Rose does discern "a spectrum of female responses to patriarchal fairy tales ranging from the critical at one extreme [i.e., Sexton] to the creative, even visionary, at the other [i.e., Carter]" (212). This diversity of voices among women's revisionist fairy tales is significant but does not address the multivocality within specific texts. So whereas Ostriker finds the heroines "in women's revisionist mythology . . . more often fluid than solid" (88), Rose determines that revisionist tales, taken together, reflect a diversity of female responses and alternative visions.

36. On modern/postmodern fairy-tale revisions, see especially Harries, *Twice* 99–163; Roemer and Bacchilega; Walker; and Wilson, *Margaret Atwood's Fairy-Tale Sexual Politics*. See also the dissertations by D'Uva, Fullerton, Green, and Lappas. Myth and fairy tale in contemporary women's fiction from England, Ireland, and the United States is the subject of a book published in 2001 by Susan Sellars. While the study draws on feminist theory, it does not take into account significant works of feminist fairy-tale scholarship. For a good summary and critique of Sellars, see the review by Harries.

37. In her second edition of *Mirror, Mirror on the Wall* (2002), Bernheimer expanded the number of writers represented from twenty-four to twenty-eight. For additional personal reflections of this type, see also Atwood; Hyman; and Yolen, "Brothers Grimm."

38. For more on productive and passive reception, see Link 85–108.

39. Stone's findings concerning the gender-specific nature of fairy-tale response have been borne out in another context by the Kristin Wardetzky's studies of children in the former East Germany (*Märchen*; "Structure").

40. See Stone, "Burning Brightly" and *Burning Brightly*, in addition to her essay in the present book. See also Gordon for another storyteller's account of this reclamation.

41. Kolbenschlag 3, 4. Claudia Opitz, in considering "what women think about fairy tales," suggested that the Grimms' tales, despite their misogyny, can be salvaged by women through subversive, critical reinterpretation.

42. For other models of studying fairy-tale reception, not necessarily from a feminist point of view, see Haase, "Response" 239–43. See B. Davies on feminist rewrites and preschoolers.

43. See, for example, Peters.

44. See, for example, Apo; El-Shamy; Friedl, Beck, and Keddie; Glazer; Gobrecht; Hooker; Lichtenberger; Mills; Mooijman; and Rappoport. See also the individual essays on fairy tales in the following compendia devoted to gender and folklore more generally: Apo, Nenola, and Stark-Arola; Handoo and Bottigheimer; and Köhler-Zülch and Cardigos.

45. On film, see Bacchilega, *Postmodern Fairy Tales* 66–69, 129–38; Bell; Bernikow; Cooks, Orbe, and Bruess; DeGraff, "From Glass Slipper"; Dika; Haase, "Gold into Straw"; Hawkins; Hyams; Jeffords; Jenkins; Madison; Murphy; Sells; and Zipes, "Breaking the Disney Spell" and *Happily Ever After* 61–110. On art and illustration, see Bottigheimer, "Fairy Tale Illustrations" and "Iconographic Continuity"; Wilson, "Bluebeard's Forbidden Room" and *Margaret Atwood's Fairy-Tale Sexual Politics*; Zipes, "Epilogue"; and the catalog from an exhibit of women's art, *pixerinaWITCHERINA* (Blinderman and Porges), as well as the three essays included in it: Conger; Susina; and Tatar, "Invocations."

46. For just two of numerous examples, see Windling, "Ashes" and "Women."

47. See, for example, Conrad; Dégh, "Beauty"; Ganas; and Haase, "Television."

2
Fertility Control and the Birth of the Modern European Fairy-Tale Heroine
Ruth B. Bottigheimer

etween 1400 and 1700—that is, during most of the early modern period—girls' and women's literary roles in novella collections shifted dramatically in ways that set the stage for the emergence of the modern fairy-tale heroine. At the beginning of this period, novella heroines held their own against a world brimming with antagonists, using mother wit to sustain their social and sexual independence. Two centuries later, girls had become frightened damsels, their mothers had retreated into the shadows, and maids and sisters who had formerly lent their mistresses a helping hand had disappeared. Since Alice Clark's pathbreaking study of 1919, *The Working Life of Women in the Seventeenth Century*, historians and literary critics have more often than not attributed the kinds of changes I discuss here to the advent of capitalism. In turning to recent studies in women's history, sex, sexuality, and family formation to attempt to decipher this remarkable and complex literary phenomenon, this essay represents a fundamental departure in efforts to interpret the status of historical literary heroines.

By the nineteenth century, the most influential body of popular tales, the Grimms' collection, labeled a girl bad and a boy bold for one and the same deed (Bottigheimer, *Grimms' Bad Girls*). That curious polarization corresponded to social assumptions about gender in nineteenth-century Germany and in Western culture as a whole in that period. The Grimms' nineteenth-century German tales contrasted sharply with German tale collections of the sixteenth century, which—like French, English, and Italian medieval tale collections—show much less of the gender polarization that has become familiar in modern fairy tales. Sometimes, in fact, they manifest qualities opposite to modern ones.

In my exploration of the differences between medieval, early modern, and modern tale heroines, I will describe the way in which sex and sexuality have been thematized, and then I will analyze how that treatment changed radically in the early modern period. Finally, I will incorporate what has been learned about the historical conditions that shaped real women's experience in an effort to understand the relationship between historical women's diminishing control over their own fertility and the birth of the modern fairy-tale heroine.

No one is likely to argue against the proposition that sex and sexuality, gender and gender roles are of central social significance, "omnirelevant circumstances of action" that vary from one culture to another. This phrase comes from Candace West and Sarah Fenstermacher's 1993 article, "Power, Inequality, and the Accomplishment of Gender: An Ethnomethodological View," but the point has been repeatedly and persuasively argued over the last few decades.

People are born biologically female or male. Close acquaintances as well as complete strangers incorporate that aspect of a person's identity into their perception of individual people. The concept of gender is so deeply rooted in human awareness that the extent to which it conditions social expectations and emotional reactions long went largely unrecognized.

An ever-expanding number of publications, both scholarly and popular, on the subject of gender and gender roles has made these twin concepts so familiar a category that they need no footnote references. In this state of broad awareness, it is not necessary to provide technical definitions for "sex" and "gender," except to say that I subscribe to a conceptualization of sex as a biologically given and physically visible characteristic and gender as a socially constructed set of attributions that is recognizable as part of a highly elaborated semiotic system within communities.

The relationship between sex and gender has occupied men's (*sic*) minds for millennia. Misogynistic biblical commentators alluded to women's penchant—beginning with Eve—for talking and sinning. In the last three hundred years, dozens of tracts, more often than not Protestant, have been devoted to characterizations of the sexes and the hierarchically appropriate relationships between them. The pen, nearly always held by a male hand, inked directions for what women should and should not do and what constituted feminine and unfeminine behavior. Such were the descriptions, injunctions, and explanations of the German Georg Brandes in 1787, and they continued to characterize the genre into the twentieth century (Feyl).[1]

How and why the female sex was verbally constructed as it was, and in particular why that happened so decisively between 1400 and 1700, is a tantalizing subject. In my view, European tale collections contain hints about the changing nature of femaleness and maleness and contribute to explaining the enormous differences that exist between Europe's first modern fairy-tale heroines in sixteenth-century Italy and their descendants three and four centuries later.

Tale collections appeared again and again, decade after decade, century after century (Clements and Gibaldi), some reprinted for centuries. Contemporary readers find occasional familiar stories among late-medieval tales, but in two categories that at first glance appear unrelated—work and sexuality—readers far more often encounter alien attitudes and foreign practices. That is because, over time, fundamental alterations took place in the common understanding of the economic functions considered proper to women and to men at the same time that changes were taking place in defining the social categories of sex and sexuality.

Human physiology has determined that in heterosexual sexual relations, a man penetrates the body of his female partner.[2] Anatomical penetration was long understood as active and male, while being penetrated represented passivity and femaleness. That was both the customary and the normative vocabulary of sex and gender theory from 1700 onward, and it remained an unstated principle throughout most of the twentieth century (R. Davis 52, 744–45, 186). I would argue, however, that in historical terms it was not penetration in and of itself that defined passivity and femaleness but the real-world consequences of that penetration. It was and is the impregnating potential of genital penetration that made it logical to equate penetration with passivity and to further equate passivity with femaleness and femininity.

Before 1500, sex, sexuality, and sexual relations as they were portrayed in tale collections had little to do with familiar gender roles. Historians have detected a sea change in attitudes toward sex and sexuality before and after 1500 (Briggs 277–338), and gender roles in tale collections both reflect and incorporate that change. The transformations were geographically irregular, temporally slow but unidirectional. Since approximately 1700 it has been the consequences of sexual relations—that is, a nine-month pregnancy and concomitant personal and economic dependence (Leapley 35–39, 72)—that determined an entire set of female gender roles (Dawson 102–04). A literary aspect, indeed a consequence, of this historical development was the emergence of the modern fairy-tale heroine.

Let us for a moment try to think our way clear of the conditions of twentieth-century Western urban society. Remember that except for a tiny minority of Europe's population, conditions of daily life were grimly harsh in cities, towns, and country villages. Comforts such as heating or hot and cold running water, which we now achieve effortlessly by turning a knob or pressing a button, then required cutting, hauling, and chopping wood, removing ashes, hauling water, boiling it, and pouring it out. Most people lived at or near a subsistence level, which meant that either they worked for their bread or they died. Under conditions like these, it seems self-evident that a woman who wished her child to survive (and many did not!) had first to reorient her attention to that child (only the well-off farmed their children out to wet nurses) and then to comport herself in ways that would ensure the presence of a steady breadwinner and shelter provider. Single motherhood meant social ostracism, even banishment; widowhood for most meant extreme poverty.

Let us return to the female protagonists of tale collections. What if no baby resulted from sexual congress? What if not only did a nine-month pregnancy not follow repeated sexual intercourse, but no pregnancy at all occurred? What if pregnancy could be terminated? What if girls and women controlled their own fertility? What if a baby were born but could be spirited away?

It was around 1700 that modern attributions of femininity took firm shape and led to the construct of a femininity that until recently was regarded as normal. Increasingly, evidence indicates that four, five, and six hundred years ago women and men thought and acted in ways that differed profoundly from our assumptions and expectations about that past. Recent research suggests that until up to 1450, 1500, or 1550, with the help of knowledgeable midwives, women in much of Europe were able to control their own fertility to a very large extent (Riddle 117–19).[3] Subsequently that ability diminished; and after 1700 the principal forms of control left to women were either abstaining from sexual relations or spacing births by breastfeeding. In other words, Western European women gradually lost control over their own fertility between 1450 and 1700. Put another way, "fecundity . . . right up to the eighteenth century, ha[s] marked the contrast between married love and love outside marriage" (Ariès 133). That is, the physical consequences of sex, or "love," as Philippe Ariès gallantly expresses it, before or outside marriage could be controlled, and *were* controlled, by many females.

HISTORICAL FORCES AND CHANGES IN WOMEN'S STATUS

In the late Middle Ages options had existed for a woman to live and to support herself on her own. A woman of virtuous life and good habits, whether poor or rich, widowed or never married, might eschew (re)marriage and join a *béguinage*. Such communities had existed at least since the early twelfth century, originally housing unmarried daughters of urban patriciates. By the late twelfth century they sheltered impoverished women, and gradually they became places for gainful employment, with parallels to the male-centered guild system (Wehrli-Johns 16, 26–27). Widespread in Northern Europe, *béguinages* could be found in large numbers in the Rhenish towns of Mainz, Strasbourg, Basel, and Cologne, where there were well over a hundred (Schmitt), as well as farther east in Germany (in the towns of Hamburg, Bremen, and Lübeck), throughout the Low Countries, in France in Paris and in Marseilles, as well as in scores of French commercial centers in between, such as Cambrai, Lille, Douai, Arras, Béthune, and St. Omer (McDonnell 82–87, 270–77; Le Grand 10–13). In a *béguinage* a woman lived in complete safety and with relative freedom and personal independence, as satirical verses by Rutebeuf make clear (Le Grand 21). Many *béguinages* disappeared during the economic boom of the late 1400s, but the institution reappeared in the 1600s.

At the other end of the spectrum was the sex trade, another important avenue to economic independence. Even very small communities had officially protected places for fornication outside lawful wedlock. Often constructed at municipal expense and frequently managed by widows or wives of craftsmen, they were stocked with pâté, wine, and servants. All levels of male society frequented the *prostibulum publicum*, especially at their zenith between 1440 and 1490 (Rossiaud). In the Venice of Giovanfrancesco Straparola, the "courtesan was not a phenomenon on the margin of society, but one of its essential components . . . and constitute[d] an important stage in the diversification of social roles and of labour" (Olivieri 95–96). Moreover, for Venetian girls and women, "eroticism [was] one of the numerous instruments for the creation of capital" (96). But the "French evil," worsening economic conditions, and eventually effective strictures against birth control changed the availability and commodification of childless sex. Easy access to municipally and socially sanctioned sex outside marriage dwindled beginning in 1490–1500 in France, somewhat later in Venice. Such radical changes in long-accepted sexual practices must have been accompanied by equally

Illustration by Dora Polster for "The Juniper Tree" from *Deutsche Märchen gesammelt durch die Brüder Grimm,* ed. M. Thilo-Luyken (Ebenhausen bei München: Langewiesche-Brandt, 1916; n.p.: Brentano's, n.d.) 184.

radical changes in public perceptions of sex and sexuality. In any event, attitudes in popular tale collections changed, and the heroines of fairy tales embodied the result.

When Joan G. Kelly considered the question "Did Women Have a Renaissance?" she concluded that women had instead "experienced a contraction of social and personal options" (20). Consider, for example, that celebrations peculiar to women's lives were downplayed in the course of the 1500s, that women's participation in lay female confraternities came to be forbidden, that women were forbidden to travel unaccompanied, that many crafts in which women had previously predominated, such as the making of votive candles (Wiesner, "Nuns, Wives, and Mothers" 14, 20, 23) or brewing ale (Bennett, *Ale, Beer, and Brewsters* 77–78), diminished dramatically in the 1500s. In terms of choosing between marriage to man or God, the distribution of convents' property and the dispersal of female religious in Protestant-ruled areas eliminated a vital refuge for women. At the same time, trials and executions for witchcraft began their two-hundred-year reign of terror for marginal individuals, the majority of whom were women. Reading against the grain, we must conclude that women before 1500, or at least many women, had belonged to a confraternity, had been active in the money economy, or had lived in relative emotional and intellectual independence in a convent or *béguinage*.

Popular practice in the late Middle Ages had offered women opportunities to express themselves piously. The church itself provided female role models such as the Virgin Mary and her mother, Saint Anne, within the Holy Family, within the life and governance of convents, and among its pantheon of saints (Jacobsen 51). That, too, changed with Europe's successive religious reformations—Lutheran, Calvinist, and Catholic. In addition, "the Lutheran Reformation brought with it an emphasis on women's place in the home" in Germany (Karant-Nunn 40) as well as in the Nordic countries (Jacobsen 47).

In the fourteenth and fifteenth centuries some women had held membership in women's guilds in Paris and Cologne (Herlihy 162). Others had belonged to men's guilds as wives or as widows (Bennett and Kowaleski). A few hundred years later, however, the guild system excluded women almost entirely. After 1500 the generally lower capitalization of women's businesses worked even more to their disadvantage as markets became increasingly long-distance and capital-intensive. Inferior in status, women's businesses were also generally restricted to the home (Bennett, *Ale, Beer, and Brewsters* 145–57, esp. 146, 148). As Merry Wiesner puts it in a translation of sixteenth-century language, a "masterless" woman was increasingly denied the ability to support herself after the Reformation (Wiesner, *Working Women in Renaissance Germany* 1–2, 8, 149–85).

All of the tendencies outlined in the previous paragraph were exemplified in the brewing business. Women—single, widowed, or married— had dominated the craft in the Middle Ages, but with the widespread introduction of hopped beer, brewing was reorganized along large-scale lines of production and distribution in which single women and widows rarely found a place (Bennett, *Ale, Beer, and Brewsters* esp. 83; N. Davis 187–89).

Like brewing, cloth making had also slowly evolved from a medieval woman's craft, to a late-medieval joint enterprise in which both men and women participated, to an early modern male-dominated industry (Herlihy 185–86). Outside the domestic economy, it became increasingly difficult for women to become either equal economic partners or economic partners with equal rights with their fathers, sons, or brothers, or even independent entrepreneurs among their male peers (Shaw 248–53).

Sexual diseases, such as syphilis (Arrizabalaga, Henderson, and French 34–36, 123, 129–30; Foa 26–45), became public health problems and complicated the social and sexual congress of women and men from 1493 onward (Frascatoro [1547] in Rosenberg 370). These profound changes made themselves felt in the lives of girls and women and provided a force for shifts in girls' and women's gender roles.[4] The extent to which any individual girl or woman experienced these changes depended on her religion (Catholic or Protestant[5]), her family's social class (patrician, artisanal, or laboring), and her residence (urban or rural). The literary significance of the changes discussed here is that as plots caught up with daily life they also marked the beginning of radical change in the kinds of stories that were retailed to a popular readership.

Gender Roles and Pregnancy in Brief Narrative Texts

If we subject pre-1550 narrative texts to gender-based analysis, unanticipated gender roles emerge. Take, for example, the late-twelfth-century *Alexandreis,* in which Queen Talestris of the Amazons appears before Alexander the Great and asks him, an exemplary male, to impregnate her to produce a genetically superior heir (Townsend 137). The Middle English poem *Cleanness* celebrates and endorses heterosexual loveplay as God's own design (Keiser esp. 65–79). These treatments of sex and sexuality as a social trope differ recognizably from their guises between 1700 and 2000!

What underlay such fearless sexuality? Was the astonishing lack of progeny among famous lovers a fictional trope? Or did it correspond to couples' actual experience? If that is so, should we conclude that unauthorized intercourse led to few (or no) social or economic consequences? Is it possible that unlegitimated sexual congress might not bar a woman from providing her own sustenance or practicing a craft (Wiesner, *Working Women in Renaissance Germany*)? If this were the case, then a woman might comport herself physically and psychologically in a manner that contemporary women have relearned only in recent decades.

Where might we begin in a search for alternative gender roles, ones that preceded the formulation of the modern fairy-tale heroine? French fabliaux, a beloved and widespread narrative form in English, French, Italian, and German in the thirteenth and early fourteenth centuries (Noomen and van den Boogard; Montaiglon and Reynaud; Muscatine), illuminate old gender roles, even as we recognize that they thrived on fixed tropes. Fabliaux were brief versified stories whose content often centered on body parts and body functions (Burns 31–70; Nykrog 3–19). Were these stories funny because their language broke taboos (Beyer 101–04)? Was their delirious obscenity the result of "the inability of language to name the sexual relation" (Leupin 83)? Did the fabliau ironize (Gaunt) a publicly acknowledged and jolly sexuality (Muscatine 164), which Boccaccio (in 1353) more politely named "dulcet kisses and amorous embracements and delightsome couplings" (1: 290)? Or was the fabliau a burlesque form that parodied courtly epics (Nykrog)? Developed in the high Middle Ages around 1250, elements of fabliau content in both prose and verse remained a strong presence all over Western Europe for over four hundred years (Hines 250–76).

Fabliau content speaks volumes about social assumptions. In "The Fisherman on the Seine Bridge" the first sentence prepares listeners for the story's conclusion, as its French original baldly states:

> *Quar jone fame bien peüe*
> *Sovent voudroit estre foutue.*
> (Muscatine 121)

The verse says, rephrased, that it is precisely a well-brought-up young woman who often wants sexual relations. This arresting opener initiates a story about a young wife who takes a lover because her husband spends too much time fishing. The narrator not only accepts the wife's behavior but also presents it as a necessary response to domestic neglect. Other characters in the story similarly lay blame squarely on the husband, who, instead of fishing, should have been satisfying his wife.

In other fabliaux, authors state that sexual relations are as important as eating and drinking[6] and that they should give pleasure to both partners.[7] Many stories rest on an assumption evidently shared by the audience that women will sometimes take the initiative in lovemaking[8] and that furthermore it is self-evident that a woman will abandon a husband who has lost his male member, or the use of it, no matter how it has happened.[9]

For contemporary readers it is perhaps surprising that fabliaux, which speak so much of sexual intercourse, say so little about babies. It is a phenomenon that the noted American fabliau scholar Charles Muscatine commented on (Muscatine 131). Everything suggests that far from being limited to the French, this Gallic childlessness existed throughout the leisure reading public of Western Europe.

Additional examples may be necessary to persuade readers of the broad validity of my observations. One famous textual descendant of crude country fabliaux were Giovanni Boccaccio's refined urban stories. Within his *Decameron* plots, "utmost delight" recurs repeatedly between ardent Guismondas and willing Guiscardos, yet their unwed intercourse never produces pregnancy. One hilarious example is Pampinea's story (4.2) about the lecherous Brother Alberto:

> Berto della Massa, an Imola "man of lewd and corrupt life," had thieved, pimped, forged, and murdered until he had to flee his hometown. Making a new life in Venice as a Franciscan priest named "Brother Alberto da Imola," he lived in conspicuous austerity and wept loudly at the altar, his pious habits soon making him a trusted counselor throughout the city. As an old reprobate, he was a knowledgeable and indulgent confessor. Consequently he was most sought-after, in particular among women of the highest rank.
>
> One day he rebuked the beautiful but featherbrained Madonna Lisetta da Ca' Quirino, for her vainglory, but secretly he plotted how he might seduce her himself. Ten days later he came to her with the news that the Archangel Gabriel had beaten him mercilessly for disparaging her "celestial charms," had lamented that heaven with all its glories was as nothing since he'd seen her, and that he'd die for love unless he could visit her. This heavenly report immensely flattered the silly woman, who immediately agreed that the archangel should come the next day and that he should borrow a human body from Fra Alberto so that she too would have pleasure.

"Fra Alberto paid her many visits in angel-form, without suffering any
hindrance," until she boasted to a neighbor that her angelic lover performed
"better than my husband . . . and comes very often to lie with me." (My
paraphrase; quotations from Boccaccio 1: 305–11)

It is worth pausing to consider Madonna Lisetta's conduct and its
consequences. From the *Decameron's* telling, it is evident that she enjoyed
a long-term liaison with the "archangel" and that he was not her first lover.
Despite the length of their dalliance, neither babies, pregnancy, nor fear
of pregnancy spoiled their amorous pleasure.

With respect to its nonexistent pregnancies for unmarried lovers,
Brother Alberto's story is typical for the *Decameron*. In England Geoffrey
Chaucer's band of pilgrims similarly told one adulterous (but childless)
adventure after another in the *Canterbury Tales,* which was equally true of
fifteenth-century literary descendants such as *Cent nouvelles nouvelles* (ca.
1460).[10]

Faced with these fourteenth- and fifteenth-century stories from
England, France, and Italy, one has to inquire whether Western and
Southern European peoples knew something of which stalwart north-
erners had no inkling. It would appear, however, that people north of the
Alps were just as informed as were their neighbors to the south and west,
for adulterous German heroines enjoyed their lovers for long periods of
time without producing little Tristans or baby Isoldes, while Guinevere
and Eufame refused motherhood equally successfully in their liaisons
(McCracken 38, 43).[11] Cuckolded husbands and cheated wives exist
aplenty. An active female sexuality is thematized, but pregnant adulter-
esses do not exist.

I would like to note here that pregnancy plays a role in two genres.
It occasionally occurs in the punch lines of ultrabrief narratives, which
are, essentially, anecdotal jokes, and it also plays a part as a character indicator where ignorance of the potential consequences of sexual intercourse
marks one or another character as preternaturally stupid. In neither of
these cases, however, is there a narrative in the ordinary sense, nor can one
speak of a narrative "heroine" in either genre.[12]

It should come as no surprise that tales told in medieval collections
differ in content from theologians' tracts and priests' sermons. Historian
Jean-Louis Flandrin contested the easy assumption that church teachings
accurately reflected social practice in the Middle Ages. After all, tale collections were not sold among choir stalls in churches but in bookstalls in
marketplaces. Like all merchandise, they were salable only if they offered

stories that contemporaries wanted to read, stories that fit their life and their experience and made them laugh.

Story plots also had to make sense without interpolated explanations. The plots in these tale collections testify to sexual activity among women and men, both within and without a marital bond. Their stories include spirited heroines who marshal their friends and their wit to evade the consequences of the sexual transgressions, of which they are fully conscious.[13]

The period during which the modern fairy-tale heroine—and fictional heroines in general—took shape, 1500–1700, is now upon us. As befits a transitional period, sixteenth-century tale collections send mixed messages about sex, sexuality, and gender. Giovanfrancesco Straparola's magic tales (1550–1553) are exemplary for the genre, particularly since they exerted so lasting an influence on the form and content of European fairy tales.

Straparola took most of his tales from earlier Italian tale collections, and these retold stories maintain the old values concerning men, women, and sexuality. But a handful of his tales were new creations, the first modern European fairy tales (Bottigheimer, "Straparola's *Piacevoli notti*"). In examining these tales with an eye to the heroine's sexual exposure, pregnancy under other characters' control and the fear of such a pregnancy leap off the page. In the first story of the second night, the long-childless Queen Ersilia is impregnated by three mischievous fairies as she lies sleeping in the garden, and her mud-besmeared pigskinned son takes a wife who is pregnant soon after the wedding night. In another tale of magic, Pietro the Fool (3.1) impregnates a ten-year-old princess by simply wishing it. The unexpected sight of the fairy-tale hero Fortunio in her bedchamber (3.4) makes Princess Doralice shout in terror as if wild animals were tearing her to bits. "I have not come to despoil you of your honor," Fortunio assures her (*Facetious Nights* 1: 352). The lost honor that Princess Doralice fears is the same that Marmiato the miller suspects in another tale when he finds three abandoned babies (4.3) and concludes that "some noble lady had committed this crime to hide her shame." In the fifth story on the seventh day, three brothers rescue a princess but can't decide which of them should have her; *she*, apparently, has no choice in the matter. And finally, when Dionigi (8.5) materializes magically in Princess Violante's chamber, he lays his hand on her young, barely swelling breasts. She would have screamed in terror, but he covered her mouth. He had not come to shame her, he explains, and she begs him to respect her honor.

In Straparola's tales of rags to riches through magically made marriages, the balance has tipped in favor of men. Men act on women's bodies. In these stories women no longer scheme to admit men to their beds. Instead, boys and men intrude their bodies into the private space of terrified girls or women.

By the time Giambattista Basile's *Pentamerone* was published (2 vols., 1634–1636), *all* of his stories—not just a handful, as was the case with Straparola—reflect a changed world. His entire collection of stories hinges on a pregnancy in the frame tale that follows a girl's first sexual congress with her royal husband. What's more, Basile's stories describe further pregnancies—above all, unavoidable ones. For instance, the ninth story of the first day regales listeners with a dragon's heart that causes reproduction on every hand: the big bed gives birth to little beds, the great stool to little stools, and the cook, the queen, and her maid all give birth too! The first story of the second day, "Petrosinella," concerns a pregnant woman. The next story has a no-fault and no-fear sexual relationship between Nella and her princely lover, but the following one returns to involuntary pregnancy, when the narrator notes that "some students say that in Spain mares had been known to become pregnant by the wind" (*The Pentamerone* 1: 149).

Literary examples like those in Basile's *Pentamerone* continue into the eighteenth century, whose increasingly urbanized and bourgeois society Jürgen Habermas characterized as divided into two spheres. One was masculine, public, dominant, held to be rational and to exist on a higher intellectual plane; the other was feminine, reserved, natural, contained, and subservient, considered irrational and close to nature, which meant, among other things, exposed to the risk of pregnancy, whether wished for or not.

One of Germany's most famous eighteenth-century pregnancies was that of Goethe's Gretchen. Impregnated by Faust, she descends into madness, kills her child, and is herself executed for infanticide. And yet Renaissance Faust books have no pregnant Gretchens. Why, we must ask, was it only with Goethe's *Faust* that the heroine's belly swells? (One inevitably thinks here of the Grimms' earliest version of "Rapunzel" with its tightening bodice!)

In the nineteenth century the weaknesses ascribed to women also characterized the majority of German or German-influenced tale collections. That was above all the case with the Grimm collection, where "strong" or "speaking" women were defined as "wicked" (Bottigheimer, *Grimms' Bad Girls* 51–80). Most girls and women suffered, and suffered far more than male characters in similar tales. Condemned to years of silence, numerous heroines had to wait out their exile in a wilderness, their clothes slowly rotting away.

Why did the Grimms' girls suffer? In part it was because popular "knowledge" willed it so. The proverb was "Männer tun, Frauen leiden" (men act, women are acted upon).[14] The proverb meant that women are passive, but the word "leiden" allows a second meaning, "suffer," and it was more often than not understood in the latter sense and was justified from pulpit and podium as the just consequence of Eve's folly.

Once the majority of early modern women had lost control over their own fertility, old concepts took on a new force and came to dominate sexual discourse. Women in tale collections no longer survived by their wits and had sexual pleasure along the way. Instead, their bodies became vehicles of "honor" and "dishonor" (Ferrante; Cavallo and Cerutti).

Coincident with women's loss of fertility control was the emergence of the new literary genre, fairy tales. As the genre developed toward its modern form, two notable changes occurred in their plots. Men became a danger to women, and newly disempowered women cowered in fear. They had lost their wits, quite literally. The dangers that men posed sexually were generalized into a fairy-tale world in which women suffered wicked abductors, relentless captors, long captivity, and increasing isolation. In short, the modern fairy-tale heroine was born.

Notes

1. Rare exceptions among German Protestants were the enlightened and sympathetic views of Theodor Gottlieb von Hippel, *Über die Ehe* (1774) and *Über die bürgerliche Verbesserung der Weiber* (1792).

2. In all cultures, whether American, Moroccan, Mexican, or German, the penetrating partner is recognized as the "male" participant, the one penetrated as the female, a distinction that remains whether the sexual pair consists of a man and a woman, two men, or two women. See Trexler, as well as any number of studies of prison culture.

3. There is a remarkably widespread assumption that women did not or could not control their own fertility then or later. See, for example, Dawson 108, with reference to Baroness von Zay.

4. In a 1992 essay, "Medieval Women, Modern Women," Judith Bennett argues against the idea of major changes in women's work experience between 1350 and 1600. While acknowledging her thought, I want to stress that literary evidence corroborates the historical narrative of change in women's economic status in this period.

5. I do not consider the lives of Jewish girls and women in this context, because there is at present no evidence for their participation in the production or the consumption of secular tale collections in Italian, French, or German in the late medieval or early modern period.

6. "Bovin de Provins" (Muscatine 121).

7. "La Dame qui aveine demandoit" (Muscatine 122).

8. Muscatine 123.

9. "Le Pescheor seur Saine" (Muscatine 122).

10. One exception is a husband's murderous revenge on an illegitimate child in no. 19, "The Snow-Baby." Only in Matteo Bandello's *Novelle* (4 vols., 1554–1573) does abortion appear, and then reportedly at the request of Lady Ippolita Sanseverino. See Clements and Gibaldi 176–77.

11. It is important to take contraception and abortion seriously as a set of practices whose results are evident in literature. Otherwise one is led to needlessly recondite theorizing. McCracken, for example, understands the adulterous queen's not producing children as a "sterility" that McCracken characterizes as "sexual containment." She comments as follows: "The ritualized sexual containment of the queen is both an isolation and a penetration, simultaneously a closing of her body to other men and an opening to her husband" (52).

12. Etienne van de Walle discusses much the same primary material and also acknowledges the relevance of genre to the incidence of narrative pregnancy in an article that appeared in the winter of 2001. More recently, in 2003, Holly Tucker drew attention to the treatment of reproductive issues in the fairy tales written by women in early modern France.

13. Clements and Gibaldi tell a different story by citing an unidentified 1350 passage: "young ladies hold their amorous flames hidden" (Clements and Gibaldi 181). In my view this passage antedates and previews changes that will emerge two centuries later.

14. For one example among scores, see Ewald, where for boys religion meant "tun," for girls, "leiden" (1: 263).

3

On Fairy Tales, Subversion, and Ambiguity: Feminist Approaches to Seventeenth-Century *Contes de fées*

Lewis C. Seifert

*O*nce upon a time, critics who devoted themselves to the study of seventeenth- and eighteenth-century French literary fairy tales were condemned to the margins of scholarly life. *Contes de fées,* according to a widely held prejudice, belonged to that vast category of what was not infrequently called "sous-littérature" (subliterature). Associated with children's literature and popular culture, they could not possibly rival all the venerable literary masterpieces of the ancien régime. For much of the twentieth century, then, French fairy tales were caught in an infernal cycle of pedagogical and canonical exclusion: they could not be taken seriously because they were not taught; and they could not be taught because they were not taken seriously. Compounding the problem was the fact that modern editions of these tales—with the notable exception of Charles Perrault's *Contes*—were, until just a few years ago, virtually nonexistent.[1] So, even if critics had had enough curiosity to take a look for themselves, it would have been extraordinarily difficult for them to do so short of a trip to one of a handful of rare book libraries. For a long time it appeared as if the corpus of "classic" French literary fairy tales as a whole would remain an odd curiosity for footnotes or, at most, a paragraph or two in reference works,[2] in spite of several groundbreaking studies.[3]

But then a fairy godmother, of sorts, appeared on the scene. Feminist criticism, I would argue, is owed a great deal of the credit for the revival of interest in seventeenth-century French fairy tales. Scholarly books, articles, conference papers, undergraduate- and graduate-level courses (both inside and outside of French departments), preliminary exam lists, and dissertations all testify to a new awareness and appreciation of this corpus. In the space of just over a decade, at least some of

the *conteuses* (female fairy-tale writers)—Marie-Catherine d'Aulnoy,
Louise d'Auneuil, Catherine Bernard, Catherine Bédacier Durand,
Charlotte-Rose Caumont de La Force, Marie-Jeanne Lhéritier de
Villandon, and Henriette-Jule de Murat—and *conteurs* (male fairy-tale
writers)—Jean-Paul Bignon, François-Timoléon de Choisy, François de
la Mothe-Fénelon, Eustache Le Noble, Jean de Mailly, François-Au-
gustin de Moncrif, Paul-François Nodot, Jean de Préchac, and Charles
Perrault—have gained name recognition among scholars and students.
It is telling, though, that especially tales by several of the *conteuses* have
been the object of modern editions and increasingly numerous studies.[4]
Beginning in the 1980s, the footnotes and paragraphs devoted to the *contes de fées* caught the eye of North American critics eager to rediscover
and reexamine the place of women and women's writing in early modern France. Here was a (rare) literary movement dominated by women
writers (approximately two-thirds of the seventeenth-century *contes de
fées* were written by the *conteuses*). It was yet another example with which
to prove the often obscured truth that women had played a central role
in this period's literary field. Here, too, was a corpus that lent itself well
to the study of *écriture féminine* (construed as the textual specificity of
women's writing) and the practice of "reading in pairs," to use Nancy
Miller's influential term (48–49). The obvious (and regularly noted) differences between Perrault's better-known *Contes* and the lesser-known
tales by the *conteuses* and, further, the existence of several pairs of *contes
de fées* based on the same folkloric tale type by male and female writers
were perfect material for such critical enterprises. Now, at the beginning
of a new millennium, when feminism and feminist criticism are in crisis,[5] it is worth taking stock of what feminist approaches have contributed
to our understanding of seventeenth-century French fairy tales. As the
euphoria of those initial years of rediscovery wanes, the tale spun by feminist interpretations, it would seem, is far from coming to an end. But
what, exactly, has the proverbial fairy godmother done for us?

    Of course, fairy godmothers don't exist, or at least they don't have
magical powers. So, we should begin by acknowledging that feminist
approaches must share the credit for the new visibility of this corpus.
Feminist readings of the *contes de fées* would scarcely have been possible
were it not for the nitty-gritty biographical, bibliographical, and literary
historical work of Mary Elizabeth Storer (1928), Marc Soriano (1968),
Jacques Barchilon (1975), and Raymonde Robert (1982). Of these,
Robert's study is particularly noteworthy. Establishing a definitive bibliography for seventeenth- *and* eighteenth-century French fairy tales, pro-

posing a heuristic narratological definition of the genre, sorting out the extent and limits of its debt to popular folklore, uncovering its intertextual connections to other genres, and elaborating many of the tales' contextual meanings are but a few of the fundamental insights her rich study offers all students of this corpus. If Robert's is not an overtly feminist work, it nonetheless examines closely tales by both the *conteuses* and the *conteurs* that scholars before her had by and large dismissed out of hand.[6] *Le conte de fées littéraire* is also eloquent on the largely aristocratic class consciousness reflected in the corpus and metacommentaries on it. It is not difficult to see why Robert's study found a receptive audience among critics open to recovering neglected works by women and to pondering the textual construction of "class" alongside "gender." Both of these topics were high priorities in the late 1980s, and *Le conte de fées littéraire* lent itself readily to analyses along these lines. More generally, though, this study demonstrates that to judge the seventeenth- and eighteenth-century *contes de fées* according to aesthetic criteria derived from Perrault's *Contes* (e.g., concision, linearity, litotes, symmetry), as the vast majority of critics before her had done, was to miss not only their rationale but also their complexity. Robert provided a fruitful starting point for rediscovering these lesser-known texts, first among them those by the *conteuses*.

In the wake of Robert's but also Barchilon's French-language studies, one might have thought that France would have been host to a revival of interest in the *contes de fées*. In spite of recent scholarly and publication activity on the eastern side of the Atlantic,[7] the word "revival" seems far more apt for describing the situation in North America. Whatever the reasons for this disparity (a rigidly canonical and hierarchical conception of seventeenth-century literature is at least a partial explanation for the situation in France), more articles, dissertations, and books have been produced by North American than by French (or European) scholars. Among the North American studies, feminist approaches have clearly been dominant, and this has been true from the very beginning. Thus, a 1987 special session of the Modern Language Association, one of the first North American meetings devoted to the *contes de fées*, was titled "Women's Fairy Tales in Seventeenth-Century France."[8] And three years later, the 1990 meeting of the North American Society for Seventeenth-Century French Literature included a panel with the topic "Approaches to the Literary Fairy Tale: Questions of Gender and Genre," organized with the express intention "to celebrate the tricentennial of the literary fairy tale and women's preponderant contribution to the genre."[9] It is hardly insignificant that the inspiration for this session was the tricentennial of the publication of d'Aulnoy's *Histoire d'Hypolite, comte de Duglas* (1690), which included the first French fairy tale, referred to as "L'isle de la félicité" ("The Island of Happiness"). Celebrating, as it did, the *conteuse*, this session reminded scholars that a woman—and not Perrault—initiated the vogue of fairy-tale writing that lasted, roughly, from 1690 to 1715.

By the time these scholarly meetings were organized, feminist studies of the *contes de fées* were well under way, and what was to become their central "theme" had already been delineated. Beginning with Marcelle Maistre Welch's "La femme, le mariage et l'amour dans les contes de fées mondains" (1983), subversion in the women's fairy tales emerged as the crucial topic of investigation. Committed to exploring this subversion, numerous articles and a growing number of books have focused on thematic elements of the *conteuses'* corpus, among others: female characterization (Jasmin 368–89; Welch, "Le devenir de la jeune fille"), feminine desire and sexuality (M. Farrell, "Celebration"; Welch, "L'Eros féminin"), and motherhood and family relations (Hoffmann; Tucker). Other studies have sought to define this subversion through consideration of the sociohistorical context in which the *contes de fées* were produced (Jasmin; Mainil; Marin, "Pouvoir"; Raynard; Seifert, *"Les fées modernes"*; R. Simpson; Warner, *From the Beast;* Zuerner). Still others have approached subversion through the reception of the *conteuses* (Harries, *Twice;* G. Verdier, "Figures").

With different methodological concerns but the common aim of exploring subversion, feminist studies of the women's *contes de fées* tend to be divided into two different camps. Some critics emphasize especially the various manifestations of subversion in this corpus (e.g., Raynard; Warner, *From the Beast*; Welch). Others, however, are more circumspect and accentuate the limits of this subversion (e.g., M. Farrell, "Celebration"; Hoffmann). Upon reading these studies, then, one comes away with an ambiguous or ambivalent understanding. This lack of critical consensus can certainly be taken as a measure of the richness of the women's *contes de fées,* but it ultimately stems from opposing interpretations of key ambiguities within this corpus. To examine these ambiguities in some detail, I will turn to two books on this subject—Patricia Hannon's *Fabulous Identities* and my own *Fairy Tales, Sexuality, and Gender*—that are, to date, the most extended feminist readings of the *contes de fées.* Since they diverge on some central points, it is worth rehearsing their arguments.

In my *Fairy Tales, Sexuality, and Gender in France, 1690–1715: Nostalgic Utopias* (1996), I examine the meanings of the marvelous in not only the women's but also the men's *contes de fées* from this period. Through analyses of the marvelous—its theoretical underpinnings, its textual construction, its social functions, and its role in portraying sexuality, masculinity, and femininity—I argue that the genre assumes ambivalent desires. The subtitle conveys what I take to be the seemingly contradictory impulses at work in this corpus: nostalgia, an idealized vision of the past taken as a hope for the future, and the utopian impulse, which, following Ernst Bloch, I define as the envisioning of yet-to-be-articulated ideological and social orders. In my view, these desires—nostalgia and the utopian impulse—explain many of the central ambiguities both within the corpus as a whole and within individual tales. Thus, in the first part of the book, I interpret the production of seventeenth-century fairy tales on the one hand to be a reaffirmation of aristocratic values through, among other things, the recycling of many early-seventeenth-century literary *topoi*. On the other hand, this same corpus demonstrates the superiority of "modern" (versus ancient classical) *mondain* culture and the potential of women as writers. Ideological tensions are likewise apparent in the representations of sexuality and gender, which are examined in the second part of my study. The vast majority of the tales reaffirm the well-worn tenets of Western romantic love by insisting on the complementarity of male and female heterosexual desire and by featuring marriage closures (of the "happily ever after" variety). Yet some of these same tales exceed literary and ideological conventions with (thinly) veiled eroticism; and other tales cast doubt on the very myth of romantic love through "tragic" endings and cynical final morals. Similarly, heroes and fathers throughout the *contes de fées* afford an ambiguous portrait of masculinity. If many of them exemplify the mythic self-mastery and self-sufficiency of patriarchal masculinity, others fall short of these goals, some even becoming the object of metanarrative critique. Compared to masculinity, though, femininity is even more ambivalent. In the *contes de fées* (and a good many other fairy tales), the polarization of good and evil princesses, mothers, and fairies is at the epicenter of narrative attention and reiterates a host of misogynistic stereotypes. As I argue, however, such binarisms are blurred if not rejected in a number of tales by the *conteuses* that explore uncharted territories for motherhood, female authority, and feminine virtue. Notwithstanding the above-mentioned ambiguities of contextual meanings and representations of sexuality and gender, the vogue *as a whole*, I claim, demonstrates more of a propensity toward nostalgia than the utopian impulse.

Patricia Hannon's *Fabulous Identities: Women's Fairy Tales in Seventeenth-Century France* (1998) argues, basically, the opposite point. Influenced by recent historical scholarship that has emphasized the ambition and individualism of seventeenth-century French nobles, Hannon finds precisely these traits in the tales of Perrault and the *conteuses*. In her view, these writers created "experimental identities" (16) that reject nostalgia, social constraints, and, in the case of the *conteuses*, the conservative definitions of female "nature" in male-authored prescriptive literature of the period. Focusing first on Perrault, Hannon argues that the *Contes* "destabilize traditional forms of social stratification" (76) through misalliances of bourgeois and noble characters and the redistribution of power within the family unit. However, Hannon also finds that the treatment of women is fraught with ambiguity. If many of the *Contes* advocate the pursuit of female self-interest (e.g., the heroine at the end of "La barbe bleue"), there are also numerous instances of violence against female characters. Hannon concludes that Perrault's "feminism" is anything but unequivocal. By contrast, d'Aulnoy's metamorphosis tales offer a stridently unconventional vision of femininity. Hannon claims that shape shifting makes it possible for d'Aulnoy's heroines to explore identities that are at odds with the prevailing seventeenth-century ideology that enclosed women in the domestic sphere and associated them with the body and disorderly sexuality. Recognizing that these *contes* are not entirely free of ideological conflict, Hannon stresses that d'Aulnoy's metamorphosed heroines privilege personal interest over the courtly and the social. In her view, personal interest is likewise crucial to understanding the fairy-tale aesthetics and authorial identities of the *conteuses*. Through analysis of male- and female-authored *contes* based on the same tale type, Hannon notes the *conteuses'* predilection for *mise en abyme*, the play of self-reflection, which in her view explains the often noted (and criticized) amplifications of their tales and, further, "discourage[s] conventional ways of 'making sense' of the narrative" (160). *Fabulous Identities* closes with a reconsideration of the *conteuses'* authorial identities. Hannon acknowledges the collective identity they forged through writing fairy tales, but she argues that they used it to fashion individual personae that parallel the independently minded heroines of their tales. She concludes that "the *conteuses* elect the risk involved in the unpredictability of writing and publication over the nostalgia so long attributed to a presumably dejected aristocracy" (215).

Among the many points on which Hannon and I agree are the ideological ambiguities of the women's *contes de fées*, which she and I both go to great pains to establish. To be sure, our approaches to this question are different (albeit complementary, I would contend). Where, on the whole, Hannon refers at greater length to historical setting and the "moralist" literature on women in order to describe these ambiguities, I rely more heavily on literary historical antecedents and textual structure, as well as the notions of "nostalgia" and the "utopian impulse." Yet the final outcome, at least at certain moments in our books, is not dissimilar. Speaking of the *conteuses'* fairy-tale aesthetics, Hannon asserts that their "heroines are at once active and passive, their tales simultaneously conformist and subversive" (160). And in my introduction, I state that "[the seventeenth-century fairy tales] represent an unstable middle ground between . . . ideological surplus and anticipatory illumination on the one hand and nostalgia and distressed genres on the other" (18). These assertions notwithstanding, it seems to me that in the long run both of us tend to contradict the argument for the ideological ambiguity of the women's tales. As stated previously, I stress the nostalgic leanings of the fairy-tale vogue, especially in my afterword, whereas Hannon highlights the "outward thrust" (214), the forward-looking vision of the tales by Perrault and the *conteuses*. If part of this disagreement can be resolved by the fact that my own conclusion is based on a broader corpus of tales than Hannon's,[10] there are nonetheless several specific points for which we offer rather different accounts. In what follows I would like to consider three problems: the expression of personal autonomy, the question of nostalgia, and the interpretation of narrative closure in the tales. Examination of these questions demonstrates not only how complex the women's *contes de fées* are, but also how difficult it is to account for their ideological ambiguities.

Personal Expression and the "Self"

A long-standing commonplace holds that early modern Europe witnessed the emergence of the modern "self." Philosophical reflections, literary expressions, and social transformations all provide ample evidence for this notion. Recently, historians have given renewed attention to selfhood in early modern France through studies of private life (Ariès and Duby) and the aristocracy (Dewald; Mettam; Motley; J. Smith). Over and beyond the epistemological problems of any attempt to study the "self,"[11] there seems to be a general consensus that individualism was gaining ground in the early modern period and that social interaction (through class, family, and religious association, among other things) still

constrained individual identities more than in later periods.[12] The case
of early modern French aristocrats is especially noteworthy. Against the
backdrop of an increasingly centralized absolutist state, they continued
to wield considerable political and cultural power. More pertinent here,
though, is the fact that they increasingly took advantage of their privileged status to express individual ambitions, sometimes disregarding if
not contradicting the various forms of allegiance owed to lineage and
caste. Until recently, however, such signs of the aristocracy's vigor have
been overshadowed by a focus on its subjection to (and loss of *relative*
independence from) monarchical authority. Literary critics have been
particularly prone to assert this understanding of aristocratic identity,
especially because it would seem to explain the "pessimism" of so many
neoclassical French texts.

Interpretations of the late-seventeenth-century *contes de fées* hardly
escape this tendency. Almost all of the major studies of this corpus view
it, to some extent at least, as a compensatory reaction to the supposedly
gloomy atmosphere during the twilight years of Louis XIV's reign.[13] In
light of the recent historical work on aristocratic identity, such an interpretation, although not entirely invalid, is clearly insufficient. Even before
the advent of these new historiographical perspectives, Robert's study had
shown the limits of the "compensatory reaction" thesis. According to
Robert, these fairy tales uphold "the image of an exclusive social group
arrogantly turned in upon itself" (341; my translation). Expanding on this
insight, I argue that the late-seventeenth-century fairy-tale vogue offered
a means of defending the values of *mondain* (worldly) culture and, for
women writers, a venue for staking out positions within what Pierre
Bourdieu calls the "literary field." Hannon goes a step further to claim
that individual ambition and not group solidarity was the ultimate aim of
the women fairy-tale writers and that expression of this ambition is found
throughout their tales.

Hannon makes a compelling case for reinterpreting the motives
behind women's production of fairy tales—and indeed all literature—in
late-seventeenth-century France. Her analysis of the few available metacommentaries on fairy-tale writing by the *conteuses* brings into clearer focus
the individual authorial personae they hoped to attain via publication
(164–91). This is an important insight for the history of women's writing
in France because it suggests not only the vitality of aristocratic culture but
also, and especially, the possibility of a new individualistic writerly identity among elite women. However, it is less clear that the textual inscrip-

tion of this authorial self-consciousness—the *mise en abyme* of textual production—is a distinguishing trait of the women's fairy-tale aesthetic. To be sure, as Hannon convincingly demonstrates, many of d'Aulnoy's tales and selected others (Lhéritier's "Les enchantements de l'éloquence" ["The Enchantments of Eloquence"], for instance) do explicitly foreground the process of writing and/or authorial self-reference. Yet such is not the case for many other tales by the *conteuses,* and, more importantly, several of the male-authored fairy tales also feature similar *mises en abyme* (e.g., tales by Mailly, Perrault, and Preschac).[14] In the wake of Hannon's analyses, it is incontrovertible that the fairy-tale form often served as a means of self-expression and self-assertion, but I would argue that this was not a gendered phenomenon.

A related but separate question concerns the expression of individualism and personal autonomy in the plots and characters of the female-authored *contes de fées.* Hannon asserts that the *conteuses* reaffirm "prestigious class identity with a nod in the direction of the monarchy, all the while expressing the desire to become one's own authority figure" (208). Not only through their *mises en abyme* but especially through their heroines, Hannon argues, they privilege an emerging sense of personal autonomy that contradicts the social constraints inherent in the period's norms of sociability and civility (214–15). Several tales, especially those by d'Aulnoy, seem to support the validity of this claim.[15] Upon closer examination, however, these expressions of individualism and personal autonomy are perhaps more ambiguous than one might initially conclude. Not only are heroines more frequently than not reintegrated into a courtly society at the end of the tale (a question to which I return later), but also the values their adventures are intended to illustrate are often precisely those that are highlighted by sociability and civility. To cite but two examples, Blanche's celebrated *doux langage* (sweet language) in Lhéritier's "Les enchantements de l'éloquence" and Cendron's magnanimity at the end of d'Aulnoy's "Finette-Cendron" are qualities that certainly underscore the heroines' individuality. Through them, they stand out as exceptional women and gain social recognition as such. Yet these qualities are also very much prized by the prevailing codes of sociability and civility. There is (from our perspective) a paradox at work here: these heroines—and many others created by the *conteuses*—attain their identities as individuals by exemplifying par excellence values ordained to facilitate social interaction. These heroines are not, then, individualistic in the modern sense of rejecting entirely social norms and their accompanying constraints. Rather, if they often stand out as exceptional individuals who defy the definitions of femininity promoted by seventeenth-century French "moralists" and antifeminists, they do so, paradoxically, by embodying values enshrined by society at large. Affirming their individuality, they simultaneously reinforce their ties to the fairy-tale societies in which they exist.

Reading the female-authored *contes de fées* as expressions of a desire for personal autonomy raises yet a larger interpretive question. Fairy-tale characters are widely assumed to be, in Max Lüthi's words, "one dimensional" or lacking in psychological depth (4–10). In this perspective, they are archetypes more than individuals, and they are characterized by exterior traits more than by interiority. To be sure, such critical assumptions are hardly valid across the board. One has only to think of tales by Angela Carter or Robert Coover to realize that characterization in many contemporary fairy tales is anything but one-dimensional. But what of the seventeenth-century *contes de fées?* The answer, I would suggest, is far from straightforward. In her analyses of tales by the *conteuses,* Hannon argues that male, and especially female, protagonists experiment with alternative identities, yearn for personal authenticity, explore their private selves, and assert individual (as opposed to familial) interest. These are hardly traits one associates with "one-dimensionality," and one of the important byproducts of Hannon's work is to underscore the limits of this critical assumption when applied to the *conteuses'* characters. This said, not all of these characters display the same psychological depth. Interior dialogue and psychological description are featured regularly in d'Aulnoy's and Bernard's fairy tales, but much less so in those of the other *conteuses.* Here again, then, it is difficult to come to any quick conclusions about the gendered specificity of the female-authored *contes de fées.* The larger (and unresolved) question that deserves still further consideration is the extent to which even d'Aulnoy's and Bernard's characters exhibit a psychology comparable to that found in late-seventeenth-century French novels.[16] To measure the precise extent to which fairy-tale characters can be said to be "individualistic," it would be necessary to compare them to characters in novels of the period as well as characters in the Italian precursors that influenced the vogue. In fairy tales as in life, the "self" is always a fiction created by combining bits and pieces from preexisting models. The result is necessarily ambiguous—both distinct from its models and recognizable because of them. Seventeenth-century fairy-tale characters require further scrutiny before we can conclude just how much they affirm a private, individualistic self.

NOSTALGIA

It has become commonplace for critics to emphasize the nostalgic tendencies of the seventeenth-century *contes de fées*. These fairy tales have routinely been interpreted as an imaginary escape from an oppressive reality. More recently, critics have nuanced this assertion by highlighting the creative initiative found in the vogue. Thus, Robert, noting the reductive nature of Storer's "compensatory reaction" thesis, speaks of this corpus as a "mirror" that allowed an elite social group to revel in an idealized portrait of their milieu (16–18, 341). My own work on the *contes de fées* has attempted to further refine this observation by using Norbert Elias's concept of "aristocratic romanticism" and the allied notion of nostalgia. I contend, as I have already stated, that the vogue can be understood *in part* as a reworking of a mythic, idealized past (*Fairy Tales* 73–78). By invoking and reframing literary *topoi* of the past, seventeenth-century fairy-tale writers engaged in a decidedly *creative* enterprise, the result of which was, after all, a new genre. Like Robert's and my own work, Hannon's recognizes the creativity of the *conteuses* and the *conteurs*; however, she stresses (what she calls) the "forward-looking impulse" of Perrault's and the *conteuses'* tales. In her view, critics have overemphasized the "compensatory reaction" thesis, leading them to neglect the philosophically and socially innovative aspects of the *contes de fées* (193, 211). Instead, Hannon argues that the *conteuses*, especially, critique if not reject pastoral and chivalric *topoi* so as to explore "experimental identities" that, in particular, include unconventional roles for women.

Hannon's thesis that the *contes de fées* are more than nostalgic reiterations of the past is a convincing one. Indeed, in its broadest features it is precisely what Robert and I, among others, have argued. What is open for debate, though, is the extent and the ways in which nostalgia influences this corpus and more specifically its representation of femininity.

Now, it is hardly unusual to invoke nostalgia as an explanation for storytelling. Not only have critics repeatedly recognized its importance, but writers of all sorts of tales (and not just fairy tales) invoke nostalgia as a central motivation for tale spinning. Yet this obviously does *not* mean that tales by Chaucer, Boccaccio, Marguerite de Navarre, or fairy tales by Basile, Straparola, Perrault, or the Brothers Grimm (to name but a few authors who explicitly invoke nostalgia as a pretext for storytelling) are little more than reiterations of the past. Even if it could be claimed that nostalgia permeates to the core the tales of these writers—a claim that no one, I think, would make—it is important nonetheless to recognize that nostalgia does not simply "reiterate" the past. Rather, as Susan Stewart has shown, nostalgia should be understood as a three-part process: first, a rejection of the present as corrupted; second, an expression of desire for an idealized, mythic past; and third, a projection of this past into the future (x–xi). In its own way, then, nostalgia does indeed look to the future. It too is "forward looking." But of course the future conceived from a nostalgic perspective is one that projects a certain *vision* of the past. Even the most nostalgic storytelling is oriented toward the future. It is all the more important to recognize this forward-looking impulse because it helps to explain how many of the seventeenth-century *contes de fées* exceed nostalgia—that is, how they are more than nostalgic rewritings of past literary *topoi*. Both grounded in the past and oriented toward the future, nostalgia can be grafted onto forward-looking perspectives that are *not* rooted in the past (or that are what might be called the "utopian impulse"). Nostalgia is not incommensurable with future-oriented perspectives, and many of the *conteuses'* fairy tales can be read as both nostalgic and something more.

An example of how such ambiguity expresses itself in the *contes de fées* can be found in d'Aulnoy's "La Princesse Belle-Etoile et le Prince Chéri" ("Princess Belle-Etoile and Prince Cheri"). Ostensibly, this tale incorporates both pastoral and chivalric motifs. Pastoral settings recur throughout the tale: at the beginning, when an impoverished queen and her three daughters find solace in the countryside; later, when the queen's infant grandchildren, after being wrested from their parents at birth, are taken in by a kindhearted pirate couple; and finally, when these same children, as young adults, return to their parents' kingdom (unbeknownst to themselves or their parents) and are given a country estate away from court. Throughout this tale, each instance of pastoral setting is accompanied by explicit denunciations of court life (d'Aulnoy, *Contes* 2: 349, 356, 362–63). Critiques of the duplicity and corruption of courtiers are commonplace in the literature of seventeenth-century France and much of early modern Europe. Moreover, they are congruent with the pastoral ethos, which provides an imagined refuge from the constraints imposed on courtiers and, especially, an alternative means of (re)affirming aristocratic essence.

Such is certainly the case for the leading characters of this tale—Belle-Etoile; her brothers, Petit Soleil and Heureux; and their cousin Chéri—who embark on a quest to discover their true (aristocratic) identities once they learn the pirate couple are not their biological parents. Lacking the genealogical details provided the reader, they are nonetheless convinced of their innate nobility. Their adoptive parents had provided them with teachers befitting what they presumed to be their high social standing. On the open sea, after leaving the pirates, they are reassured by a siren that their vessel will lead them to their destiny. And when they unknowingly arrive at their father's kingdom, they are immediately received and treated as royals. Before they find the missing proof of their elevated social station, though, they must find dancing water, the singing apple, and the green bird that tells all. At first, the quests that ensue for these magical objects are of the most conventionally chivalric sort. Chéri braves mortal danger to bring his beloved Belle-Etoile the dancing water and the singing apple. But when he embarks on his mission to capture the green bird that tells all, he falls into a pit and is frozen. One after the other, Belle-Etoile's two brothers encounter a similar fate. It is at this point that the tale's nostalgic rendering of chivalric adventures gives way to the unconventional. Belle-Etoile herself takes on the role reserved for the chivalric hero by cross-dressing as a knight, capturing the green bird, and delivering her brothers and Chéri (as well as three hundred other knights). Nostalgia gives rise to something decidedly different—female chivalry— and yet it is not rejected. After all, Belle-Etoile dons the armor of the chivalric knight. She affirms an unconventional feminine identity in the trappings of a nostalgic topos.[17]

Like Belle-Etoile, the *conteuses* often (but not always) exploit nostalgia to unnostalgic ends—but without completely breaking away from nostalgia. It is precisely this sort of ambiguity that makes their fairy tales so difficult to interpret. But it is also precisely this sort of ambiguity that characterizes many liminal epistemic moments, not least of which is late-seventeenth- and early-eighteenth-century France. Looking to a different future with one proverbial foot in the past, the *conteuses* can accurately be said to reproduce nostalgia without being confined by it. To make this claim is most definitely not to deny the subversiveness of the "fabulous identities" they create but rather to resituate these within the complex cultural, ideological, and intertextual forces of their time. Writing at the origins of the genre, the *conteuses* show both the difficulty and the necessity of extricating the literary fairy tale from nostalgia. This, perhaps, is one of their most important legacies.

CLOSURES AND CONVENTIONS

Of all the features of the seventeenth-century *contes de fées*, their endings are undoubtedly the most difficult to interpret within a feminist perspective.

Quite plainly, there seems to be no critical consensus about how to under-stand them. Of course, those (relatively) few tales whose endings or morals defy what we now take to be stereotypically "fairy-tale-like" pres-ent no such problems. Bernard's "Riquet à la houppe" ("Riquet with the Tuft") and Murat's "Anguillette"—to name two striking examples that stridently reject marriage—lend themselves well to feminist commen-tary. But these are exceptions. As critics widely acknowledge, the over-whelming majority of the *conteuses'* stories end with a "happily ever after" marriage. For some critics (notably Hannon), these endings are ironic if not superfluous; at most they provide cover for the more subversive mes-sage of the narrative.[18] For others, they are transparent acknowledgments by the *conteuses* of the social and familial constraints on women of the period.[19] For others still (myself among them), they constitute an impor-tant limit to the ideological subversiveness of these *contes de fées* and a key element of their textual ambiguity.[20]

All of these critics would seem to agree that the marriage closure is conventional. Yet at the heart of their different interpretations are diverg-ing understandings of what a convention (or at least *this* convention) means. For those who view the marriage ending as ironic or superfluous, a convention is unoriginal and thus of limited significance.[21] For other critics, this type of closure is conventional in the sense that ideology is conventional. It is the reflection of a received truth and thus must be taken seriously. Given the frequency of the final marriage closure in the *con-teuses'* fairy tales and the opposing interpretations feminist critics have offered, a reconsideration of this convention is in order.

To speak of conventions in the seventeenth-century *contes de fées* raises complex problems, both historical and theoretical. From the per-spective of literary history, it is somewhat problematic to refer to the generic features such as the final marriage as conventions. To be sure, Straparola's and Basile's collections preceded the first "vogue" of *contes de fées* and offered models that were to a certain extent followed in late-seventeenth-century France. However, the *contes de fées* are not only different in style and tem-perament from their Italian antecedents, they also inaugurated many of the features that we now consider to be stereotypical of the fairy-tale form. Among other things, the (pseudo)chivalric adventures and marriage clo-sures are far more central to the *contes de fées* than they are to the earlier Italian tales, which purport to reproduce the "lowly" tone of popular tales. More to the point, the very form of the French fairy tale was in the process of being defined by the men and women who published *contes de fées* between 1690 and 1715. Thus, if one accepts the inaugural status of this corpus, it is contradictory—and anachronistic—to consider certain of its features as *fairy-tale* conventions. That a small subgroup of the *contes de fées* do not include the marriage ending highlights further still that the features of the genre were not entirely fixed. The *conteuses* did not simply reproduce a well-established literary convention; they deliberately chose the marriage closure for the majority of their tales.

If the *choice* of the marriage closure cannot be explained away as conventional, the marriage closure is of course itself conventional. Yet the fact that it is a stock feature of comedies and much prose fiction does not make it somehow superfluous. Nor does this fact by itself make the marriage closure ironic, as some critics have asserted.[22] For, as I would argue, it does indeed matter *how* the peripatetic fairy-tale adventures end, *how* (to use structuralist terminology) narrative equilibrium is reestablished. One way or another, the adventures of fairy-tale characters—narrative disequilibrium—must come to an end. In this sense, all narrative endings are entirely conventional. But this does not mean that they serve only a formal function. Like many literary endings, the conventionality of the marriage closure imposes, as Frank Kermode puts it, "order on chaos" (24). What this means is that, like many conventions, it offers the reassurance of familiarity.[23] Of course, such reassurance, borne of familiarity, requires allegiance to what I have called the myth of "heterosexual complementarity" (*Fairy Tales* 101–02, 108–09). The marriage ending is the illusion of a mutually satisfying relation between men and women in patriarchy. But what then of the *conteuses'* unconventional plots and characters, which often contest this illusion?

To take the marriage endings seriously is not to discount the subversiveness of many of the *conteuses'* plots and characters. This is not an "either/or" choice. What this means, rather, is that many of their *contes de fées* are fundamentally ambiguous or, more precisely, ambivalent. From our own vantage point, competing ideological visions coexist. Thus, for instance, Belle-Etoile's self-assertive, chivalric stance clears the way at the end of the tale for her marriage with Chéri (predestined as it were by the very title of the tale: "La Princesse Belle-Etoile et le Prince Chéri") and her reunion with her long-lost father and mother. It can certainly be argued that the heroine's heroic actions make it possible for her to marry the man of her own choosing, in short, to illustrate a vision of female selfhood inimical to conservative social commentators of the day. But through the "conventional" final marriage, this assertive female self, like many others created by the *conteuses,* is reintegrated into the family unit and courtly society. Belle-Etoile, like many other heroines, submits at least partially to patriarchal dominance. Perhaps this type of closure is an idyllic attempt to resolve the tensions between self and society, the "feminine" and the patriarchal, the unconventional and the conventional. Or perhaps this sort of ending invites readers to reflect on the uneasy coexistence of these opposing terms, both within this tale and in the nonfictional world beyond it. The marriage closure does not clearly privilege one or the other of these interpretive options, but it does create them. It does not close down but rather opens up interpretive possibilities. Recognizing the ambiguities of the marriage ending is an important step toward accounting for the historical and textual complexity of the fairy tales by the *conteuses*.

Feminist criticism has done much for the seventeenth-century *contes de fées*, especially those authored by women. Once confined to the periphery of literary and fairy-tale studies, this corpus is becoming increasingly prominent, and feminist critics deserve a good deal of the credit for this. But if feminist approaches are to continue to be productive, it is imperative that they take into consideration the ideological ambiguities of this corpus. Products of their time, seventeenth-century French fairy tales bear witness to a period of philosophical, political, and social ferment in which women writers played a prominent role. Products of their time, they also reveal the ambiguities of a period rife with ideological conflict and contradiction. Feminist readings must keep both of these horizons within their purview. In short, they must be attentive to the folkloric, historical, and literary intricacies of this corpus so as to avoid the ever-lurking dangers of anachronism and overdetermined interpretations. The desire to revalorize women's fairy tales should not cause us to exaggerate their subversion. But we should also not overemphasize the limits of this subversion. A delicate balance needs to be struck, a balance that responds to feminist objectives as well as to historical and textual ambiguities.

As we look forward to a new era of feminist fairy-tale studies, much about the seventeenth-century French fairy tale remains to be explored. Critics should continue to reflect on the "self," nostalgia, and the marriage closure. They should also investigate individual tales by both women and men, integrate the *contes de fées* into other literary and cultural forces of this period, explore the rewritings/adaptations of these tales in subsequent periods, and compare them with other periods and national traditions. From whatever viewpoint, it is doubtless time to adopt other approaches alongside the typological one, which attempts to describe the features of the entire corpus. Typologies have—and will continue to have—an important, even crucial role to play in the study of this and any genre. However, to the extent that typologies tend to set a particular genre apart from others, they can also have potentially negative consequences, including (but not limited to) overgeneralizations and, at worst, marginalization of a genre and its specialists. Perhaps part of the reason why it has been so difficult for feminist critics to account for the ambiguity of the *contes de fées* has been our desire to devise an all-encompassing typology. Different interpretive questions also need to be explored. And, in particular, feminist and other critical approaches need to enter into dialogue with each other. Doubtless, still more ambiguities will be uncovered. The net result, though, promises to be anything but ambiguous.

NOTES

1. Apart from a few early-twentieth-century anthologies (all of which are difficult to find), virtually none of the *contes de fées* were republished in modern French-language editions until the 1990s. Since 1978, scholars have been able to read most of the seventeenth-century fairy tales in the Slatkine facsimile of the eighteenth-century *Cabinet des fées* (*Nouveau cabinet des fées*). However, being extremely expensive, this edition is primarily a library resource, and for large research universities at that. Far more accessible editions have begun to appear (d'Aulnoy, *Contes* and *Contes de Madame d'Aulnoy*; d'Auneuil; and selected tales by other authors in Lemirre's edition of *Le cabinet des fées*), but most of this corpus is still readily available only through the Slatkine *Nouveau cabinet des fées*. It is a sign of differing critical, editorial, and readerly priorities on either side of the Atlantic that more of the seventeenth- and eighteenth-century *contes de fées* are available in English translation than in the French original. See Zipes, *Beauties;* Warner, *Wonder Tales.* It should be noted that in France considerable energy and resources are regularly expended on promoting Perrault's tales, which are available in several annotated paperback editions (Folio, Garnier, Garnier-Flammarion, Livre de Poche) and numerous editions for children.

2. For instance, Antoine Adam's standard five-volume *Histoire de la littérature française du XVIIe siècle* devotes only two pages to this corpus (5: 318–19). This treatment is typical of most similar literary histories.

3. Thus, for instance, Marc Soriano's *Les Contes de Perrault: Culture savante et traditions populaires* received wide attention upon its publication, both by literary scholars and historians of *mentalités.* If it sparked a revival of interest in Perrault, it was perhaps more influential as a methodological experiment in psychoanalytic criticism and a reconsideration of the relations between "popular" and literary traditions (see Velay-Vallantin, "Les *Contes*"). Soriano's study did little to rekindle interest in fairy tales written by Perrault's contemporaries.

4. On this count, d'Aulnoy, the most prolific writer of seventeenth-century fairy tales, takes the lead; but most of the other *conteuses* have seen republication or translations of individual tales and/or articles devoted specifically to them, as noted earlier. See, for example, note 1 above.

5. See Gubar for a penetrating overview of the history and the current crisis of feminist criticism.

6. Jacques Barchilon's *Le conte merveilleux*, published a few years before Robert's study, also examines a wide range of seventeenth- and eighteenth-century *contes de fées* and argues passionately for their reevaluation.

7. The 1990s saw two monographs on d'Aulnoy (Defrance; Thirard) and republications of tales by d'Aulnoy, d'Auneuil, and several other *conteuses* (see Lemirre). The proceedings of a conference devoted to the tercentenary of Perrault's *Contes* include several articles of interest to feminist critics (Perrot). More recently, Sophie Raynard has published a comprehensive study of the *conteuses* from 1690 to 1756, and both Nadine Jasmin and Jean Mainil have written major studies of d'Aulnoy. While all of these French-language studies address feminist questions, they consider other aspects as well. With the exception of Raynard, they are not primarily feminist in approach.

8. Organized by Faith Beasley (Dartmouth College) at the 1987 MLA Conference, San Francisco.

9. G. Verdier, "Approaches" 141. The ten papers presented at this session appear in the volume edited by Hilgar.

10. My book covers the entire corpus of French fairy tales, by both women and men, published between 1690 and 1715. Hannon's is restricted to the women's tales, although she also considers Perrault's *Contes* in chapter 2. She makes brief mention of six other male-authored tales (three of these by Perrault) in chapters 4 and 5.

11. In simplistic terms, two approaches can be discerned. Work by anthropologists and sociologists (such as Elias and Arditi) concentrate, understandably, on the social and cultural construction of the individual, whereas historical and literary studies have often tended to emphasize individuality.

12. Mettam and J. Smith, while demonstrating the ambition of seventeenth-century nobles, also show their social connectedness. Dewald recognizes a similar tension and argues "for seeing the connectedness of individualistic, liberal assumptions and the apparently more ancient, atavistic warrior culture that liberalism ultimately overthrew" (10). He also claims that "many French nobles combined qualities that we might suppose incompatible" (10).

13. Storer offers the most straightforward version of this interpretation. Barchilon (xiv) and Zipes (*Beauties* 4–12) concur.

14. In a suggestive analysis, Hannon herself shows just such a *mise en abyme* in Perrault's "Riquet à la houppe" ("Riquet with the Tuft"); see especially Hannon 140–41.

15. These include d'Aulnoy's metamorphosis tales: "La chatte blanche" ("The White Cat"), "L'oiseau bleu" ("The Blue Bird"), "Le pigeon et la colombe" ("The Pigeon and the Dove"), "Serpentin vert" ("The Green Serpent"), and "Le mouton" ("The Sheep"). See Hannon, ch. 3.

16. Jasmin studies the numerous intertexts that inform d'Aulnoy's *contes* and sheds much light on the psychological dimension of the *conteuses'* characters. Still, more work needs to be done on the comparative psychology of characters in fairy tales and novels of the period.

17. Belle-Etoile's cross-dressing is, of course, not without literary precedent. Fictive female warriors (such as Corinda in Tasso's *Jerusalem Delivered*) were well known to readers in seventeenth-century France and, in all likelihood, to d'Aulnoy herself. Belle-Etoile's cross-dressing is thus part of a long-standing literary tradition. However, female knights are far and away less frequent than male knights both in the *contes de fées* and romance, and Belle-Etoile's chivalry can still be considered unconventional.

18. Hannon states: "While it is true that the vast majority of all seventeenth-century fairy tales, men's as well as women's, conclude with the traditional marriage that

reintegrates the heroine into the kingdom from which she was temporarily exiled, one must qualify this closure as it relates to women's narratives: when the body of the text and that of the heroine are in constant flight, one can at best refer to a merely ironic closure" (162). Defrance makes a similar argument concerning d'Aulnoy's final morals, which she designates as a "subterfuge" (326–28); at the same time, she states that "[late-seventeenth-century] tales do not yet serve to openly unsettle the established order" (330; my translation).

19. This thesis has been advanced notably by Marcelle Maistre Welch ("Rébellion et résignation"), who analyzes d'Aulnoy and Murat.

20. See, among others, M. Farrell, "Celebration" 58; Hoffmann 294–95; Seifert, *Fairy Tales* 103–09. Jasmin emphasizes the interpretive ambiguity introduced by d'Aulnoy's *dénouements* and *moralités* (480–503).

21. Speaking of d'Aulnoy's tales, Hannon asserts: "As for the conventional marriage endings, the brief concluding lines that allude to marriage must be put in context with the 20–60 odd pages devoted to the transformative adventure" (120n104).

22. In a few *contes de fées* (e.g., d'Aulnoy's "La grenouille bienfaisante" ["The Beneficent Frog"]), the final moral explicitly undercuts the marriage closure, which then becomes ironic. However, to consider all of the *conteuses'* marriage closures as conventional and, thus, ironic is ultimately to posit authorial intention and to fall into the trap of overdetermined readings.

23. Speaking of the repetitious closures of sixteenth-century French *nouvelles* (novellas), Mortimer describes the "reassuring conventionality of [their] endings" (29; my translation).

4
German Fairy Tales: A User's Manual.
Translations of Six Frames and Fragments
by Romantic Women

Jeannine Blackwell

*F*airy tales were subjected to personalized readings long before readings by Sigmund Freud, C. G. Jung, Marie-Louise von Franz, Bruno Bettelheim, William J. Bennett, and Robert Bly. Our understanding of personal interpretations, however, is so imbued with the reception and history of the standard tales and their readings by modern psychologists and critics that it is difficult to envision what the tales might have meant to earlier readers. Since feminist reinterpretations of fairy tales have so altered how we look at the traditional tales, it is instructive to look at earlier women's use and interpretation of tales. Today's critics might ask how women, and specifically women writers, used fairy tales for their own purposes before and during the time of the Brothers Grimm. Did they rewrite fairy tales? Did they reshape them with an eye toward their emancipatory potential, recast them as autobiography, or dream out the passive plot of rescue by Prince Charming? Did they see themselves as assistants to their male counterparts—friends, lovers, or family members? Did they see fairy tales as part of an aesthetic agenda, a ground for introspection, or as a cash cow?

The answer to these seemingly contradictory queries is positive in every case. The earliest known female authors of German fairy tales— Catherine the Great, Philippine Gatterer Engelhard, Benedikte Naubert, Isabelle von Wallenrodt, Sophie Albrecht, Frederike Helene Unger, and Caroline Auguste Fischer—used the fairy tale for a dizzying number of purposes.[1] They sought to educate and instruct their children or grandchildren, as in the cases of Catherine and Engelhard; to profit from renewed interest in the French tales and to enhance revenues, as did Unger for the family publishing house; and to spin a great yarn in the traditions

73

of late *Empfindsamkeit* (Sentimentality) or adventure writing, as did Naubert and Wallenrodt. They also had aesthetic and cultural aims: Naubert rewrote many tales and legends highlighting positive female development, while Fischer and Wallenrodt stressed the exotic orient in many of their tales.

For this first generation of German women authors of fairy tales, the story was the heart of the narration, and there was authorial intervention in the tale only in fleeting comments about character morality, hints to the reader, and summation of the outcome. Already in these works, however, authors talk about their reasons for choosing and using the fantastic. One example is Benedikte Naubert, who explained in 1790 the difference between *Geschichte* (history) and *Sage* (legend) to her readers: "History, according to a writer of the past century, is a well-behaved matron too proud or too modest to display charms which cannot bear the serious scrutiny of truth; legend, on the other hand, is a saucy little thing eager to please, and doesn't care where she borrows her baubles as long as they do the trick. Since I confess openly to you, dear readers, that my guide is not the former, but the latter, supported underway by her sisters, then you know what to expect in these pages and which hours of the day you should spend reading them" (*Werner, Graf von Bernburg* 5). For at least some of the writers of the first generation, then, the fairy tale, with its sisters legend and myth, offered a fantastic flexibility unavailable in other genres and did not require the pretension to knowledge and verisimilitude of high poetry and history.

In the next generation of women writers, whose works come into view from 1800 to 1818, readers can see this flexibility displayed. Fairy tales are used for introspection, life narration, as metaphor for traumatic psychosocial events, social criticism, and—above all—entertainment. Five different types of crafted fairy tales by the writers Karoline von Wolzogen, Bettina von Arnim and Karoline von Günderrode, Ludowine von Haxthausen, and Annette von Droste-Hülshoff, as well as that productive writer "Anonymous," are presented here in their first English translation.

ANONYMOUS

In the first translation presented here, the anonymous author of the *Feen-Mährchen* (1801; *Fairy Tales*) assumes the pose of a castaway, possibly a girl, living on the fictional island of Dardesia with her family.[2] "She" describes how her aunt, an archetypal "schöne Seele" ("beautiful soul"), uses tales as a calming restorative in a stormy life of troubles. Her fictional tales, like her aunt's, are intended to restore composure for the beleaguered, to bring refreshment to overworked housewives, to bring back memories of past happy times. The idyllic setting of the foreword, no doubt a combination of the Dardanelles and Indonesia, conjures up the tall tales of shipwrecked survivors like Robinson Crusoe. Was anonymous a woman? The evidence is not clear, but her role model definitely was.

Foreword to *Feen-Mährchen* (1801)

Back in the happy years of my early youth when I was still growing up on the quiet island of Dardesia—as my days came and went in sunny enjoyment—my aged aunt was my dearest company. From her mouth flowed streams of wisdom; she had suffered much on the twisted paths of life, experienced much, and salvaged from all the storms which crashed in on her from every side a beautiful equanimity and a loving heart. She felt most at home in the circle of us children. Her heart was attached to these innocent creatures and she was never happier than when a large circle of them had gathered round. Then she was inexhaustible in telling her stories and set us back into the times of giants, fairies, witches and goblins. Since I liked hearing them more than anyone else, I soon became her favorite. I listened with passion and eagerness to the fairy tales; my brain absorbed them quickly, my imagination was fired, and my fantasy was given a particularly adventuresome turn. Often, after I had listened for hours to this wise old aunt, I hurried away from her into the darkest thickets surrounding our little island, and in the shadow of an oak threw myself into the gravel-bottomed river that cut through lush meadows and I thought about what I had heard. Then I was gripped with a peculiar feeling; I saw a dryad in every tree, an enchanted princess in every flower I did not recognize, and constantly floated in the higher realms. I destroyed whole scenes in the fairy tales I had heard and created new ones, or kept changing them until they took on the form of my glowing imagination and matched the idea which I had at that moment. Of course, I was not always happy with my own creations, but the time back then when I was creating fairy tales passed by very pleasantly. I assumed the character of my hero for a long time after that, and stuck with him, until another came along to replace him.

Since I was insatiable in listening, and since my aunt had such a treasure house of ancient lore, she fulfilled my numerous demands, and so much of it remained fast in my soul that the time thereafter with all its troubles and cares was never really able to displace the impressions of my early youth, and now, in the autumn of my life, it remains a pleasant memory to recall those happy hours and to hold in memory my aunt, long since released from all the storms of life. Because I am thoroughly convinced that today's young people need the miraculous as much as, and possibly even more than, youths of the previous century, I have sketched out, in my leisure hours for the enjoyment and entertainment of souls like my own, some of the fairy tales from those days which gave me such unspeakable joy as a child. It is true, the rough winds that often blew around me have made my senses duller, and I have painted the scenes in less glowing colors than I felt them as a child. But in these mature years one loses almost at every point the lovely bubble which separated the child from the big world and which the child can never burst soon enough. Alas, how many shadowy images did I seek after! How they all disappointed me! And how happily I set myself back into those years when a bright ball, a new fairy tale, and a piece of cake satisfied all my desires.

But these pages are not only for the young. Good and cheerful women and girls, page through this book! Perhaps some small scene will win your approval, and perhaps I can steal an hour from you with my pleasantries, just when you need such reading, after you are tired from household duties.

KAROLINE VON WOLZOGEN (1763–1847)

The fairy tale serves as a healthful tonic for yet another female protagonist, the eponymous heroine of Karoline von Wolzogen's *Agnes von Lilien* of 1798. Unbeknownst to Wolzogen's heroine, abducted and held prisoner, her true parental heritage among the nobility is about to come to light. She will also find love at the end of her story with the dashing yet serious older Sentimental hero, Nordheim. A first stage in her emergence into a new self is her recovery from the attack: a dream and then fairy tales. The prescription is literally just what the doctor ordered.

From *Agnes von Lilien* (1798)

I fell into a fever, then into listlessness and weakness, and finally I lost consciousness.

When I awoke from this condition, I was lying in a small bleakly dark room. A woman sat at my bed, a small shriveled-up figure; her facial features bore the signs of adverse circumstances and the friendliness she tried to assume made her face look totally like a mask. "For the last eight days," she told me, "you have lain here without giving a sign of consciousness. You have been entrusted to me, and I am very concerned about your condition."

"But where am I?" I asked again and she replied: "Do not trouble yourself; you are in a place where you will soon make a full recovery. The locale is lovely, the air is healthy, and people here consider it a pleasure to do everything for your amusement, as circumstances allow."

I heard from her voice that she was not a German, but French. The man had withdrawn. My youthful strength and my good constitution had overcome the power of the illness, my blood circulated calmly once again, and my memory gradually began to separate out the threads of real events from the confusion of dreams which my imagination created during my fever.

I felt the separation from my friends was cold and destructive. A feeling of the strange and unknown seized me with dread, wild pains cramped my breast, and my state threatened to return to that senseless stupor, when a good genius livened my youthful fantasy anew, and my heart was wonderfully strengthened in faith and hope.

An endearing young boy entered the room and brought a platter of beautiful fruit. I felt inmost joy at this sight; he seemed an intricate part of one of my recent dreams during the fever, and now that dream appeared as a lovely image in my soul again. All those dream figures presented themselves before me in unspeakably bright colors; only an airy veil of mist seemed to separate them from reality.

I sat next to Nordheim in a blooming garden. He held my hand earnestly and silently. A large many-colored bird of the most brilliant hues flew toward us and held a basket of splendid fruits in his beak. We both reached for the fruits, but the bird fluttered past us, laughed, and shouted to Nordheim: "Not yet, not so soon, for she loves you not!" Nordheim pulled his hand out of mine and rushed to leave, I threw myself weeping at his feet and wanted to hold him back, but in vain, he had disappeared. I searched for him, but everywhere I fled, a circle of hedges, most made of wild roses, hemmed me in and blocked my exit. When I slipped though a break in the hedge, then a new circle would form, growing up to a frightening height. Julius stood in the middle of such a circle and he wore the armor of an old knight, and over his breast was a broad white band covered with spots of blood. I approached, he tore the bandage open and from his breast there grew a flower of exquisite form and color which I had never seen before. "Pull the flower out of my breast," he said to me gravely, "and I will liberate you." I tried as hard as I could to break the flower, but in vain. He watched me, smiling, touched the rose hedge surrounding us with his sword, and a small footpath opened. Soon the undergrowth parted, and before us lay Nordheim's castle. Nordheim himself approached us congenially, and when the three of us stood close together, the same many-colored bird flew toward us. Slowly he descended over us, and as he touched the ground, we saw not him, but a handsome young boy. He held the same platter of fruit which the bird had first denied us, and all three of us rushed to embrace the boy.

The magic of these dream images had a lively effect on my spirit, like the presence of a friend, and the old woman was happy about the singular change that seeing this child brought about in me.

Shortly thereafter the doctor appeared, a middle-aged man with a gracious education and hearty demeanor. He approached me courteously and asked about my health with modest questions.

I soon noticed that the presence of the old woman hindered his free conversation with me; when she had to leave for a few moments, he said softly: "Above all your convalescence will be helped if you can stop worrying about your—I must admit—peculiar situation here. Take courage and just concern yourself with your convalescence." The old woman returned before I could answer, and the doctor's behavior toward her made me suppress any more questions in her presence.

When she tried to refer to my emotional state and told me to take courage, I answered coldly that I knew of nothing which I had done to earn a horrible fate, and thus did not fear encountering one.

The doctor replied that the whole cure depended on eliminating every gloomy idea, and occupying my thoughts with pleasant things. He suggested that the old lady read me light and graceful stories which would provide my fantasy with friendly images. "You have the key to the library," he said, "and there are plenty of books in the fairy tales section."

BETTINA VON ARNIM (1785–1859) AND KAROLINE VON GÜNDERRODE (1780–1806)

If the fairy tale around 1800 had positive medical effects on the female body, it was even stronger tonic, though sometimes deadly, for the soul. The therapeutic use of fairy tales as a means of working through emotional trauma has been analyzed before. Here is an early example from Bettina von Arnim, who uses the fairy-tale structure to tell her own childhood autobiography in the third person (*Frühlingskranz* 88–91). It is concerned primarily with the death of her mother, Maxmiliane von La Roche Brentano, who died quite young, possibly of complications from her many pregnancies. It is noteworthy that Bettina tells this tale to her brother, also a distant witness to this family tragedy. Although *Clemens Brentanos Frühlingskranz* (*Clemens Brentano's Spring Wreath*) was not published until 1844, the probable date of the original correspondence from which this narration was developed was around 1801 to 1803, when Bettina von Arnim was in her late teens.

Bettina von Arnim's Autobiographical Fairy Tale from
Clemens Brentanos Frühlingskranz (1844)

Today I decided to write my life story. I'll start it right here on this page.

Once upon a time there was a child who had many brothers and sisters—
a Lulu and a Meline, they were younger—and the others were much older. The
child counted up all her siblings and found that there were thirteen all told, and
Peter was the fourteenth and Therese and Marie fifteen and sixteen, and then
even more, but she hadn't known them, they had already died. There were at
least twenty of them, to be sure, possibly even more. Brother Peter died when
the child was three, but she still knew a lot about him. He had dark eyes sparkling
with blazing fire and the child often lost herself totally in them.

Brother Peter often carried the child up to a small turret on their house
where he fed all sorts of birds, doves, and a hen with her chicks, and the child
sat with him and made up fairy tales for him. Those were moments that glisten
still in splendor from her earliest childhood. And what other crazy things did
Peter do with the child? He was deformed, and too small for his age and at
Christmas he took her secretly to church, but since no one was to see her, he
took a big bearskin throw and held it in front of them; people could see neither
head nor hand of her, but only four feet tripping along and they wondered what
kind of shenanigans were afoot, walking across the street.

Once her dear brother built something in the garden, and led the child
out to see it. A small hill had been dug open, he moved a stone and a stream of
water spurted up for a time, and then stopped. You did all that out of love for
your little sister, my brother Peter! And she loved you very much. When she
woke up in the morning you were standing before her bed, and she laughed with
you before she had even opened her eyes. She learned to climb steps with you,
and she always came to you.

Once when it was quite late, the sun was just going down, and he stood
on a circular stair with the child; the last rays of the sun shining on his deathly
pale face; the child hugged him fiercely, he said in a faint whisper, "let go," and

fell down the stairs. The child had held his clothes and fell down with him. They carried Peter to his bed, and the child never saw her beloved brother again. When she asked, they always said Peter had been buried, and she didn't understand what that meant. Sometimes she yearned for her brother and sometimes she sat in her corner in the evenings where the lamplight didn't reach, and she saw that his dark eyes shone on her. Or was that only her imagination?

Her father loved her very much, possibly more than the other children, for he could not resist her sweet compliments. Whenever her mother wanted something from her father, she would send the child and plead for him to say yes, and she was never refused. In the afternoons when her father took a nap and no noise or disturbance was allowed, the child would run into the room, throw herself onto her slumbering father and snuggle up energetically, wrap herself up in his robe, and fall asleep on his breast. He would lean her softly to one side and give up his spot to her, and never tired of being patient. He showed her much tenderness and, when they went for a walk, he would wait for her to gather every flower in the meadow to make a big enough bouquet. There was no end to it, night fell, and since the giant bouquet was too large for her tiny hands, her father carried it for her.

Oh, how many lovely things happened back then and how much fun was woven into the rich carpet of life. All the bustle on the street! In the house across the way, an open hall where from May until autumn the neighbors camped out the whole day long, the children played with the puppy, the parrot on its perch shouted "rascal," we could have listened to it all day. How delighted we children were with the primroses that the milkmaid brought along every morning! Oh, the country life! The road to the open air! The kids shinnied down the city wall into the deep grass. And in Klapperfeld, where a ghost haunted the house and the mayor had set up a watch, with ten men inside and ten men outside, and the ghost had thrown them all to the ground at the stroke of midnight. Doctor Faust was said to have lived there, and the ghost had appeared only after he had died. And people told the wonders of Doctor Faust late into the night, how he could make trees bloom in winter, so fast that you could see the flowers bursting open.

The child did not sleep; she heard everything from her little bed, and was delighted by all the impossibilities.

Once there died in the city an elegant woman from far away who had lain long ill from an incurable malady. She often had the child brought to her bed and given her many playthings. A long, mournful requiem sounded through the streets of the city; men in black carried the casket. The elegant woman is to be buried, they said, and much could be said about her painful death!

What does that mean, death?

Buried! Not here anymore!

The child could not understand how someone could simply not be there anymore. And even today, she cannot believe in that: no longer being. No! Only like the butterfly that breaks out of its shroud into the floral essence, and does not think, but only staggers drunk with light, rushing with joy—that is the way the sick and the weary rise from their bodies up into a purer life of freedom. All this is what is invisible to our senses. Just as the lowly worm can ennoble and transform itself, so too can we mortals change.

The next spring comes, led gently by the hand by Death, and takes the loveliest of all mothers, the mother of that child, and leads her to the grave. There is desolation in the house, among her loved ones!

Tears of gratitude flow freely. The father cannot bear it; wherever he turns he must wring his hands, everyone shies from his grief and pain.

The children flee from him when he enters the room; only the little child stays and holds his hand and he lets her lead him away. In a dark room, barely lit by a street lamp, where he wails before the portrait of the mother, the child hugs him tightly and holds her hands over his mouth and says, don't cry so loud and sadly, Papa!

Blessed was the little head that rested on his breast, washed by his tears, and gave him solace.

Try to become as good as your mother, said the Italian father in his broken German.

Oh, dear Clemens, today I can no longer write on this story of my childhood. And what I have written here is really only nothing. And even still I am shaken and must weep for the dead. My light is ready to go out, it is so cold in the room—I feel only now that I've been writing with bare feet at my desk. When I write again, I will tell about the cloister school where we were taken soon after my mother's death. Adieu, Clemens; if we come to Frankfurt again, I'll go straight to the Carmelite Church and see how things are, it has been so long since I visited our parents and the children; if they could feel it, they would wonder at how their child has neglected them.

Your Bettine

The fairy tale helps Bettina von Arnim give voice to her grief, even if it does not still it; in the case of Karoline von Günderrode, the fairy tale does not help its creator to overcome her deadly melancholy. In her epistolary novels *Die Günderode* and *Goethes Briefwechsel mit einem Kinde* (*Goethe's Correspondence with a Child*), von Arnim reports about a certain fairy tale written by her close friend. No clue remains about this tale in Günderrode's oeuvre, although I surmise that it might be part of her reworkings of Ossian that appeared in 1804.[3] What is left is one letter from Günderrode to von Arnim and the possibly fictional, yet autobiographical trace of the tale in Bettina's epistolary novels. The letter from Günderrode to Bettina (probably from 1802) states: "I have been writing on the fairy tale diligently for some time. But I cannot now produce the light and colorful thing that was my first plan. Melancholy often overcomes me, and I don't seem to have power over these moods" (von Arnim, *Die Günderode* 526). Bettina incorporated this extant letter into her epistolary novel *Die Günderode* and had her own character in this work respond to Günderode: "Write about the fairy tale" (132). The fictionalized Günderode answers that she is not writing on it anymore (152).

Bettina took this tale and crafts it as a partial explanation of Günderode's suicide of 1806 in a letter to Goethe's mother (originally written around 1808), which in turn was incorporated into her novel *Goethe's Correspondence with a Child* (1835). She speaks of Günderode in a contemporary British translation that is probably her own ("Report on Günderode's Suicide"):

She made a journey to the Rheingau; from thence she wrote me a few lines, once or twice—I have lost them or else I would insert them here. Once she wrote as follows: "When one is alone upon the Rhine, one becomes quite melancholy; but in company, the most awful spots become just the most charming. I, however, like to greet alone the widespread purple sky of evening; then I invent a fairy tale as I wander on, which I will read to thee. I am every evening curious to know how it will proceed; sometimes it becomes quite awful and then rises to the surface."

When she returned and I wished to read the tale, she said: "It is become so mournful that I cannot read it; I dare not hear any more about it and cannot write any more on it—it makes me ill," and she took to her bed and stayed there several days; the dagger lay at her side; but I paid no attention to it, it lay right next to the night-lamp, when I came in.

LUDOWINE VON HAXTHAUSEN (1795–1872)

Fairy tales were also social and family events for Romantic tale gatherers, including the families Brentano, Droste-Hülshoff, Hassenpflug, Haxthausen, and Wild. The numerous young women in these families— some thirty all told, some aristocratic, some of the educated middle class— had a range of strategies in their tale telling. Some tales were taken from peasant sources or servants or retold from the store of tales told and retold by the families. Some of these were actually from book fairy tales that had submerged in oral culture, as is the case in the following translation of "Schöneblume, Fienetchen und Leiseöhrchen"—"Prettyflower, Finette, and Tiny Ears."

Ludowine von Haxthausen was the second-oldest daughter in this aristocratic family of sixteen children. A canoness in the town of Geseke, she established and ran an orphanage (1832–1848) in the former convent Brede bei Brakel. She later established an educational institute and nursing home at the family estate of Bökendorf. She also provided the Grimms with a large selection of stories.

"Prettyflower, Finette, and Tiny Ears" bears similarities to Mme d'Aulnoy's tale "Finette Cendron." A frantic combination of motifs from "Hansel and Gretel," the ogre in the skies of "Jack and the Beanstalk," "The Robber Bridegroom," and "Cinderella," this tale tells how a cruel (step)mother takes her three daughters into the forest, purportedly on a groom quest, but really to abandon them. On their quest to find a groom, they climb a magic oak tree and find an ogre's castle, where they survive by their wits. After defeating the ogres, they live peacefully, find treasures behind the locked golden doors, and go to the ball of the handsome prince, as the youngest, Tiny Ears, wins the competition for beauty and becomes queen.

The breathtaking pace of multiple narratives differs greatly from the Grimms' one-plot tales, which explains why this story remained part of the Grimm brothers' unpublished collection of tales. The Grimms wrote a simple statement on Ludowine von Haxthausen's contribution: "Some parts of Cinderella. Everything put together" ("Von Aschenputtel etwas. Im ganzen zusammengestellt" [*Märchen aus deutschen Landschaften* 173]). By presenting the three sisters sometimes as collaborators, sometimes as enemies, Haxthausen shows the complex relations of sisters. The narrative also shows the operation of the oral tradition, in which stories are embedded in or connected to other stories and imbue each other with new meanings in these changing contexts.

In this translation, I have retained the original shifting tenses of the narrative, which show the immediacy and breathlessness of the oral tradition: such tense-shifting occurs in texts by Bettina and Gisela von Arnim as well.

"Prettyflower, Finette, and Tiny Ears" (ca. 1818)

Once upon a time there was a King who had three daughters, Prettyflower, Finette, and Tiny Ears. They tolerated much abuse from their stepmother. One evening, when they were all in bed, the Queen waked her husband and poured so much evil into his ears about his children and finally said that she could not swallow one more day of their nuisance and would take them the next day into the deep forest. The King wanted to calm her down, but it did no good; she always had more to add, until he finally chose to hold his tongue.

Tiny Ears lay in her little bed and heard everything that her father and mother discussed and wept so bitterly that it would have made a stone weep. She stuck her blanket in her mouth so that her mother could not hear her sobbing and finally cried herself to sleep.

She wakes up again the next morning with this on her heart, and it is as if God had put it into her head that she should take refuge with her godmother—

who was an enchantress—and tell her all her woes. The godmother gave her a ball of yarn and said:

"If your mother takes you out into the forest, then you must fasten this thread to the lock and put the ball of yarn into your basket, and then you can find your way back home again, but you must not bring back your two sisters with you, or else they will cause you disaster."

When the afternoon comes, the Queen says: "Come children! I know a handsome young suitor; let me take you to him." The two eldest sisters are delighted and say: "Yes, we would love to, so we can get out sometime!" They rush off, dress in fine clothes, and put their finest gowns in a small basket they carry on their arms and talked of nothing else but how they would please this suitor.

When they were ready to leave, the King was very melancholy, especially because of Tiny Ears, for he loved her more than all the others, more than life itself. She stayed one blink of an eye longer and said farewell to the King once more. And then she tied the thread onto the lock so that the ball of yarn would unravel.

After they had wandered a long time in the great forest, and it is beginning to turn to dusk, the Queen says: "Let us sit down for a time on the ground, and I will delouse you." And while she was doing it, the three daughters fell asleep and the Queen creeps away. Tiny Ears was a light sleeper and woke up instantly. Nevertheless she did not follow her mother right away, but lay still until she could no longer see her. Then she stood up and followed the thread, winding it back into a ball as she went. The two other sisters woke up as well and followed her.

They come to the castle door, but it is shut tight and they had to keep knocking long enough to wake everyone inside. Then Tiny Ears begins to call: "Father, open up for us!" The King comes out and is filled with joy that he had his Tiny Ears again. The Queen was angry and was beside herself with vexation. Yet she let her daughters have two days respite. The third evening she again speaks with the King about taking them deeper into the forest the next day. But

arrives at the palace, the gentlemen immediately take her up and try on the silver shoe. And then the rejoicing and jubilation are great in the palace. The Prince regains his health and there is a joyful wedding. Tiny Ears's godmother, a witch, had sent the horse. And Tiny Ears becomes the Queen.

ANNETTE VON DROSTE-HÜLSHOFF (1797–1848)

While Anna and Ludowine von Haxthausen were among the most productive contributors to the Grimms' collecting efforts, not all of their female acquaintances delivered acceptable tale versions. With some frustration, scholars have noted that even though in 1811 or 1813 the Grimms already knew Annette von Droste-Hülshoff, cousin of the Haxthausens, there is little record of collaborative fairy-tale projects between her and the Grimms. The sole tale from her in their archive of transcribed tales—"König Einbein" ("King One-Leg")—shows an unhappy interaction in the physical evidence between scribe and informant.[4] On 28 July 1813, Wilhelm Grimm reported to his brother Jacob on his visit to Bökendorf, the country estate of the Haxthausens, landed aristocrats with six daughters and one son. He had sat, possibly in the garden house, with a gangly, unattractive sixteen-year-old girl, a cousin of the Haxthausens; she had dictated the story as he transcribed it. But the narrative had been apparently interrupted at three points. The first time (indicated by "POINT A" in the text), one word was crossed out: the gender of the possessive pronoun was changed on the word "virtue" from "her" to "his," so that the sentence read: "The girl who takes the ugliest man because of his [rather than her] virtue, she shall have this handsome sleeper." The second breakdown ("POINT B") comes when Grimm stops writing and Droste takes up the pen. According to Schulte-Kemminghausen, the manuscript shifts to her hand at this location. It continues in her hand until the words "back into the forest" ("POINT C"). Wilhelm Grimm continues writing until the name of the fairy Turbulentia (in German "die Fee Ungestüm"), at which point he ends the manuscript with a sentence fragment ("POINT D").

The story was never finished, but there were two additional comments written on the page. From Wilhelm Grimm, there is a note to his older brother about the tale, written at the bottom: "etc. I consider it to be contrived" ("usw. Ich halte es für gemacht"). His comment was confirmed in the same words in Jacob's hand at the top of the manuscript.

This apparently refers to similarities to Mme d'Aulnoy's tale and characters and is the reason such a tale was not accepted into the printed collection.

"King One-Leg" (22–26 July 1813)

A king had two daughters, he was named King Silkspinner because he was always working with his silkworms. The queen was so angry about this that she withdrew to a country estate with her two daughters. The youngest was happy with their quiet life, the oldest not, and that is why she abused the oldest daughter. The youngest was good and modest and when there were serenades she always shut the window. Once the youngest was out walking and [thinking] to herself, and suddenly she heard a loud scream, as she looked down she saw that she had stepped on the head of a snake. The snake began to talk and said: Princess, you almost kicked me to death, but I will forgive you if you will hang me up again on that branch. The prin. was amazed that the snake could talk, but picked it up and got out of there fast. The same day the other princess was also out walking, came to a large tree, tried to lean on it, and there fell a golden key from its bark. She looked at the bark and the key, touched them together and in that moment the tree opened up and she saw a large marble staircase, up above it was bright, but as she went down it got darker; she came to a door and when she opened it, she came into a large room that was lit not with lamps but with diamonds. There stood also a bed, and on it lay a prince who slept deeply, she went further and next to bed was a tablet on which was written: The girl who takes the ugliest male because of his [POINT A] ["her" scratched out] virtue, she shall have this handsome sleeper. At that, she turned at that back to the bed, and in that moment there came a number of large spiders who wove a thick curtain; she wanted to tear it down, but it wasn't possible. She went back and climbed up again, when she was out of the tree, the tree closed up by itself and she could find no trace. [POINT B] [Droste's hand] She kept on going, and when she stepped out of the forest, she saw her sister who was carrying a large diamond in her hand that she had found on the banks of the lake. As soon as the oldest princess saw the diamond, she wanted to rip it from her sister's hands, when suddenly someone tapped her on the shoulder from behind, she looked around and saw a man with only one leg and red hair and small green eyes and his nose and mouth looked almost like a pig's snout. The princesses ran away full of terror, yet the oldest soon reconsidered and thought that this might be the ugliest male, who she was supposed to love for his good qualities, so she stopped, she couldn't force herself at the beginning to look at him, he came closer, and she asked in a friendly way what he wanted and why he had tapped her on the shoulder. "I have often seen your bad behavior toward your good sister and wanted to give you a little reminder that you should be nicer next time.

"You are listening to me with an open heart, and that is why I am called Openheart," then he turned around and limped [POINT C] [Grimm's hand] back into the forest. The princess went back on the following day, [to see] whether she could find the prince again, he was actually there again. She asked him why he didn't come to the castle. He didn't want to and said he [preferred] to live in solitude. The other girl went there and wanted to convince him. Then she went home and told her sister, who thought, she has invited him to the court only to make fun of him. The other girl went into the forest and advised him not to come to the court. He said, "I see your good intentions," he didn't want to go to the court, and she should keep the ring she had found, it could be of help to her, it was meant to be hers. On the way home she saw a ball rolling on the ground, it sprang up and a blue mist rose up, and from it there formed a wagon with dragons. And there formed a fairy who said, I am the fairy Turbulentia [POINT D]

etc. I consider it to be contrived.

What, if anything, do these fairy tale fragments and frames have in common? What do they tell us about German Romantic women writers? What narrative elements do they share? Why aren't they true, finished fairy tales? We can speculate on a few notions, based on these tales and current research.

First, the tales framed by the foreword of *Feen-Mährchen,* as well as the tales by Haxthausen and Droste-Hülshoff, show us the deep influence of fairy tales by Mme d'Aulnoy and the French tales in general on a whole generation of women readers and writers in the late eighteenth and early nineteenth centuries. The changes that these authors make in the tales indicate a kind of oral reception or presentation in narration (drastic simplification of plot; combination of several tales; shifts back and forth in tenses to heighten dramatic effect). Do these markers of orality mean that the German women writers and tale tellers heard the tales told, by mothers or other relatives, friends, servants, or country folk? We cannot know this except from anecdotal evidence, but those anecdotes are numerous. Let three examples suffice. The anonymous author of *Feen-Mährchen* presented among her tales "Der Riesenwald" ("The Giant Forest"), a rollicking version of Mme d'Aulnoy's "The Bee and the Orange Tree" in which the heroine Aurora not only performs the magic transformations but also takes back the sympathetic ogress to be the nanny of her own children. Second, Schulte-Kemminghausen maintains that Droste-Hülshoff's tale of "King One-Leg" was transmitted via a French governess to Westphalia during the Napoleonic occupation (Droste-Hülshoff and Grimm 45). A third example is from the Grimm archive: In 1792–1793, Maxmiliane von La Roche Brentano (Bettina von Arnim's mother) told her five- or six-year-old daughter, Ludovica Brentano Jordis, a much shorter, juvenalized variant of Mme d'Aulnoy's "The Beneficent Frog" (Zipes, *Beauties* 545–63); Jordis passed it on to the Grimms on 31 May 1814. They included it in one edition of the tales but later removed it. The number of French-influenced tales by women is substantial, and it is unfortunate for later research that these tales did not have adequate acceptance in the changed political atmosphere of the years of French occupation and thereafter. With little positive reception and republication, these tales died on the vine.

Framed tales and "bunched" collections of tales are characteristic of German women writers and fictionally female surrogate authors in this period. Writings by Naubert, Sophie Tieck Bernhardi von Knorring, and Caroline Auguste Fischer combine and overlap tales to layer their meanings and to deepen the characters presented. In the tales presented here, the author of *Feen-Mährchen* and Ludowine von Haxthausen give their stories depth by having characters shown as both child and adult, ogress and nanny, or sisters as both evil and cooperative—each at different points on life's path. They all follow a long Asian and European tradition that has run counter to the presentation of short, one-plot stories as the model for children's literature. The tale-within-a-tale or sequential-yet-related tales did indeed become a part of the tradition of Romantic irony, but authors who used these forms for the sheer entertainment value of the fantastic, as did most women writers of the nineteenth century, were gradually relegated to popular fiction for the masses and eliminated from the ranks of recognized authors of the *Kunstmärchen* (literary fairy tale).

Some of these tales are intentional fragments in the style of German Romanticism, such as Bettina von Arnim's autobiographical tale and her re-creation of the fictional Günderode's tale as a metaphor for failed life. It is significant that Arnim had artistic control over both of these projects and thus could shape them for artistic purposes. The larger number of fairy-tale fragments by women, however, does not carry the aesthetic import of fragment usage in German Romanticism. They show instead the *lack* of control and fragmentation in their lives and writings at that time. Whether it is the vastly underreported, failed fairy tale of the historical Günderode or the abruptly ended dialogue of Droste-Hülshoff and Wilhelm Grimm, we can see that some fragments are not artistic choices but rather are the result of strictures from a society where women poets were cut off, emotionally or verbally. Reading these fragments is a different kind of Romantic experience; the unfinished contours make these fragments neither *Volks-* nor *Kunstmärchen*—neither folktales nor literary fairy tales—but rather disturbing and even tragic examples of stories that should have been.

The translations provided here show the lush variety of fairy-tale elements coursing through German women's writing before the second edition of the Grimms' tales in 1819. There is a strong autobiographical (or fictionalized autobiographical) usage of fairy-tale elements in this wide range of works. They depict adept heroines and influential storytelling women. They show cooperation as well as competition between women, as fairy-tale heroines as well as friends and authors. They show the need to expand the unsatisfactory historical record into legend and fairy tale, as Benedikte Naubert explained it in the generation previous to theirs. And they expose the rough edges and even the pain, as German women begin to appropriate the fantastic.

NOTES

1. Works cited by these authors include fairy tales, legends of the fantastic, and gothic novels with fairy-tale elements. See the following sources for more information

on their works: on Catherine the Great and women fairy-tale authors in general, see Jarvis and Blackwell; on Albrecht: Royer; on Fischer: Runge; on Naubert: Blackwell, "Die verlorene Lehre"; Dorsch; Jarvis, "Vanished Woman"; Schreinert; Sweet; Toauillon; Runge; Vogele; on Wallenrodt: Runge.

2. The translation is the foreword to the anonymous *Feen-Mährchen* (iii–viii), which has been published in a new edition prepared by Ulrich Marzolph.

3. See Günderrode's *Gedichte und Phantasien* (*Poems and Fantasies*). One of these tales, "Temora," is translated in Jarvis and Blackwell 105–09.

4. I have used textual information presented by Schulte-Kemminghausen, who discovered this tale in the Grimm collection in Berlin and published its transcription in 1936 (see Droste-Hülshoff and Grimm).

Bibliography of Early Fairy-Tale Writings by German Women

This bibliography offers a convenient overview of the earliest fairy-tale writings by German women, which are listed here separately. Critical works cited in this essay are listed in the bibliography at the end of this volume.

Albrecht, Sophie. *Graumännchen oder Die Burg Rabenmühl: Eine Geistergeschichte alt-deutschen Ursprungs von S. A.* Altona and Leipzig: Buchhandlung der Verlagsgesellschaft, 1799.

———. *Legenden von S. A. Erstes Bändchen.* [= *Das höfliche Gespenst.*] Altona and Leipzig: Friedrich Bechthold, 1797.

———. "Die reiche Anna." *Trümmer der Vergangenheit: Vol III. Erzählungen aus dem Dunkel der Vorzeit.* Hamburg: Benjamin Gottlob Hoffmann, 1801.

Anon. *Feen-Mährchen zur Unterhaltung für Freunde und Freundinnen der Feenwelt.* Braunschweig: Friedrich Bernhard Culemann, 1801. Ed. Ulrich Marzolph. Hildesheim: Olms, 2000.

Arnim, Bettine von. *Clemens Brentanos Frühlingskranz aus Jugendbriefen ihm geflochten wie er selbst schriftlich verlangte.* 1844. Leipzig: Reclam, 1974.

———. *Die Günderode: Mit einem Essay von Christa Wolf.* Frankfurt: Insel, 1983.

———. "Report on Günderode's Suicide." *Goethe's Correspondence with a Child.* London: Longman, 1839. Rpt. in *Bitter Healing: German Women Writers, 1700–1830. An Anthology.* Ed. Jeannine Blackwell and Susanne Zantop. Lincoln: U of Nebraska P, 1990. 465.

[Catherine II, Empress of Russia = Sophie Auguste Friederike Prinzessin von Anhalt-Zerbst-Dornburg]. *Das Mährchen vom Zarewitsch Chlor.* Berlin and Stettin: Friedrich Nicolai, 1782. Trans. as *Ivan Czarowitz, or The Rose without Prickles That Stings Not: A Tale.* London: Robinson and Sons, 1793.

———. "Märchen vom Zarewitsch Fewei." *Erzählungen und Gespräche. Von I. K. M d. K. a. R.* Pt. 2. Berlin and Stettin: Friedrich Nicolai, 1784. 179–228. Trans. as "The Tale of Fewei." Trans. Jeannine Blackwell. Jarvis and Blackwell 17–26.

————. *Obidah, eine morgenländische Erzählung. Obidag, vostocnaja povest' se nemeckago na rossijskoj jazyk perevedenaja Semenom Velikim, prileznym k naukam junoseju, v Sankt Peterburge, pecatano s dozvolenija ukaznag u Snora, 1786 goda.* [*Obidag, an oriental tale translated from the German into Russian by Semen Veliki, for the encouragement of youths, printed with permission in St. Petersburg by Snor, 1786*]. Trans. as "Obidah, or The Journey of a Day. An Eclogue. Time, Morning." Printed as addendum to: *The Forsaken Infant, or, Entertaining History of Little Jack.* By Thomas Day. Philadelphia: B. Johnson, 1806. 30–37.

Droste-Hülshoff, Annette von, and Wilhelm Grimm. "König Einbein." In "Annette von Droste-Hülshoff and Wilhelm Grimm zeichnen ein Märchen auf." Segment of "Volksüberlieferung aus dem Nachlaß der Brüder Grimm." By Karl Schulte-Kemminghausen. *Westdeutsche Zeitschrift für Volkskunde* 33 (1936): 41–50.

Engelhard, Philippine Gatterer. *Neujahrs-Geschenk für liebe Kinder von Philippine Engelhard, geborne Gatterer.* Göttingen: Johann Christian Dieterich, 1787.

————. *Spückemährchen.* Göttingen: Johann Christian Dieterich, 1782.

[Fischer, Caroline Auguste]. *Mährchen.* Journal der Romane 10. Berlin: Johann Friedrich Unger, 1802.

[Günderrode, Karoline von]. *Gedichte und Phantasien von Tian.* Hamburg and Frankfurt: J. C. Herrmann, 1804.

Haxthausen, Ludowine von. "Schöneblume, Fienetchen und Leiseöhrchen." [1818?] *Märchen aus deutschen Landschaften* 91–97.

Jarvis, Shawn C., and Jeannine Blackwell, eds. and trans. *The Queen's Mirror: Fairy Tales by German Women, 1780–1900.* Lincoln: U of Nebraska P, 2001.

[Knorring, Sophie Tieck Bernhardi von]. "Der Greis im Felsen" and "Die Hölle." *Bambocciaden.* Pt. 3. Berlin: Friedrich Maurer, 1800. 149–216.

————. *Wunderbilder und Träume in Eilf Märchen von Sophie B.* Königsberg: Friedrich Nicolovius, 1802.

Märchen aus deutschen Landschaften: Unveröffentlichte Quellen. Ed. Karl Schulte-Kemminghausen. Vol. 2. Aschendorff: Aschendorffer Buchdruckerei, 1976.

[Naubert, Benedikte]. *Almé oder Egyptische Mährchen: Mit dem Bildnis der Alme.* Parts 1–5. Leipzig: Johann Gottlob Beygang, 1793–1797.

————. *Amalgunde, Königin von Italien oder das Märchen von der Wunderquelle: Eine Sage aus den Zeiten Theoderichs des Großen.* Leipzig: Weygandsche Buchhandlung, 1787.

————. *Gebhard Truchses von Waldburg Churfürst von Cöln oder die astrologischen Fürsten.* Leipzig: Weygandsche Buchhandlung, 1791.

————. *Heitere Träume in kleinen Erzählungen, von der Verfasserin des Walter von Montbarry, Fontages u.s.w.* New ed. Leipzig: Weygandsche Buchhandlung, 1809.

————. "Die Minyaden." *Journal für deutsche Frauen* 1 (1806): 8–31; and 2 (1806): 1–38.

————. *Neue Volksmährchen der Deutschen.* 4 vols. Leipzig: Weygandsche Buchhandlung, 1789–1792.

————. *Velleda: Ein Zauberroman.* Leipzig: Schäferische Buchhandlung, 1795.

————. *Wanderungen der Phantasie in die Gebiete der Wahrheit.* Leipzig: Weygandsche Buchhandlung, 1806.

————. *Werner, Graf von Bernburg.* 1790. Frankfurt and Leipzig: n.p., 1791.

[Unger, Frederike Helene]. *Prinz Bimbam: Ein Märchen für alt und jung.* Berlin: Johann Friedrich Unger, 1802.

————. "Prinzessin Gräcula: Ein Mährchen." *Albert und Albertine.* Berlin: Johan Friedrich Unger, 1804. 63–124.

Wallenrodt, Isabelle Eleonora von. *Die drei Spinnrocken oder Bertha von Salza und Hermann von Tüngen: Aus dem 12. Jahrhundert von Frau der Frau v. Wallenrodt.* Bibliothek der grauen Vorwelt 1. Leipzig: Voß und Leo, 1793.

————. *Prinz Hassan der Hochherzige bestraft durch Rache und glücklich durch die Liebe: Eine morgenländische Urkunde.* Leipzig: Kleefeldsche Buchhandlung, 1796. Münster: lit, 1989.

[Wolzogen, Karoline von]. *Agnes von Lilien.* Berlin: J. F. Unger, 1798. Pt. 1: 419–30.

5

The Mirror Broken:
Women's Autobiography and Fairy Tales

Elizabeth Wanning Harries

> To the uncritical eye, autobiography presents as untroubled a reflection of
> identity as the surface of a mirror can provide.
>
> Bella Brodzki and Celeste Schenck, *Life/Lines*

> We were truly illegitimate, outside any law of recognition: the mirror bro-
> ken, a lump of ice for a heart.
>
> Carolyn Kay Steedman, *Landscape for a Good Woman*

*I*n the great feminist fairy-tale debates of the 1970s, all the participants assumed that tales have a direct effect on women's lives and
dreams, presenting "romantic paradigms that profoundly influenc[e]
women's fantasies and the subconscious scenarios for their real lives"
(Rowe, "Fairy-born" 69). Even Alison Lurie, who sparked the debates with
her 1970 article "Fairy Tale Liberation," assumed a fairly direct relationship between women's lives and the tales they read or were fed. She argued
that "the traditional folk tale" offered women—as heroines and as
storytellers—active roles and powers that the everyday Dick-and-Jane
stories of her childhood denied them: "To prepare children for women's
liberation, therefore, and to protect them against Future Shock, you had
better buy at least one collection of fairy tales" (42).

But other feminist literary critics would have none of this. They
argued that most popular fairy tales, like "Cinderella," "Snow White," and
"Sleeping Beauty," had heroines who were passive, apparently dead or
sleepwalking, dependent on the arrival of the prince for any animation and
for entry into a real life—though a real life that never was given any contours after the obligatory royal wedding. As the earliest feminist critics of
fairy tales all agreed, women in the best-known tales were either beautiful,
slumbering young girls or powerful, usually wicked and grotesque older

women. Though there might be a muted tradition of tales in which women were admirable, active, clever, and self-assertive participants, the dominant tradition (particularly the tales popularized by Andrew Lang in his rainbow fairy-tale series and later adopted by the Disney industry) prescribed harmful roles for women that little girls could not help but imitate. As Vivian Gornick says in a recent essay, "We were in thrall to passive longing, all of us—Dorothea [Brooke, from *Middlemarch*] and Isobel [Archer, from *Portrait of a Lady*], me and my mother, the fairy tale princess. Longing is what attracted us, what compelled our deepest attention" (166). Rather than design a life for themselves, the women "in thrall" to fairy-tale patterns wait for male rescue, or at least for something to happen. They half-consciously submit to being male property, handed from father to suitor or husband without complaint or volition. And it is the gender economy of the often-repeated fairy tales that has betrayed them. As one of Margaret Atwood's characters replies to the question "'Did you believe that stuff when you were little?' 'I did, I thought I was really a princess and I'd end up living in a castle. They shouldn't let kids have stuff like that'" (*Surfacing* 8).

In 1975, in the thick of the fairy-tale debates, Hélène Cixous wrote in "Sorties":

> *Once upon a time . . .*
> One cannot yet say of the following history "it's just a story." It's a tale still true today. Most women who have awakened remember having slept, *having been put to sleep.*
> *Once upon a time . . . once . . . and once again.*
> Beauties slept in their woods, waiting for princes to come and wake them up. In their beds, in their glass coffins, in their childhood forests like dead women. Beautiful, but passive; hence desirable: all mystery emanates from them. (65–66)

Cixous uses these fairy-tale patterns as one focus of her attack on the binary organization and hierarchy of gender in the West. She believes it is precisely the repetition of the "once upon a times" that has helped create women who cannot value themselves, who are most themselves precisely and paradoxically when they are absent or not themselves, "the same story repeating woman's destiny in love across the centuries with the cruel hoax of its plot" (67). As Lurie pointed out in her second article, "Witches and Fairies," in 1971, the heroines of novels from Gwendolen Harleth to Lady Chatterley to Nicole Warren in Fitzgerald's *Tender Is the Night* all fit this type; we could multiply the literary examples endlessly. But both people who argued that fairy tales are dangerous for girls and women and people who argued that fairy tales are essential reading focused on the power of their "images of woman" to shape or deform real lives, like most feminist critics of the time. Lurie sums up this belief in her offhand, Wildean remark about "real life, which as usual imitates art" ("Witches and Fairies" 7).

Women's autobiographies, however, often suggest more oblique and complex responses to the tales that supposedly govern our lives. Though many writers testify to the power certain patterns and roles continue to have, others show that fairy tales have symbolic resonances that work against, or even contradict, the dominant models. The formation of the female subject, if such a thing exists, takes place in many indirect and mediated ways.[1] Many autobiographies assume that there is an "essential self" that the autobiography as mirror can reflect. As Felicity Nussbaum has suggested, the ideology of the genre traditionally demands a stable "I": "In first-person narrative, the 'I' arbitrates reality through cultural codes to make 'experience' intelligible and to place it in a familiar framework" (15). But many modern autobiographers, from Gertrude Stein to Roland Barthes, have avoided or elided the "I," deliberately thwarting our desire for a unified subject we can recognize and for reiterated cultural codes that help us make it make sense.

In the pages that follow, I will often refer to *Mirror, Mirror on the Wall* (1998), edited by Kate Bernheimer, a collection of essays by various contemporary women writers who were asked to reflect on the function of fairy tales in their childhood, "how fairy tales affected their thinking about emotion, the self, gender and culture" (xviii). The wildly different answers suggest some of the many ways fairy tales can mirror and form versions of the female self. But I will focus on Christa Wolf's autobiographical meditations on her Nazi childhood, *Kindheitsmuster* (1976), and on Carolyn Kay Steedman's innovative double biography/ autobiography, *Landscape for a Good Woman* (1986), both shot through with fairy tales. Neither text presents a stable and coherent self. In both books, fairy tales become what Steedman calls "interpretative devices," stories to think with, stories that do not necessarily determine lives but can give children (and adults) a way to read and to understand them. As Walter Benjamin says, in his review of a book called *Alte vergessene Kinderbücher* (*Old, Forgotten Children's Books,* 1924), "Children are able to manipulate fairy stories [*Märchenstoffen,* or tale elements] with the same ease and lack of inhibition they display in playing with pieces of cloth and building blocks" (408).

Christa Wolf calls her autobiographical text *Kindheitsmuster: Roman* (*Patterns of Childhood: A Novel*—the subtitle is omitted, significantly, in the English translation.)[2] The difficulty of making contact with her childhood self is one of the themes and problems of the text; Wolf refers to this self as "Nelly," never as Christa, and only in the third person. She does not pretend to be able to breach the distance between them, to claim that the "auto" in "autobiography" represents a continuous and stable self, or to avoid the sentimental nostalgia of what she calls "der Tourismus in halb-versunkene Kindheiten" (14; "the tourist trade in half-buried childhoods" [6]). She further complicates the problem of the continuous self by inter-weaving scenes from her childhood during the Nazi era and the Allied occupation (from roughly 1933 to 1947); from a trip she makes with her husband, brother, and fourteen-year-old daughter to her hometown, now in Poland, in 1971; and from her meditations on current events (the Vietnam War, for example) during the writing of the book from 1972 to 1975. She consistently refers to her adult self as "du" ("you") stressing her own distance even from the self that is experiencing and writing in the present. Only in the last few paragraphs does Wolf use the pronoun "I" instead of the second-person "you"—and there it is the "I" of the writer looking back on what she has written.[3] The subtitle "Roman" suggests the impossibility of bringing her selves together, even at the end:

> Und die Vergangenheit, die noch Sprachregelungen verfügen, die erste Person in eine zweite und dritte spalten konnte—ist ihre Vormacht gebrochen? Werden die Stimmen sich beruhigen?
> Ich weiß es nicht. (Wolf 519)

> And the past, which can still prescribe rules governing speech, which can still split the first person into a second and third—has its supremacy been broken? Will the voices be still?
> I don't know. (406)

Early in the book, Wolf stresses the inauthenticity of her attempts to remember, to recapture her childhood self. There are a few moments when she seems to begin to approach the child doing childlike things:

> Da hättest du es also. Es bewegt sich, geht, liegt, sitzt, ißt, schläft, trinkt. Es kann lachen und weinen, Sandkuten bauen, Märchen anhören. (13–14)

> You've got it, then. She moves, walks, lies down, sits, eats, sleeps, drinks. She can laugh and cry, dig holes in the sand, listen to fairy tales. (7)

This list of the child's activities is strangely mechanical, almost like an advertisement for a doll with many talents (accentuated in the German by the neuter pronoun "es" for "das Kind"). This child can do the things any three-year-old can do—and one of those things is to listen to fairy tales, as any good German child should. References to the Grimms' tales run throughout the book: snakes who might be fairy princes, frog princes, "Hänsel and Gretel," the hedge of thorns around Sleeping Beauty's castle. When her father returns, wizened and unrecognizable, from a Russian prisoner-of-war camp, "Nelly" has half-expected his transformation:

> Merkwürdigerweise hatte Nelly es geahnt. Märchen bereiten uns von klein auf darauf vor: Der Held, der König, der Prinz, der Geliebte wird in der Fremde verwunschen; als ein Fremder kehrt er zurück. (507)

> Strangely enough Nelly had foreseen it. Fairy tales prepare us for it from childhood on: The hero, the king, the prince, the lover falls under a spell in foreign lands; he returns as a stranger. (398)

Fairy tales often provide "Nelly" with a way of reading and even predicting the world, as "interpretative devices."

But, though the Grimms' tales are one ground of her existence, she also constantly plays variations on them. She mentions the hedge of thorns around Sleeping Beauty's castle, but she never sees herself as the sleeping princess. Snow White ("Schneewittchen") becomes the name of a witch; the story of Hänsel and Gretel's parents plotting their deaths becomes a reason to try to overhear her own parents' conversations about politics; when she and her brother act out "Mary's Child," she refuses to confess to opening the forbidden thirteenth door as the truthful child of the tale does. Living in a broken-down castle at the end of the war makes her think "sie würde nie wieder in einem Märchen lesen können: 'Und er nahm sie mit auf sein Schloß . . . ,' ohne laut lachen zu müssen" (425; "she'd never again be able to read a fairy tale which said: 'And he brought her home to his castle . . .' without bursting out laughing" [336]). Often "Nelly" finds herself acting in opposition to the tales she knows, refusing to act out their plots "wie vorgeschrieben" (152; "according to the script" [116]). These refusals, in fact, become dry runs for her instinctive opposition to some (though certainly not all) Nazi political doctrines, like the expectation that all young girls should be happy to bear Aryan children for the fatherland. Fairy tales provide scripts for living, but they also can inspire resistance to those scripts and, in turn, to other apparently predetermined patterns.

Very early "Nelly" begins to object to the happy endings of fairy tales:

> Es war dieselbe Irritation, die sie von den Märchenschlüssen her kannte,
> wenn sich die Befriedigung, daß alles sich so wohl gefügt . . . doch, kaum
> eingestanden, ein kleines bißchen Enttäuschung beimengte, spätestens bei
> der Schlußbemerkung: Und wenn sie nicht gestorben sind, so leben sie
> heute noch— . . . Wer war sie, an den Schlüssen der Märchen herum-
> zumäkeln? (118)

> It was the same irritation that came over her at the end of fairy tales, when
> the satisfaction that everything had turned out all right . . . was nonethe-
> less mixed with a barely admitted touch of disappointment, especially at
> the conclusion: And they lived happily ever after . . . Who was she to find
> fault with the endings of fairy tales? (89)

The traditional German ending is even more pat and irritating than the
English: literally, "and if they haven't died, they're living still." Yet Wolf's
early resistance to that ending suggests that children don't always accept
fairy tales as a package, or as packaged. Throughout her book she stresses
the tension between the richness of some elements of the tales and the
sham finality of their closure. Shattering the typical practices of conventional autobiography, she also breaks fairy tales into parts. Just as her text
becomes a collage of scenes and thoughts from different eras of her life,
a "novel" rather than an "autobiography," so the fairy tales she remembers
are fragmented and woven apparently at random into her text. They do
not have the compelling force of coherent myths but rather provide scat-
tered models for resistance and for interpretation.

Steedman's book, published ten years later, is an attempt to tell the
stories of the lives she and her mother made for themselves, stories that
contest the existing templates for narratives of British working-class life
and of female psychological development. She is the daughter of
Lancashire parents who migrated to London in the mid-1930s, looking
for better work and opportunities, fleeing family and perhaps other threats
in the north. Her mother's mother was a weaver and a weaver's daughter,
precariously self-sufficient after her husband's death at the Somme; her
father's parents had once owned, and lost, a corner sweet shop. Only when
Steedman is an adult, after her father's death, does she discover that her
parents had never married, because her father already had a wife and child.
Her illegitimacy becomes a confirmation of her continuing sense of exclusion from dominant, middle-class British culture. Her book is an attempt
to trace the "*development* of class-consciousness (as opposed to its expres-

sion) . . . as a *learned* position, learned in childhood, and often through the exigencies of difficult and lonely lives" (13).

Much of Steedman's book is her story of her mother's life, whose stories and dreams disrupted and deformed Steedman's own: "stories designed to show me the terrible unfairness of things, the subterranean culture of longing for that which one can never have" (8). Like the women and fictional characters Gornick talks about, Steedman's mother longed for things that she half-knew were unattainable and yet longed them for all the same: "a New Look skirt, a timbered country cottage, to marry a prince" (9). The New Look skirt would have taken far too many yards of material to make in postwar Britain; the timbered country cottage was always just out of reach, in spite of the thousands of pounds she saved in building-society funds; the prince never came. One of the more amusing as well as telling passages in the book is Steedman's father's account of how difficult it was to live with her mother during the abdication crisis of 1936: "Mrs. Simpson was no prettier than her, no more clever than her, no better than her. It wasn't fair that a king should give up his throne for her, and not for the weaver's daughter" (47).

As Steedman sees it, her mother believed what fairy tales like the Grimms' "Goose Girl" told her: that if she were good and patient and long-suffering, a prince would recognize her worth and carry her off, off into a different social world, a world that was "fair." She is never the dependable emotional center of the home, as working-class "Mums" are supposed to be, but always off-center, yearning for a life that is denied her.

And yet, like many interpreters reading the story of Cinderella, Steedman never mentions one basic fact about the goose-girl story: that the goose girl is the true princess in disguise, displaced by a scheming maid. As Joyce Carol Oates reminds us, "In a crucial sense fairy tales work to subvert romantic wishes, for they repeatedly confirm 'order' and redress dislocations of privileged birth while leaving wholly unchallenged the hierarchical basis for such privileging" (250–51). Steedman believes that her mother has been betrayed by the false hope that fairy tales like "The Goose Girl" give, but she (and perhaps her mother) has misread the story or tailored it to fit other, perhaps more compelling patterns. As Oates and many others have pointed out, there are very few stories of heroic adventure for women in the usual fairy-tale repertoire; only male characters like Dick Whittington, Jack the Giant-Killer, or Tom Thumb rise from rags to riches through their own ingenuity and courage. Most of the stories that seem to point to such social movement for women are actually reaffirmations of social status and reenactments

Illustration by H. J. Ford for "The Snow Queen" from *The Pink Fairy Book*, ed. Andrew Lang (London: Longmans, 1897) 99.

of Freud's "family romance": "My real parents were a king and queen; I was really always a princess."

Trying to articulate her mother's longings, then, Steedman reaches for a fairy-tale pattern that actually undermines them, reaffirms their impossibility. She attributes conventional hopes and fairy-tale expectations to her mother, confirming her continuing estrangement from her. In the last scene in the book, returning to her childhood home for the first time in years, she sees her mother as a witch who looks just like the witch in illustrations for "Hänsel and Gretel": "[she] opens the door of the gingerbread house; she stands there; you look at her face: she is like my mother" (140). Again Steedman places her mother in a conventional, polarized role.

When Steedman talks about her own life, however, she chooses different patterns, usually from Andersen's tales that she read over and over early in childhood. Rather than see herself as the central female figure of the tales, she oscillates from identification to interpretation of symbolic structures. Emphasizing her middle name, Kay, a name she doesn't use in signing her other books, she insists on the parallels between herself and the "Kay" of Andersen's "Snow Queen," a boy who is emotionally frozen by the shards of a broken mirror: "Kay was my name at home, and I knew that Kay, the boy in 'The Snow Queen,' was me, who had a lump of ice in her heart" (46). She also repeatedly returns to Gerda, in many ways the active heroine of Andersen's tale—the faithful girl who searches for Kay throughout the world and finally redeems him from the powerful and icy Snow Queen. The little robber girl Gerda meets, who will not sleep without her knife, becomes a central image in Steedman's interpretations of her parents' life together: "Each had a knife, sharp-edged with a broad yet pointed blade, and what they did with the knife, what the grown-ups did, was cut each other . . . Downstairs I thought, the thin blood falls in sheets from my mother's breasts; she was the most cut, but I knew it was she who did the cutting. I couldn't always see the knife in my father's hand" (54). This bloody scene becomes the key to her understanding of her parents and their relationship to each other and to their children. Her mother uses the knife primarily to hurt herself, "displaying to my imagination the mutilation involved in feeding and keeping us" (82). Her father lacks the phallic power of the knife, the power of the father to name, to give laws, and to control. As Steedman says, "the fairy-tales always tell the stories that we do not yet know" (55).

Throughout the book, Steedman stresses the ways in which her family constellation differs from the dominant middle-class fairy-tale and

Freudian norms. Middle-class women have a "central relationship to the culture. The myths tell their story" (17): "In the fairy-stories the daughters love their fathers because they are mighty princes, great rulers, and because such absolute power seduces. The modern psychoanalytic myths posit the same plot, old tales are made manifest: secret longings, doors closing along the corridors of the bourgeois household" (61). Excluded from the world of dominant fathers and big houses, Steedman cannot love or fear her absent and powerless father: "He did know some rules, but he didn't embody them: they were framed by some distant authority outside himself" (57). She also knows that her feelings for her mother are a tangled mixture of resentment and guilt. Unlike her mother, or at least unlike the mother she has created in her autobiography, she does not long for the unattainable, as expressed in "The Goose Girl," or attempt to insert herself into the dominant fairy-tale framework. Rather she reinterprets the tales and case studies she reads to fit her own childhood on the social margins.

Another tale of Andersen's, "The Little Mermaid," becomes talismanic for Steedman's understanding of her own emotional life. Though in this case she sees both her mother and herself as the central mermaid figure, rather than the witch who advises her or the emotionally distant prince, she does not make either the heroine of a romance plot. Both she and her mother are little mermaids, but neither is in thrall to conventional longings: "The Little Mermaid was not my mother sacrificing herself for a beautiful prince. I knew her sacrifice: it was not composed of love or longing for my father, rather of a fierce resentment against the circumstances that were so indifferent to her. She turns me into the Little Mermaid a few years later, swimming round and round the ship, wondering why I was not wanted, but realizing that of course, it had to be that way" (55). The Little Mermaid removes herself from the world of her sisters, who are at home in the water, but she is never at home in the human world on the land. The tale becomes a metaphor for emotional dead ends and repetitions, the mermaid's voicelessness a sign of inability to speak in a way that might change things.[4] Her mother's circumstances remain unaltered; both her parents remain distant and essentially unavailable.

For Steedman herself the tale is also a lesson in enduring suffering: "I knew that one day I might be asked to walk on the edge of knives, like the Little Mermaid, and was afraid that I might not be able to bear the pain" (46). The knives, so prominent in her renderings of her parents' lives, here are turned against her, crippling her emotionally. (It was only after reading Steedman that I began to notice how often knives figure in Andersen's tales, all their repressed violence rising momentarily to the surface.) Like her mother, she chooses a kind of self-mutilation, violently cutting herself off from meaningful human contact.

Very early Steedman begins to feel distanced from herself as well. She sees herself in an old photograph when she was about four and remembers that "things were wrong; there was a dislocation between me and the world; I am not inside myself" (51). The shift into the present tense here (from "was" and "were" to "I am") suggests her continuing self-estrangement. Like Wolf, Steedman splits her "self" into various "selves": the academic self from the working-class self; the self skilled in Freudian analysis from the emotionally frozen self; the childhood self from the self who is trying to remember, interpret, and understand. Writing an autobiography, combining her autobiography with a biography of her mother, is part of her attempt to see continuities between those selves, to "compose" a self for herself, to reunite the observing eye and the feeling "I." Her readings of Andersen's tales, as well as of "The Goose Girl," are part of that complex and often fragmentary project. At the end, again like Wolf, she must acknowledge "the irreducible nature of all our lost childhoods" (144). There is no existing narrative structure that can contain her particular story, no existing "structure of political thought" that can recognize "all these secret and impossible stories" (144). The meaningful fragments of fairy tales can only suggest some of those nearly inexpressible secrets.

As A. S. Byatt says, "These stories are riddles, and all readers change them a little, and they accept and resist change simultaneously" (83). Some fairy tales do fall into repetitive patterns, as their early feminist critics saw: tracing the longings of a goose girl or a mermaid for an apparently unattainable prince, freezing heroines in glass coffins to wait for his arrival. These repetitive plots can be reframed, as Anne Sexton, Jeanette Winterson, Emma Donoghue, and others have done, changing their significance by placing them in new and contrasting contexts.[5] But their sharply etched images (a rose, a transformation, a knife, a mirror) open them up to other readings, other ways to understand them. In women's recent autobiographical writing, these images are refracted in the splintered forms of the narratives themselves.[6] One conventional form, one unambiguous mirror cannot contain them.

Cristina Bacchilega has recently argued that "the tale of magic's controlling metaphor is the *magic mirror,* because it conflates mimesis (reflection), refraction (varying desires) and framing (artifice)" (*Postmodern Fairy Tales* 10). One could say that the controlling metaphor of recent women's autobiographies is the *broken mirror,* the mirror that does not pretend to reflect subjectivities or lives as unified wholes. As Wolf says, "Im Idealfall sollten die Strukturen des Erlebens sich mit den Strukturen des Erzählens decken" (345; "Ideally the structures of experience should match the structures of narrative" [272]). Autobiography, as we have long understood it, should be a serene and accurate reflection of a life (see my first epigraph). But even the complex layering of narrative levels that makes up Wolf's text cannot reproduce or match what she calls the "verfilztes Geflecht" (345; "tangled mesh" [272]) of her experiences. All she can do is attempt to reproduce the reflections in the broken shards of the autobiographical mirror.

Steedman's repeated references to Andersen's "Snow Queen" suggest the importance of the image of the broken mirror for her understanding of her autobiographical project. At the beginning of the tale, as we have seen, a splinter of a wicked magician's mirror pierces Kay's heart. And at the end Gerda finds Kay in the Snow Queen's ice palace, working "the ice-puzzle of reason," attempting to fit fragments of ice together. In the story the fragments finally cohere, forming the word "eternity," when Gerda, in tears, sings a song about the child Jesus, recalling Kay to the warmth of human relationship and Christian belief (Andersen 259–60). But Steedman avoids any mention of Andersen's optimistic and typically rather saccharine ending. Rather she focuses repeatedly on the splintered mirror and on the icy power of the Snow Queen to lure Kay to her cold and colorless kingdom: "The mirror breaks, just as the clock strikes five, and a lump of ice is lodged in the heart" (97). The broken mirror is a metaphor throughout for Steedman's feelings of emotional isolation and exclusion, but it also reflects the difficulty she has in creating a narrative form for her experiences. She finds it necessary to begin before the beginning, to see how her mother's stories of her life shaped her own and how their stories are interwoven; her book is "about the experience of my own childhood, and the way in which my mother re-asserted, reversed and restructured her own within mine" (8). There is no single story of individual growth and development but rather a tangle of stories caught up, like Wolf's, in cultural currents and political realities that have yet to be described in any way that can contain or explain them.

Neither Wolf nor Steedman pretends that she has solved the problem of competing, even conflicting selves, selves woven out of different material exigencies and discursive possibilities. Both accept the continuing mystery of the Chinese puzzle of identity, rejecting the false solutions and happy endings that fairy tales and traditional autobiography provide. Fractured identities demand fractured forms, a momentary self glimpsed in a remembered scene—or in a fragment of a fairy tale.

Notes

1. In thinking about the gendered subject, I have found Elspeth Probyn's arguments and imagery very helpful: "a gendered self is constantly reproduced within the changing mutations of difference. . . . One way of imaging this self is to think of it as a combination of acetate transparencies: layers and layers of lines and directions that are figured together, and in depth, only then to be arranged again" (1). Another helpful metaphor, this one from Jeanette Winterson's *Sexing the Cherry:* "The self is not contained in any moment or any place, but it is only in the intersection of moment and place that the self might, for a moment, be seen vanishing through a door, which disappears at once" (87).

2. The inadequacies of this translation have long been apparent. The original title—*A Model Childhood*—revealed the pervasive failure of the translators to catch the nuances of ordinary spoken German; though the title has been corrected to *Patterns of Childhood,* the subtitle has still not been added—and the mistaken translation still turns up in the text (36). Although I cite this English translation, I have often been forced to modify their versions of the text and to supply translations of missing passages. My thanks to Lisa Harries-Schumann for thoughtful suggestions. (The passages the translators leave out are often passages in which Wolf insists on moving between her present, writing self and her earlier selves. The omissions transform the text into a more conventional memoir.)

3. See Brodzki for a fascinating discussion of Wolf's use of pronouns, particularly pages 257–58.

4. Rosellen Brown, in her essay "It Is You the Fable Is About," interprets the story in a different way: "I know that in the mermaid's voicelessness Andersen captured one of our—I mean humans'—primal terrors . . . He gave us an implicit judgment of the limitations of mere beauty, beauty unendowed with self" (62). For Steedman, however, the absence of voice does not mean the absence of self but rather the inability to express the self forcefully in the world. Like Brown, however, Steedman suppresses the Christian "happy ending" of the tale, the possibility of the Little Mermaid's gaining an everlasting soul.

5. For recent examples of reframing, see Anne Sexton's book of poems based on the Grimms' tales, *Transformations* (1971); Jeanette Winterson's treatment of "The Twelve Dancing Princesses" and "Rapunzel" in *Sexing the Cherry* (1989); and Emma Donoghue's collection of linked stories, *Kissing the Witch* (1997). For discussion of techniques of reframing, see Bacchilega, *Postmodern Fairy Tales,* particularly pages 32–36.

6. For a helpful discussion of fragmentation in women's autobiography, see Sidonie Smith (434–35).

6

Fire and Water:
A Journey into the Heart of a Story

Kay Stone

Here are two very different story scenes:

> In a dark forest an old woman—a hag, not a granny—sits beside her fire awaiting a rebellious girl. When the girl arrives, the hag will turn her into a log and throw the log into the fire.

> In another forest a sister and her brothers are seeking the Water of Life. The brothers will fail and be turned to stone, but the sister will succeed in the quest.

The creative tension between these stories has fueled feminist studies of folktales for the last decades of the twentieth century. They seem diametrically opposed, victim and victor, but it is not so simple given the deliberately enigmatic quality of wonder tales. The mysterious nature of this genre endures, even after long years of attention by a host of writers offering their own particular interpretations. Feminist scholars especially have criticized the overabundance of passive victims and have sought out more active and resourceful women. Each new study and every re-created story opens up new patterns, perspectives, and constant variations on themes. Jane Yolen's stories, for example, always make me look again at my own favored traditional tales. Even with all of this attention, no single outlook or approach offers a final answer to the mystery of this genre, because the wonder tale at its best is multifaceted in depth and meaning, always open to new breath and breadth.

Like others who followed a feminist path, I was lured into the enchanted forest of wonder tales by an interest in the good and bad women who peopled them. I read story after story to see how folktale women fared or failed in their adventures. I was studying stories from a safe academic distance, making my own observations and assigning heroines to categories

113

I found appropriate.[1] But when I stepped over the threshold and started *telling* the tales, strange things began to happen. I could not avoid experiencing a few transformations myself, coming out of the hag's metaphorical fire somewhat different than what I was before I was thrown in. As I write this essay, I balance metaphorically somewhere between the hag's fire of death and the Water of Life, with the ever-growing understanding that this enigmatic position offers me the fullest potential for insight. But I am getting ahead of my story.

My first steps on the feminist path began with an article, the first I ever wrote, titled "Things Walt Disney Never Told Us." At that time, in the early 1970s, I was a graduate student researching my dissertation on women in folktales. I have written many articles on women and wonder tales and have since moved on to explore contemporary storytelling and tellers, but it is still that first article that continues to interest readers. This has been both blessing and curse: a blessing because it set my direction as a feminist folklorist; a curse because it seems to have cast a spell by keeping my academic image preserved like Sleeping Beauty, forever young and eternally unchanging. My original intention for this present volume was to try to break this spell by exploring where I and others have been these past few decades. However, the computer intervened by wiping out my first draft with its reflections on feminist work, expansive explanatory notes, and careful citations. It all vanished like the golden ball in "The Frog King." After a rage worthy of the elder sister that I am, I took it as a message to let the original essay go, focus on the two opening stories, and see what happened next. I was prepared to expect the unexpected.

Expecting the unexpected is central to the two stories that opened this essay. Both were memorable tales that stood out from the hundreds of others I read in the 1970s, but for very different reasons. The first one, a distressing Grimm tale called "Frau Trude," enraged me; the second, an unusual Catalan variant of "The Water of Life," delighted me.[2] They seemed like perfect opposites, one ending in destruction and the other in re-creation. Each in its own way has made its mark on my evolution as feminist, folklorist, and storyteller, and each continues to do so. Because they still speak to me, I will explore them here as literal and figurative examples of this evolution, my revolution around the figures of the victimized and the heroic women of wonder tales. Let me begin by returning to the hag as she waits for the trespassing girl.

The girl in this brief Grimm cautionary tale has been sternly forbidden by her parents to seek out Frau Trude, an evil woman with a wicked sense of humor (it took me a while to appreciate this potential in the old hag). Of course, the girl disobeys, goes off through the forest to find the crone, and on her way sees three strange men—green, black, and red—whom she describes to Frau Trude. Her big mistake is to admit that she has looked through Frau Trude's window and has seen a distressing sight, "the devil with a fiery head" (Grimm 174). She learns too late that she has seen the forbidden, "the witch in her proper dress" (174), and is promptly turned into a log and fed to the fire. There is no redemption here. Frau Trude sits down to warm herself beside her fireplace and says sweetly (I can see her smile as I write these words), "Indeed, she does burn brightly."

Since I have already written about this tale, I will be brief here (see Stone, "Burning," "Curious," and *Burning Brightly* 219–37). The story as I initially read it was a paragon of the worst victim tales in my four-category dissertation index, which sorted heroines under the headings of Persecuted, Passive, Tamed, and Heroic. Even in one of the most abusive tales in the Persecuted category, the "Maiden without Hands," the heroine survives mutilation and gains independence. But in "Frau Trude" the girl who is simply curious and disobedient is destroyed. I was enraged with the story and unaware of how deeply I would be engaged with it over the years.

I see now how this brief little story has paralleled my own work. When I began my dissertation research, women in folktales had hardly been explored in depth, and I knew of no academic models to guide my curiosity. In my quest I was going against the wishes of one of my dissertation committee members, who wanted me to do a topic on heroines in legends of the American West. But I had already been lured into the world of folktales and was determined to go on, even if it meant I was being disobedient and trespassing in forbidden territory. It is hardly surprising that I was distressed by the story of a girl who is destroyed for being too curious. I pushed on, as she had, but I was luckier; I survived the fire and completed my impossible task, with anger as my fuel.

Now, almost three decades later, I have become the crone who waits. I ponder the scene at the fireplace rather than reacting with rage. Why was Frau Trude so unforgiving? She herself admitted that she had been waiting a long time for this particular girl. Only to destroy her? (She is lucky to have missed Gretel, who would have pushed her into her own fire.) But from the crone's point of view, and my own all these years later, perhaps what she really wanted was new energy, an apprentice who could learn whatever she had to teach. That sort of girl would have to be disobedient or she would never turn up at a witch's hut in the first place. So I look back on that curious girl that I once was and wonder where she is now that I need her fresh energy. I imagine Frau Trude whispering, "Now dear, remember that fire can be a transformative element. Just stay a bit longer and warm yourself." If that girl *had* survived the fire, we can imagine her going on to new adventures.[3]

That brings us to "The Water of Life," a grand adventure indeed. The story as I first read it is a Catalan variant published by Andrew Lang (184–90). It is a complex tale, so I summarize it more fully than "Frau Trude." A sister and three brothers decide to better their lot by working hard and manage to build a fine palace and a handsome church. They are told that in order to make these complete, they need to find "A pitcher of the water of life, a branch of the tree . . . whose flowers [give] eternal beauty, and the talking bird" (185). Each brother sets off in turn to find these objects on top of a mountain, each meeting a giant who warns them about the speaking stones on the mountain path. All the brothers hear the stones scoffing and mocking, stop to respond, and are turned to stone themselves. The sister now sets off alone on the same path, gets the same advice, and succeeds in walking over the stones even though it was "as if each stone she trod on was a living thing" (188–89). She reaches the top and finds the three precious things, but as she starts down the path, she accidentally drops water on some of the stones, which take their human shape again. She continues downward transforming the stones and returns home with all of the people and her brothers. They plant a branch of the flowering tree, watering it with the magical water and releasing the talking bird from its cage to settle on the branch. A prince hears of these wonders, comes to see for himself, and falls in love with the sister. You know what happens next.

Despite the inevitable concluding marriage, this story moved me with its unusual plot. I placed it in my highest category, Heroic Heroines, quite the opposite of "Frau Trude," whose failed protagonist was relegated to the lowest one, Persecuted Heroines. When later I began to perform stories, this one came to mind immediately. I could not find the printed text at first, but I trusted my memory since the story had been so striking. Months later I found the text again and saw with surprise how far my variant diverged. I had accurately recalled the magical power of the bird and the flowering tree, how sister and brothers walked over the talking stones to find the water of life, and how she transformed the stones on the mountain. But the order and significance of these motifs had changed as my story evolved, and there were other surprises as well. Somehow a dragon had come into the story, and the prince had left it. After several years of oral telling, here is the story as it is now. It begins in a wasteland.

THE WATER OF LIFE

Once there was a land so barren that in some places only stones seemed to grow, and only the hardiest trees could survive.[4] A sister and her brothers lived there. They had little between them, but they did have one very precious thing, a tree unlike any other. This tree bloomed just once every year, in the darkest time. It put out one perfect flower on the highest branch, and every year this flower slowly formed a single flawless fruit. On the first day of each new year when the fruit was ripe, the brothers and sister would take it down, divide it, and eat it. The rest of their year would be filled with joy, which didn't mean they had no troubles, only that their sorrows did not overwhelm them.

One year everything changed. The tree did not bloom. It had no leaves, no blossoms, no fruit. The sister and her brothers stood at the base of the tree looking up, not knowing what to do. As they watched, a strange and wonderful bird flew out of the clear blue sky and settled on the highest branch. It began to sing a haunting song that entranced them all with the rise and fall of its melody. Beautiful as it was, the sister heard something more, like a soft voice whispering. "Listen!" she said to her brothers. "The bird sings that our tree has stopped blooming because we didn't share the fruit with anyone else." They heard that it would not bloom again unless they found one cup of the Water of Life and brought it to the tree. "Where?" said the older brother, and when he heard that this precious water was in a well on the top of the mountain beyond the great forest, he announced that he would go and find it.

"You all stay here and tend the tree," he said confidently.

"No," said the younger brothers. "We want to go too."

The sister agreed to stay and tend the tree, but she was careful to notice the path they took so she might follow if they failed. The three brothers set off together. She watched them disappear down the long path that led to the great forest.

They walked on and on, further than they'd ever gone in their lives, and after some time they came to the forest. There beside the path at the edge of the

woods, a red fox crouched, gnawing on a white bone. The fox looked up at them
and said politely, "Where you are going and what do you seek?"

"We've come to find the Water of Life," the first brother answered
brusquely, "on the top of the mountain beyond this forest."

"I see. But do you know that this is a dangerous road—and that the path
up the mountain is even more dangerous? I've never seen anyone come back in
all the time I've been here."

"Why?" said all the brothers together.

"This is what I know. When your feet touch the stones on the path leading almost to the top of the mountain, those stones will call out. They'll insult
you and challenge you and flatter you, and they'll even weep and wail. But anyone who stops to answer the voices becomes one of the stones. They do not
return on this path."

The brothers were disturbed to hear this but determined to go on. They
hastily thanked the fox and set off into the great dark woods. The path led them
through shimmering light and shadowed dark as they walked together. At last
they stepped out of the forest into bright sunlight, where they could see a mountain covered with evergreen trees. A narrow path of stones wound up through
the cool green woods, almost to the top of the mountain.

"The fox was right," the first brother said eagerly, and he ran to the base
of the mountain and began to climb. The very first stone he stepped on spoke
to him. "Stop!" it called. He went boldly on, and when he didn't stop, the stones
began to insult him. He grew angry as he heard the voices, but he went on. At
last their words made him so furious that he forgot the words of the fox and
turned to answer them. He stopped. He became one of the stones.

The other two brothers, each in turn, started up the path, and each climbed
a little further than the last. But they both suffered the same fate as their brother,
the second giving in to the voices that challenged, and the third to those that
flattered. None of them come back down the fox's path.

The sister waited at home for some time until she was sure that her brothers were not going to return. She prepared herself, and then set off on the path

her brothers had taken. She, too, met the fox, who asked, "Where are you going and what do you seek?"

She answered the fox politely and listened thoughtfully to what the fox said in response. She learned that the long path was dangerous, that anyone who stopped would become one of stones. She guessed what must have become of her brothers. As she listened closely, she felt that she could hear behind the fox's words the faint echoes of a tune that reminded her of the bird's strange melody. She said good-bye and went on her way.

The song cheered her as she passed through the great forest of shimmering light and shadowed dark. At last she came out into the open and saw the mountain and its stony path. She walked toward the mountain, still listening for the faint strains of melody whispering in her head.

Soon enough she came to the first stone of the path and heard it call out "Stop!" but she went on, and the music came with her. When she didn't stop, the stones began to insult her, and then to challenge her, and at last to flatter her.

"Do stop!" they called in sweet voices, "You're a remarkable woman to have come this far. Stop and share your secret with us." She was tempted to help, but even when she heard her last brother's voice among them she went on, sorry that she was now completely alone. Then the stones began to wail and to cry out in pitiful voices: "Oh please! Stop! Stop! Please don't leave us here like this, all alone. We've been lying here for so long, so very long."

She heard their anguished voices, and now she really wanted to stop and help them, but she remembered the fox's words. If she stopped now she would become one of them, unable to help at all. In tears, she willed her feet to move over the weeping stones one step at a time, up and up, with their sad voices calling out behind her as she went on.

Finally the path ended and she found herself at the top of the mountain, with the world spread out below. At her feet lay an ancient well, and on the edge of the well was a small silver cup. She reached down to pick up the cup, but as her fingers touched it she heard a deep hissing sound. The earth under her feet began to tremble and shake, then the well was filled with a deep roaring like the

Illustration by H. J. Ford for "The Water of Life" from *The Pink Fairy Book,* ed. Andrew Lang (London: Longman's 1897) 189.

sound of a fierce storm approaching. She stood there watching, and before her startled eyes the head and neck of a great golden dragon rose up slowly from the well until it towered above her. The dragon spoke in a voice filled with rolling thunder, "Where you are going and what do you seek?"

"I've come for the Water of Life," she stammered, "just one cup, for the tree."

"One cup, you say? That is much more than you think. But I will allow you to take one cup . . . if you do something for me."

"What could I do for you?" she said, her voice full of fear.

"You can polish the scales on the top of my head until each one glows like the sun. If you do that, you may take one cup of the Water of Life."

She looked at her ordinary hands, and, with nothing else to offer, she agreed. The dragon bent down his great golden head and she began to polish the scales, each one carefully. When she finished, he lifted his great head and hissed slowly, carefully, "One cup is yours—and take care how you use it."

As the golden dragon sank back down, the well filled with surging water. She seized the silver cup and filled it, turned quickly, and started back down the mountain.

When she came to the first stone she tripped, and one drop of water fell from the cup onto the stone. Before her eyes that stone turned into a human being. They looked at each other in amazement, then she looked at the water in the cup. She touched the next stone with the water. This stone, too, became a human being. And the next . . . And the next . . . And the next.

She noticed that the water in the cup did not diminish, and then she understood the dragon's words. One cup was much more. She moved down the path touching each of the stones with one drop of precious water and watched as each stone took its own human shape again. Happiest of all to see her were her own brothers. The four of them together, followed by all the people who had been stones, carried the cup back to the tree.

The people gathered in a great circle and watched as the four poured out the precious water at the base of the tree, and as it sank slowly into the earth the tree began to put out new leaves, then blossoms. As they watched, each blossom turned into perfect fruit, exactly enough for all who were there. The sister and brothers divided all the fruit and shared it with every person there. Each who tasted it found that their new year was filled with joy, which didn't mean they had no sorrows, only that their troubles did not overwhelm them. Trees began to grow in that stony land again, but only one tree bore the fruit of joy.

So it was, and ever will be, even now to this very day.

I will offer a brief sketch of how this evocative story has matured over a decade of oral performing, in order to reveal how it has come to reflect the evolution of my ideas about women and folktales. As I have already said, I was startled to see how far it had moved away from the printed text. The characters were similar, but the events had changed. I was not conscious of altering the story significantly, and two changes were particularly surprising: I wondered where the golden dragon had come from and where the prince had gone. The dragon as tester and helper seemed so natural to the story that I found it hard to believe it was not in the story as I had first read it. Dragons guard treasures, as we know, and what greater treasure is there than precious water? Such a prize could not be taken without a challenge of some sort. Yet in Lang's variant there is no challenge, no dragon.

And the prince? When I reread the story, he seemed so superfluous that it felt as if he had been added for a romantic conclusion. I simply had not remembered him at all when I began to tell the tale, so he vanished without a trace, and without protest. This was a clear reflection of my own inclinations at that time, my strong preference for heroic women who were more in need of dragons than of princes.

These were not deliberate alterations. I stress this because much of my folkloric work has emphasized the natural integrity of wonder tales, their deeply evocative and enigmatic essence.[5] As archetypal literature I insisted that they needed no conscious modifications to render them contemporary and relevant. My position was a reaction to overly zealous modernizers, including some feminists, who were often too quick to transform stories to fit new sensibilities and polemical positions. I found that if someone worked only from the surface of a tale rather than from its depths, the story invariably lost something in the translation. Archetype became stereotype and the mystery was gone. This is the problem with all of "the Disney versions," for example.

It was a shock, then, for me to see my own meddling. I had thought I was telling the story as I had read it rather than deliberately changing it to fit my preferences. This is a fine line to walk, since tellers and writers by nature are guided by their own predilections.[6] But at that time I was more scholar than teller, still anxious about interfering with a traditional story. I could see that the tale as I had been telling it made narrative sense and did not seem unfaithful to the spirit of the text since it rose up from the depths of the tale as I remembered it emotionally. Nevertheless, I felt uncomfortable with it because it was somehow not "true" to the text and tried to re-form it by returning to Lang's sequence of events. I removed the dragon, reinstated the prince, and allowed the wedding to take place. After several attempts at telling the "true" tale, I gave up on this impossible task; the story had become as petrified as one of the stones on the mountain path. It had lost its power over me, so I stopped telling it.

A year or so passed before I was motivated to tell the story again, this time as part of a workshop sponsored by a Christian feminist gathering in Toronto. I decided to take an artistic leap and return to my own variant to see if it was still capable of any life. Interestingly, when I told it to this particular group, the blossoming tree took on its own role, sharing the center of the story with the courageous and once again princeless sister. Considered in a Christian-centered context, the story revealed itself—naturally, not through my intentional manipulation—as a redemption of "the fall." The fruit of knowledge brought joy, and the serpentlike dragon was a source of power rather than an evil tempter. What he says to the woman is a question I have asked myself often: "Why did you come here and what do you want?" If she had failed to answer, her story would have ended quite differently. I, too, had to answer the question for myself. She sought the Water of Life for the tree; I sought the breath of life for the story.

I began to tell the story more regularly again and found that the sister's heroism became less of an issue for me. I saw that her test was not so much climbing a mountain and facing a dragon, but walking over the stones without letting them stop her. At this point in my told story, the stones began to speak more forcibly and in specific voices. She almost stopped for the stones that flattered her for having come so far as a "remarkable" woman, and then for the weeping stones that begged her, implicitly, to be a more traditional woman and not abandon them on the mountain. She had to leave these stones behind without seeming heartless and opportunistic, not by ignoring them but by hearing their cries and still going on, realizing that she would be unable to help if she stopped. This has been a very powerful moment for many who have heard the story.

The metaphoric image of living things that have been paralyzed, petrified, caught alive on their own rigid paths, became increasingly central to the story. I saw, too, how important it was that the eventual transformation of the stones comes about by accident, not bold action. The sister does not have a plan; she simply trips, makes a mistake, and from this learns the full power of the water. The stones find themselves alive again, no longer paralyzed by rage and despair. As a teller, I tripped when I "forgot" the Lang variant. More by accident than by deliberation, the tale took on its own life again.

After several years of telling this story in a wide variety of contexts, each one with new revelations, new perspectives on the twists and turns of the quest for the magical water, I came to a much deeper understanding of what held a wonder tale together and brought it ever-renewing life. As in a meaningful dream, all the elements of the story were necessary for its ripening, none were trivial or meaningless. As I learned from tellers I interviewed for my study of storytelling, *Burning Brightly,* a told tale is always new, always unfolding again and again over the years of its life.[7] This variability inspires ever-new paths of narrative investigation, arising from professional training in either (or both) artistic and academic disciplines. A story can begin to grow from within, like the fruit on the tree, guided in its development as much by intuitive narrative sense as by abstract rationale.

My long experience with "Frau Trude" and "The Water of Life" as told stories allowed me to experience the very real metaphoric correlations of folktale magic and mundane reality. Let me be more specific here, and playful, by using my telling of "The Water of Life" as an allegory of my work. When I began my work on women and folktales, I was following a trail first blazed by feminist writers who criticized fairy tales as sources of negative stereotyping. Like the bird in "The Water of Life," they revealed what and where the problem was and gave some idea of the path ahead. Simone de Beauvoir (1953) and Betty Friedan (1963), for example, identified and firmly rejected the overly feminine model projected by the pretty princesses who seemed to dominate so many fairy tales. These critiques kindled fire in my soul. But their images of figures like Cinderella and Sleeping Beauty were too generic, popular stereotypes rather than archetypal characters from specific stories. In contrast, later writers like Alison Lurie (1970) and Marcia Lieberman (1972) presented impassioned critiques of submissive heroines and surveyed them more comprehensively by using specific examples from popular collections. Lurie ("Fairy Tale Liberation") focused on the Grimms, while Lieberman sought her women in the multivolume Lang "fairy books." They found that heroines like the woman in "The Water of Life" were much outnumbered by their passive sisters, and they were angry about it. This further fired my own work, making my path more apparent. The two authors functioned for me like the fox in "The Water of Life," by providing more specific information about the difficulties of the path ahead.

In the following decades other scholars, among them Karen E. Rowe, Maria Tatar, Ruth B. Bottigheimer, and Jack Zipes, carried this work even further in publications exploring traditional heroines, while writers like Jane Yolen, Tanith Lee, and Angela Carter created new ones. Some of these stories gave me the creative energy to go on with my own work and challenged me as directly as had the dragon. I felt that I had an obligation, through my writing and storytelling, to carry the water of life back down the path.

Many feminist writers and authors, myself included, continued to hold fast to the dichotomy between negatively passive and positively active heroines. I still regarded "Frau Trude" and "The Water of Life" as opposites, even after I had managed to bring "The Curious Girl" out of the fire. More recently I have rethought my firm categories that held victimized heroines in disfavor. In this I was motivated by two very different storytellers (for a detailed exploration see Stone, "Burning" and *Burning Brightly* 219–37). Susan Gordon wrote about her understanding of the Grimm tale "The Maiden without Hands" (Aarne-Thompson tale type 706), gained through her retellings. This heroine, threatened by the devil, mutilated by her own father, sent into exile to suffer alone, was one I had firmly classified as "Persecuted," an example of the most abjectly abused of all heroines. Susan's words made me look again at a heroine she viewed as heroic, a resourceful woman who does not submit passively to her fate. This was an opinion I had already heard, and ignored, from a few of the girls and women I interviewed during my early research. I had glossed over these responses as aberrations, but when I reread the interviews, I was compelled to see how earnest these respondents were in insisting that "persecuted" heroines were, in fact, heroic. Similarly, Toronto teller Carol McGirr insisted that the persecuted sister, Tanya, from the Russian tale "The Rosy Apple and the Golden Bowl," was dauntlessly heroic. I had to admit that she was certainly dauntless, overcoming her own death to triumph fully over her cruel sisters in the end.

This shift of viewpoint blurred the distinct boundaries of the four categories I set up in my dissertation, most notably those that placed persecuted and heroic women at opposite ends of the scale. Telling stories for twenty-five years further softened the firm lines I placed between categories. Having brought "Frau Trude" and "The Water of Life" together here, I am startled to see how much these two have grown together over the years. The two protagonists have become more sisters than opposites, experiencing the elemental forces of fire and water. The antagonists, too, are less disparate, the crone now cousin to the golden dragon; both are awesome figures who offer challenges that open the possibility of renewed life.

You will recall that the unexpected is to be expected in wonder tales. Just when you think the path is clear, something happens that turns everything around again. So it is in the telling of tales as well. In my present retelling of "The Water of Life" the prince has surprised me by slipping back in, though not quite in the form he originally enjoyed. It happened this way: Almost at the moment I called up the story text to begin revising it for the eye, I had a phone call from a friend asking if I knew "something ecological with a love theme" for her daughter's wedding in another city. I said that the story I had just started to edit was certainly ecological, with its theme of a tree that needs pure water in order to live again, but I was not sure about a "love theme." I was willing to play with the story for a few days for this special occasion, and as I tried it out with friends the prince did indeed find his way back. This time, however, he was a commoner, a wandering musician who was more interested in the heroine's accomplishments than in her beauty. I was intrigued to see, when I reread Lang's variant, that even in the printed tale he had the good sense to admire "the courage of the maiden" and not just her beauty. This gave him more potential.

I finished this special wedding gift and went back to work on the story. The prince, I found, wanted to stay, and I saw that he had opened an archetypal slot for a character—not necessarily male—who could carry the story further. I did not want a love story with a concluding wedding celebration, but I was curious to see what might happen if I left the slot open. I wondered who might wander in. After telling the story to friends, this unknown figure became a simple traveler of unknown gender or age, with no overt romantic expectations. This left the story open-ended, with further interpretation left up to the reader or listener. The ten-year-old friend I read it to was intrigued by this unusual resolution. She still called the traveler "he" but said she could see how it could be "she" or even "it." She wanted the fox to come back into the story. A mature friend about to set off on a solo kayak voyage envisioned an older woman looking for new adventures. No one who heard the "new" ending objected to the additional character, so as of this writing, here is the concluding scene of my told story:

The fame of that tree, and of the sister who found the water that renewed it, spread through that land and beyond. One day someone from far away heard this remarkable tale and came to see if it was true. When this curious one arrived at the place where the sister and her brothers lived, they were happy to show the tree and to tell how it came to bloom again. The traveler admired the strangeness and beauty of the tree and the truth of the tale, but even more than that admired the courage of the woman who had climbed over the speaking stones and touched a dragon to win the Water of Life.

"I will play you a song in exchange for the story," said the stranger, who took out a small flute and began to play.

When the sister heard the song, she recognized the melody that had accompanied her all the way through the forest and up the stony path. She admired the strangeness and beauty of the music, but even more than that she admired the skill of the one who played it. She asked where the song had come from.

"You'll think it's peculiar," answered the traveler, "but I'll tell you. One night I had a curious dream about a fox playing a flute. My tune came from this dream."

"I see," she said, smiling. "I know that tune."

And it was true.

So it was, and ever will be, to this very day.

This story, and wonder tales in general, continue to grow as long as the telling (or rewriting) of them goes on.

When I consider how long I have contemplated folktales and heroines, I see that the lifeblood of my work has been a deep interest in resourcefulness and transformation. These features are central to the mystery of wonder tales, true even for the most downtrodden or the most aggressive of heroines. By using two very different stories as examples, I hope I have been able to show the resilience of old tales and their heroines as they continue to live and to interact in the modern world, told and retold in contemporary contexts.

Composing stories orally is as ephemeral as writing in air, and writing them is, for me, like trying to carve words into solid rock. Both are frustrating and rewarding, in quite different ways.[8] Much of the time I have felt more like a stone on the mountain path than the woman who touches each of them with transformational water. It is a struggle to keep going, keep writing, keep telling. Sometimes I have to wait for that single drop of creativity to get me rolling again. This is a challenge for us as feminist scholars and writers and tellers—keeping our voices alive even when we feel petrified, unable to continue on the path or to face the dragon even when we succeed in climbing the mountain. Eventually we find our way, meet our witches and dragons, pass through fire, and carry water back down to other thirsting stones.

NOTES

1. In my 1975 dissertation ("Romantic Heroines"), heroines were classified, according to a four-part hierarchical scheme, as Persecuted, Trapped, Tamed, or Heroic, depending on their degree of mistreatment (at one end of the scale) or resourcefulness (at the other). I have abandoned this overly simplified method of interpretation, but it was useful at the time for seeing patterns in folktales featuring women.

2. From *The Pink Fairy Book* of Andrew Lang, who identified his source as *Cuentos Populars Catalans,* by Dr. D. Francisco de S. Maspous y Labros (Barcelona, 1885).

3. This is precisely what has happened to her as this story became part of my oral repertoire. She flies out of the fire as a shower of glowing sparks and is turned into a fiery red bird by the crone, who then demands a story that has never been heard before. After searching the world for stories, the girl/bird brings them all back but finds, in the end, that it is her own story that the crone has never heard—and she, like the stones in "The Water of Life," comes to be herself again (for texts, see Stone, "Burning," "Curious," and *Burning Brightly* 235–37).

4. This text is a reworking of a printed version I contributed to a collection of Canadian folktales edited by Dan Yashinsky, though of course the words are different when I tell it.

5. This is true even when stories have been altered by collectors like the Grimms, Perrault, and Lang, who claimed to be true in spirit—if not in word—to traditional folktales.

6. The personal artistic aspect of storytelling has been a major interest of folklorist Linda Dégh, who has touched on this in much of her scholarly writing; see in particular her *Hungarian Folktales* and *Narratives.*

7. The changeability of told tales is often described as "emergent quality," a term introduced by folklorist Richard Bauman.

8. The composition of told and written stories is different, since reading is for the eye and hearing is for the ear. Thus I do not necessarily *tell* a story twice in the same words, even when I have published a written variant.

7

The Fairy-Tale Intertext in Iberian and Latin American Women's Writing

PATRICIA ANNE ODBER DE BAUBETA

INTRODUCTION

*T*his essay is, in part, a response to Donald Haase's gentle reminder at the beginning of this volume that "scholars need to expand the focus of feminist fairy-tale research beyond the Western European and Anglo-American tradition, and even within those traditions to investigate the fairy-tale intertexts in the work of minority writers" (29). For three decades feminist scholars have examined the works of English and North American authors such as the Brontës, Jane Austen, Angela Carter, Anne Sexton, and Margaret Atwood to demonstrate how fairy-tale intertexts function "as subversive strategies to contest the idealized outcomes of fairy tales and their representations of gender and female identity" (20). Less well known is that for the last seventy years or so, women writers in Portugal, Spain, and Latin America have also been appropriating and adapting the forms and content of traditional literary fairy tales—principally those of Perrault, Grimm, and Andersen—for their own specific purposes, and certainly not for a juvenile readership. Several scholars have done invaluable work in drawing attention to Spanish women writers and their works,[1] while others have carried out the same task with respect to Latin American authors.[2] Specialists in Iberian and Latin American literature, aware of Anglo-American critical theories, have produced analytical commentaries on individual authors and their works.

Nevertheless, with the exception of notable studies by Stephen M. Hart, Janet Pérez, and Fiona Mackintosh (in this volume), there has been no attempt to discern any pattern or trend, nor has anyone sketched in the broader picture of fairy-tale intertextualities in twentieth-century Iberian or Latin American women's writing. This is perhaps to be expected, given the diversity of languages, countries, and continents involved. The study that follows cannot cover the subject area exhaustively, but it does bring together several important tools for future research: First, it serves as a preliminary survey of Iberian and Latin American women writers who use fairy-tale intertextualities in their prose fiction, accompanied by a listing of significant primary texts and, where known, their English translations. Second, it suggests several provisional headings under which these narratives can be analyzed. Third, it provides brief commentaries on works of prose fiction that have received little or no critical attention to date.

In approximately chronological order, the primary texts range from *Jardín* (*Garden*), by the Cuban writer Dulce María Loynaz (written between 1928 and 1933 but published in 1951), to *Primer amor* (*First Love*), a series of essays by Laura Espido Freire, published in Spain in 2000. In the intervening years more than two dozen women used fairy-tale intertexts to a greater or lesser extent in their own creative writing. Venezuelan author Teresa de la Parra published *Memorias de Mamá Blanca* (1929; *Mamá Blanca's Souvenirs*), a nostalgic evocation of the author's childhood; María Teresa León, in Spain, wrote *La bella del mal amor* (1930; *The Beauty of Bad Love*) and *Cuentos para soñar* (1929; *Tales for Dreaming*). Initially overshadowed by her illustrious husband, Rafael Alberti, León has now come to be considered a serious author in her own right. The same decade saw the emergence of the much-studied Chilean author María Luisa Bombal, whose entire literary production is permeated with fairy-tale motifs and symbols (Agosín, "Un cuento"; V. Smith).

The intertextual trend continued through the second half of the twentieth century. As Stephen Hart (*White Ink* 56) points out, the Mexican writer Elena Garro (also initially eclipsed by an eminent husband, Octavio Paz) draws on "Sleeping Beauty" in her *Recuerdos del porvenir* (1963; *Recollections of Things to Come*). In post–civil war Spain we find the works of Ana María Matute and Carmen Martín Gaite, whose writing continues through the transition from dictatorship to democracy. Catalan authors writing in Catalan also used fairy-tale motifs: Núria Pompeia, *Maternasis* (1967); Maria-Mercè Marçal i Serra, *Bruixa de dol* (1979; *Witch in Mourning*); and Dolors Orfila i Cirach, *Petits contes cruels i breus narracions* (1981; *Cruel Little Tales and Brief Narratives*). Still in Europe, three Portuguese authors wrote within this tradition, one of them before the Revolution of 25 April 1974 that restored democratic government: Fernanda Botelho, *Terra sem música* (1969; *Land Without Music*); Hélia Correia, *Montedemo* (1983); and Ana Teresa Pereira, *Fairy Tales* (1996). At the same time, a whole series of Argentine writers, analyzed in detail by Fiona Mackintosh in the following essay in the present volume, thoroughly subverted fairy-tale conventions. These include Victoria Ocampo, Silvina Ocampo, Alicia Borinsky, Liliana Heker, Cristina Piña, Ana María Shua, Marcela Solá, and Luisa Valenzuela.

INTERTEXTUAL TECHNIQUES

The most cursory review reveals that writers manipulate the literary fairy-tale tradition in a variety of ways, many of which conform to the "intertextual tactics" identified by Sharon Rose Wilson in her book on Margaret Atwood. The most straightforward method is simply to call a collection of short stories "fairy tales," immediately setting up particular expectations in the reader. Luisa Valenzuela, for her part, simultaneously builds on and undermines the fairy-tale tradition in *Simetrías* (1993; *Symmetries*), where she transforms the term *cuentos de hadas*—"tales of fairies"—into the clever title "Cuentos de hades"—"Tales from Hades."

A related technique is to give a work a title that immediately evokes the beginning or ending of a fairy tale. For instance, the title of Ana María Moix's postmodern metafiction in *Las virtudes peligrosas* (1985; *Dangerous Virtues*) is "Erase una vez" ("Once upon a Time"). The story concerns the characters who inhabit fairy tales, nursery rhymes, and popular ballads, forever subject to human imagination or dreams. These fictional constructs live unhappily ever after in a pink house in a park, permanently on call, "imprisoned by the implacable, fatal destiny that joined them all together" (55).[3] The story refers as much to the act of writing as to the role of popular culture. "It bothered some of his brothers and sisters to be in children's imaginations. . . . But all of them hated to be read; to be condemned to exist in the dead pages of a book, in the form of the printed word, filled them with anguish" (54). Despite its rather excessive self-reflexivity, the work does have some humorous touches. Sleeping Beauty "was not only extremely homely but malicious. She drank coffee nonstop to avoid drowsiness, and to show them that she knew how to spin perfectly well without pricking herself" (44). Moix's Snow White is no better off than Anne Sexton's "little hot dogs" (6), bullied by racist, sexist dwarves: "Do you think it's so easy to find a near-sighted prince to kiss you and wake you every time someone gets the notion to tell your ridiculous story?" (44). In other examples of authors alluding to opening and closing formulas in the title of their works, Núria Pompeia calls her 1970 collection of cartoons and texts in Spanish, Catalan, and French *Y fueron felices comiendo perdices* (*And They Lived Happily Ever After*), while the Uruguayan Andrea Blanqué goes further and leaves no doubt as to the outcome of each of the seven stories in her 1990 collection, *y no fueron felices* (*and they didn't live happily ever after*).

Some writers name their work after a particular fairy tale or character in a tale. In *Los condenados* (1971; *The Condemned*), Marcela Solá titles her reworking of "Little Red Riding Hood," told from the wolf's point of view, "El lobo feroz"—"The Big Bad Wolf." Carmen Martín Gaite, doyenne of Spanish letters until her death in 2000, published *La reina de las nieves* (*The Snow Queen*) in 1994, whose male protagonist identifies strongly with Gerda. Alternatively, works may contain fairy-tale material whose presence is not signaled in the title, as is the case of Solá's 1990 short story "Bodas" ("Wedding"), a new version of Snow White, with a shift from third- to first-person narrative point of view (Wilson 32). Authors frequently use the metafictional technique of incorporating fairy-tale strands into their narratives, as for example Lourdes Ortiz Sánchez in her historical novel *Urraca* (1982), allowing her protagonist, the imprisoned Queen Urraca, mother of Alfonso VII of Castile and Leon, to comment on her predicament.

NOVEL OF FEMALE DEVELOPMENT OR NOVEL OF FEMALE DISILLUSIONMENT?

Much has been written about the relationship between fairy tales and the novel of female development, where the fairy tale may suggest "ideal" models of behavior and their subsequent rewards (Rowe, "Fairy-born"). However, research has demonstrated that contemporary women writers tend to use fairy-tale motifs to deconstruct certain discourses. This occurs with Carmen Laforet's prizewinning novel *Nada* (1945), with its Cinderella motif, set in a Spain still deeply scarred by the Civil War. Depicting the same troubled society, Matute uses fairy-tale motifs to chart the loss of innocence that characterizes the transition to adulthood in her novel *Primera memoria* (1959; literally, *First Memory*, translated as both *Awakening* and *School of the Sun*). Martín Gaite's *El cuarto de atrás* (*The Back Room*), published in 1978, after Franco's death and the relaxation of censorship, has been described by Stephen Hart as a metafictional, feminist text that uses the fairy tale to challenge patriarchal narratives and thus empower women (*White Ink* 78). This work is effectively a recasting of her earlier novel, *Entre visillos* (1958; *Behind the Curtains*).

In 1976 Rosario Ferré published "La bella durmiente" ("Sleeping Beauty") in the collection *Papeles de Pandora* (literally, *Pandora's Papers*; translated as *The Youngest Doll*). The three parts of this story are named after famous fairy-tale ballets: *Coppelia, Sleeping Beauty* (the Perrault version), and *Giselle*. At least with regard to use of musical intertext as structuring device, this is strongly reminiscent of the earlier story by María Luisa Bombal, "El árbol" (1939; "The Tree"), made up of a series of mental flashbacks that are framed by three piano pieces by Mozart, Beethoven, and Chopin. The Mozart selection transports Brígida back to a carefree childhood and adolescence, the Beethoven piece accompanies the first days of her marriage, while the Chopin *Etudes* bring back memories of her profound unhappiness. The fundamental difference between these narratives lies in the fact that Brígida resolves to leave Luis and begin a new life, while María de los Angeles, who only ever wanted to dance, is murdered by her husband, Felisberto. Ferré's narrative, like so many other works, points to the impossibility for women of reconciling development as an artist with the demands of marriage.

At the other end of the spectrum, we find works in which a disillusioned, middle-aged protagonist contrasts the sterility of her present life with the empty promises held out by the fairy tales of childhood. Nowhere is this seen more clearly than in Bombal's *La última niebla* (1935; *The Final Mist*). Interestingly, Bombal rewrote her own novella as *House of Mist,* with significant additions, many of which are direct allusions to fairy-tale characters and plots. Where the anonymous protagonist of *La última niebla* faces a lonely, frustrated old age, trapped in an unhappy childless marriage, the named heroine of *House of Mist* does have a happy ending; her fairy tale comes true. This reversal of the earlier version is easily explained—Bombal sold the film rights to this work for $125,000 at precisely the same time as Hitchcock was directing such Gothic classics as *Rebecca,* another variation on the Cinderella theme. The same themes are found in Bombal's *La amortajada* (1938; *The Shrouded Woman*) and "La historia de María Griselda" ("The Story of María Griselda").[4] In fact, it could be argued that Bombal always has the same female protagonist, although at different stages of her life—girlhood ("El árbol"), middle age (*La última niebla*), and death (*La amortajada*)—as well as the recurring figure of the cold, indifferent, undemonstrative or unfaithful husband or lover.

Esther Tusquets's *El mismo mar de todos los veranos* (1978; *The Same Sea as Every Summer*) deals with the disillusionment experienced by a member of the Barcelona haute bourgeoisie, expressed to some extent through fairy-tale allusions. Leafing through an illustrated book of fairy tales, the narrator-protagonist comments with irony on what others may perceive as her failings and inadequacies:

> I must be one of these older, haughty queens with stiff dresses of heavy, sumptuous material, wearing a huge crown on their heads, still beautiful however, although perhaps a little wizened and hard, asking silly questions of mirrors that can't be flattering and truthful at the same time, or pricking their fingertips with little gold knives in order to let three drops of maternal protective blood fall on light lace hankies . . . perhaps that is why I have never been able to assume a normal stereotypal image, so tranquilizing for a woman like me: envious and aggressive mother and/or clement, kind mother. (118)

Sofía and Mariana, the aging women of Martín Gaite's novel *Nubosidad variable* (1992; *Variable Cloud*), are, like many of Margaret Atwood's characters, frustrated artists, "always searching for some reference point in literature" (169). As a result, in their letters to one another, they make constant allusions to literary works in general and fairy tales in particular ("Cinderella," "Sleeping Beauty"), both as a way of commenting on the constraints imposed by gender and coming to terms with the knowledge that dreams do not come true. In contrast, Maria-Antònia Oliver i Cabrer uses fairy-tale elements more positively to make a feminist statement in *El vaixell d'iràs i no tornaràs* (1976; *The Ship That Never Returns*), a "study of adolescent passage to womanhood as well as of matriarchal tutelage" (McNerney and Enríquez de Salamanca 267).

EMBEDDED FAIRY TALES—*TERRA SEM MÚSICA*

If some writers weave selected fairy tale strands into their narratives, others embed complete stories, for purposes of deconstruction and subversion, or at the very least, to introduce ambiguity and thus the possibility of multiple readings and interpretations. Fernanda Botelho is a case in point. *Terra sem música* (1969; 2nd ed. 1991)—or *Land Without Music*—contains a lengthy version of "Bluebeard." While not written with a feminist slant, it does predate such key texts as Angela Carter's *The Bloody Chamber* (1979) and Margaret Atwood's *Bluebeard's Egg* (1983), with which it could usefully stand comparison. This novel, not yet studied at any length in Portugal or abroad, merits closer examination, not least because of the interlocking framing devices used to chronicle the breakdown of the protagonist's relationships and the eventual fragmentation of her personality. The novel is the story of Antónia, who is trying to write a book. The work that engages her is *O livro de Pitch* (*The Book of Pitch*), passages from which are set alongside the sections that narrate Antónia's everyday life. As the novel progresses, it seems increasingly probable that Pitch is a figment of Antónia's imagination, a kind of alter ego (her archetype, she says). Where Antónia is the ant, Pitch is the grasshopper. The work is in fact closer to autobiography, though this is initially denied, and within this work is Antónia's own version of the Bluebeard story, "a história do Barba Azul, reescrita por mim, em sua (dela Pitch) única e exclusiva intenção" ("the story of Bluebeard, rewritten by me, uniquely and exclusively for her, Pitch" [178]). Significantly, this story within a story is inserted immediately after Antónia has broken off her relationship with her married lover Sérgio.

Sérgio initially approves of her literary activity because it "limits her frustrations" (or rather, keeps her occupied while he is at work or visiting his children and the wife from whom he has separated). Antónia has always lived in a world of books and is concerned with philosophy and existential questions. From the beginning there is a clear split between the intelligent, well-educated, sophisticated Antónia, who goes to work in an international company, accompanies Sérgio to cocktail parties, is passive, dependent, and essentially frustrated by her futile existence, and the Antónia who attempts to "write back." Botelho retains the essential elements of Perrault's tale, but the reworking is remarkable for its complex language and structures, used in a humorous parody of academic discourse. Much of this story is treated like a scholarly paper that presents and weighs evidence in order to produce irrefutable results. For example, a document has come to light that clarifies an error of interpretation, authenticated by two of the most erudite researchers of the present day—"eminent Bluebeardians" ("preclaros barbazulianos" [196])—and proving that the beard was not naturally blue. Despite, or perhaps because of, the deliberately archaic tone, we find traces of fairy-tale discourse embedded in this narrative. These include the absence of individualizing proper names, apart from Bluebeard's own: repetitions such as "a-senhora-sua-vizinha" ("the lady-his-neighbor"), the line "uma delas, indiferentemente, embora com ligeira preferência pela ruiva, que era a mais nova" ("one of them, it didn't matter which, though with a slight preference for the red-head, who was the younger" [197]), and "uma das filhas, indiferentemente, embora com ligeira preferência pela ruiva, que era a mais nova" ("one of the daughters, it didn't matter which, though with a slight preference for the red-head, who was the younger" [198]).

Bluebeard's perversion is explained in pseudo-scientific terms, attributed to an excess of cholesterol. This in turn leads, in erudite language, to "gerolibidocracia" (197), or uncontrollable sexual urges, when the object is in close proximity to the subject. Contrasting with the scientific justification, the narrator offers an explanation in common language, through the medium of a proverb. In fact, only half of the proverb is given, since it is assumed that the reader will be able to supply the other half.

Bluebeard asks for one of the daughters in much the same kind of language we would expect to find in a sixteenth-century chivalric novel. This contrasts with the seemingly anachronistic list of his goods and assets, including hotel chains, steel monopolies, petrol tankers, and trusts in South America. In one of the narrator's many asides, we are told that Fouquet would be as jealous of Bluebeard's palace as Louis XIV had been of his castle of Vaux Le Vicomte. Returning from a business trip to claim his bride, Bluebeard cleverly precipitates events by suggesting that if his neighbor were not so inconsolable in her widowhood, he would ask for her hand instead of her daughter's. This produces the desired result. In fact, the sisters have been busy. Going against biblical stereotypes, the elder sister does not act like a wise virgin warning against the dangers inherent in such a marriage, nor does the younger sister, an unwise virgin, drown her scruples in a sea of economic prospects. Rather, the two have coldly calculated Bluebeard's financial situation, drawing a graph of "before-during-after," with an upward curve. This document, so the narrator writes, in legalistic language reminiscent of a last will and testament, is now in the hands of the person who has inherited the remainder of Bluebeard's goods, bequeathed by his widow to the children of her brother, the captain of dragoons, and their descendants.

From this point on, Antónia's tale diverges from the original, and indeed from the revisions, by presenting the sisters not just as venal but as cold-blooded murderers. What was previously a suspicion concerning the "lastimoso fim" ("lamentable end" [201]) of Bluebeard has now been confirmed as fact. The next section discusses an annotation, IX-123, found on the document containing the financial chart. This number corresponds to a particular chapter and page in an ancient manual housed in the widow's library. The manual contains the recipe for a purifying potion, described as odorless, tasteless, and colorless (not only undetectable but also, so it is implied, used as an abortifacient), and that brought on fainting fits. After his wedding, Bluebeard does indeed suffer fainting fits, always in the nuptial bed, after intercourse with his demanding young wife.

Following another self-conscious narratorial aside, there is a variation on what would normally be the closing words of a fairy tale: "Eram felizes e viviam bem"—"They were happy and they lived well" (204)—which is by no means the same as they lived happily ever after. Life is a succession of banquets, parties, and worldly pleasures, with one exception. Hunting is forbidden because the bride faints at the sight of blood. This information is given in italics and must therefore be significant for the outcome of the story.

As in the original tale, Bluebeard leaves his palace in order to attend to business affairs. The bride may invite her sister and their friends to keep her company. She is handed a bunch of keys (in a comically incongruous list) to the discotheque, picture gallery, periodical library, and a reliquary that contains the uneaten heart of an enemy of one King Pedro of Lusitania. This reference to Portugal's greatest love story, in which Inês de Castro was murdered, may be Bluebeard's oblique warning to his wife; certainly it allows a joke at the expense of the Portuguese, apparently a pleasant race. In any event, she is warned not to use one special key. And just so that there is no confusion, Bluebeard tells her precisely which room it opens, at the end of gallery 5, on the fourth floor, reached by lift 7. Furthermore, there is a fluorescent sign above the door case, which reads, *Lasciate ogni speranza, voi che'ntrate* ("Abandon all hope, you who enter"), the phrase invented, so he claims, by himself. In fact, this is not only a borrowing from Dante (*Inferno*, canto 3) but also an intertextual pointer to Victor Hugo's *Notre Dame de Paris*, book 8, 4, titled, *Lasciate Ogni Speranza*, in which Esmeralda is imprisoned in the Bastille dungeons, site of dismemberment and mutilation, awaiting her execution.

Despite the threat of Bluebeard's anger, the bride and her sister rush to the room and find the corpses of his previous wives. The women send for their brothers, then remember to retrieve the now bloodstained key. Here the narrative parodies Perrault's original moral, about the negative effects of women's curiosity, with an additional observation about stupidity.

On Bluebeard's inevitable return, his wife asks for time to prepare for death by praying and climbs up to the tower where her sister is scanning the horizon, awaiting the arrival of their brothers. This part of the narrative ends with the two women waiting. The next section, couched in the language of an official report, deals with Bluebeard's death. The narrator reminds us of the annotation on the graph, Bluebeard's fainting fits, and the fact that his wife could not stand the sight of blood. He was found with a sword through his heart, but not a drop of blood; his redheaded wife was calm and pink. The verdict was one of legitimate self-defense.

However, it may be that he was already dead when the sword was thrust into his heart, an act destined to obviate the need for a postmortem examination that would reveal the cause of his fainting fits. Parodying Perrault, the narrator suggests that if there is any moral(ity) to be found in this tale, it should not be lost in a world where men have lost the "verticality" of their elders and betters.

The tale as retold by Botelho raises interesting issues. The story does show a number of the textual strategies outlined by Sharon Rose Wilson (32–33)—that is to say, the female's shift from object to subject (the red-head and her sister plot very carefully and triumph in the end). The narrator shifts between different levels of language. There is a discernible movement from negative to positive, since Bluebeard does not murder his wife. The story has different levels of transgression: the bride disobeys her husband by entering the bloody chamber, but she also premeditates his murder and poisons him.

There is some ambiguity in the fact that although the writer-protagonist is a woman, the frame story and the embedded fairy tale are both narrated from the man's perspective; the latter even seems to betray a certain sympathy for Bluebeard. One interpretation is that Antónia and the other women in her social circle have become alienated to the point of losing their selfhood. Or there may be an element of wish fulfillment where Antónia identifies with the young redheaded bride and wants to "kill" her own Bluebeard, a composite of Sérgio and her late father. She still lives in her father's house, reads his books, listens to his records, and dwells in his shadow. Adrião, for whom Antónia leaves Sérgio, addresses her as "Medusa querida" ("darling Medusa" [255]), while she herself, in the final paragraph of the novel, possibly on the verge of unconsciousness or death, says: "E o meu nome. Medusa. Me-de-usa!" ("It's my name. Medusa. Me-de-usa!" [270]). In phallocentric culture, according to Wilson, the woman artist is the Medusa monster (18–20). Although Antónia tries to rewrite her story, she has not yet undergone "the female artist's transformation from patriarchal Medusa monster in Rapunzel tower to woman artist courageous enough to draw on Medusa wisdom and her own artistic vision" (Wilson 20), hence, the fragmentation and ultimate destruction of her personality.

New Creations

The final category to be considered comprises new and original fairy tales. Certain writers have veered away from rewriting the older, canonical tales, opting instead to create their own, with the result that their writing is often labeled, appropriately or not, as magical realism. This is the case of Hélia Correia's *Montedemo,* discussed at length by Owen and now part of the alter canon of Portuguese feminist writing.

Less well known is Ana Teresa Pereira, author of numerous works of children's fiction and gothic horror stories (several complete with vampires) that have been published in detective fiction series. According to Fátima Maldonado, "It is impossible to read Ana Teresa Pereira without Angela Carter, the American [*sic*] who reinvented the fairy tale, immediately appearing." Of the seven stories that constitute Pereira's *Fairy Tales,* two are particularly germane to this essay, "O ponto de vista das gaivotas" ("The Seagull's Point of View) and "O teu lugar no meu corpo" ("Your Place in My Body"). In all of her fiction, Pereira plays with intertextuality, whether literary, musical, or filmic. This work is no exception. Where Botelho has used a Chinese box structure of story within a story within a story, Pereira uses a film review as her framing device. In fact, the film that the narrator describes does not exist but has been invented for the first of the two stories and has enough elements of truth that it is very convincing. Directed by Hitchcock, it comes between *Notorious* and *The Paradine Case* in his filmography and is supposedly based on a Daphne Du Maurier short story, which links the seagulls of this text to her story *The Birds,* also filmed by Hitchcock. The screenplay is attributed to Ben Hecht, who did indeed produce screenplays of Hitchcock, and the music has been scored by Bernard Herrmann. The director has cast Ingrid Bergman and Humphrey Bogart in the key roles. James Stewart, so we are told, would not have been believable in the role of wife killer. Hitchcock himself appears in the opening sequence, a wedding, in which he takes a photograph (a frame within a frame). In the next scene, Bergman is looking at the photograph, afraid. There is also a housekeeper, "a bruxa má presente em tantos filmes de Hitchcock" ("the wicked witch who is present in so many of Hitchcock's films" [34]), strongly reminiscent of Mrs. Danvers in *Rebecca,* and a tower, as "no conto do Barba Azul" ("in the Blue Beard story" [35]). The main intertextualities are Hitchcock's films and references to fairy tales. All of these are quite explicit and serve to blur the boundaries between reality and fiction, reality and dream. The film that frames the narrative may itself be a nightmare.

The second Pereira tale is longer but has many of the same themes. The beginning of the story could perfectly well be the opening sequence of a Hitchcock film, with the male protagonist/camera moving through an old iron gate toward a junglelike garden. A journalist falls in love with a

writer of detective stories and goes to live with her in her isolated country
house, something he must not divulge to anyone. Unlike Atwood's characters, however, this writer is in no way frustrated. Looking like a princess
in a fairy tale with waist-length red hair, she does her work in a circular
tower covered by climbing plants, with a front door at the bottom and a
tiny window at the top. The journalist engages her attention when he says,
"Rapunzel, Rapunzel," and they discover a shared love of fairy tales as well
as the fiction of William Irish, from which she quotes at length. Irish,
though we are not told in the story, was the pseudonym of Cornell
Woolrich, prolific writer of pulp fiction, murder stories, *romans noirs*, gothic
and vampire tales, and tales of the macabre, who coined the phrase "First
we dream, then we die." In fact, Irish was the author of *Rear Window*,
adapted for film by Hitchcock, and a story titled, like the apocryphal film
in "O ponto de vista das gaivotas," *Nightmare* (1950). The mention of Irish
as a favorite writer inevitably foreshadows some gruesome outcome. The
journalist is forbidden to visit the tower and asks her if that is where she
has buried her husbands, to which comes the reply that they are in the garden. Once he has moved into her house, the journalist begins to have strange
dreams. In one of these, he finds himself before a dense hedge of thorns,
which opens up and allows him admittance to a castle, in which he finds a
sleeping beauty. In another dream, he watches her as she stands framed in
the tower window, like an icon, with her unbound hair. The woman is
described as a fairy-tale figure, not an intellectual, more a witch, an
enchanted princess or an elf that can disappear into the earth or the garden ponds. She does not eat meat, rarely sleeps, and can see in the dark.
Eventually the journalist gives in to curiosity, in a reversal of the normal
convention whereby it is the woman whose curiosity brings about her down-
fall. He goes up into the tower and in a desk drawer finds photographs of
two men, one a painter who disappeared two years previously and one a
younger man. The writer returns to find the journalist in her privileged
space and prepares a special meal, with roast meat. She also dresses for the
occasion, so that he compares her with Cinderella going to her first ball.
After dinner they make love and he falls asleep. She crushes a rose in her
hand, and three drops of blood (recalling Snow White) fall on the white
sheet. Now everything makes sense, as she leans over him with a silver knife
in her hand, telling him, "You'll always be inside me" and "I love you" (46).
    The one fairy tale that is crucial for our understanding of this story
is never mentioned explicitly, yet what we have here is a reversal of "Barba
Azul," or "Bluebeard." Instead of a red-haired woman as victim, the victim is the man. Ruth B. Bottigheimer has observed that "the single most

pervasive image evoked in the popular mind by the word fairy tale is probably that of a maiden in distress leaning from a tower window and searching the horizon for a rescuer" (*Grimms' Bad Girls* 101). This Rapunzel is
not trapped in her tower, but she uses it as her refuge, in which she is able
to pursue her artistic activities, emerging periodically to sate her physical
appetites. The writer's relationship with her garden should not be under-
estimated. From the beginning, it is made clear that she is completely in
tune with nature, giving out a perfume like roses or peach blossom, apparently melting into the luxuriant vegetation. The writer draws her strength
from her garden, from the world of nature, and this enables her to write;
she is like an Earth goddess who requires sacrifices and thus kills her lovers
to nourish the earth, which in turn feeds her artistic powers. He will always
be in her body, because she is the garden, which gives a new meaning to
the concepts of *écriture féminine* and "writing the body."

ANDREA BLANQUÉ'S *Y NO FUERON FELICES*

The Uruguayan writer and cultural journalist Andrea Blanqué has seven
tales in her collection *y no fueron felices* (*and they didn't live happily ever after*).
The text has been printed in cursive script, and to bring the contemporary
reader closer to the experience of reading a traditional fairy-tale book, all
of the stories open with "Había una vez" ("Once upon a time"), complete
with dropped capital. Each tale also has a full-page drawing to illustrate a
key moment in the narrative. In addition to these external indications, the
internal characteristics confirm the stories' status as fairy tales. The language used is deliberately archaic in flavor, and all are narrated in the omnis-
cient third person. The narrative is linear, there are no place-names or
references to particular moments in time, and characters are not given individual names but are referred to by their social position (the King, the
Prince, the Princess), by their profession (the Warrior, the Captain, the
Shepherd), or even by their species (the Mermaid, the Bird).

Although the collection's title already foreshadows unhappy endings,
the brutality depicted in some of the tales may still have a shocking effect,
especially when contrasted with the traditional fairy-tale elements that are
so apparent. A page boy is tortured with fire to make him reveal the secrets
of the royal bedchamber in "La dama sabia y la reina bella" ("The Wise
Lady and the Beautiful Queen"), while in the same story the king is physically and verbally abused by his profoundly unhappy wife. In "El hombre
que volvió de la guerra" ("The Man Who Returned from the War"), a

princess who succumbs to a handsome warrior first swallows rat poison in an attempt to abort the child she may have conceived; in the end, the pregnant princess and her lover are slain by her husband, the Seneschal, while they lie asleep in each other's arms. The cook, a witch figure, slits her belly open with the Seneschal's sword and holds up a living girl child.

The flute-playing shepherd of "El pastor del cordero" ("The Shepherd of the Lamb"), who demonstrates great tenderness toward his animals, is unable to live with the countess who loves him, because she reads manuscripts, writes, and mixes potions. When he asks, "What kind of woman are you who, instead of bearing children, steep yourself in this foulness?" (71), the countess strikes him. In response, he beats her with tremendous savagery, destroys her papers, smashes the bottles, ruining all her work, and goes back to the woods where she met him. The impact of the story derives from the incongruity between its title, suggestive of nurturing and warmth, and the violent denouement, as well as from the message it appears to transmit—that a loving relationship is incompatible with female intellectual activity.

The story with the most obvious intertextual echoes is "El capitán y la sirena" ("The Captain and the Mermaid"), which ineluctably reminds the reader of Andersen's "The Little Mermaid" (1837). A mermaid follows a ship because the captain is a wonderful raconteur and has the gift of making everyone laugh, even a mermaid, when it is well known that "all mermaids are unhappy" (24). The mermaid is captured and taken on board, where she lives in a bathtub in the captain's cabin. As time passes, they fall in love, and the mermaid reveals that if the captain thrusts a knife through her at precisely the moment when she is laughing at one of his anecdotes, she will be transformed into a mortal woman and they will be able to consummate their love. However, the captain is unable to use his storytelling skills to make her laugh. Instead, he stands, dagger in hand, and is incapable of recalling any of his jokes or witticisms. The mermaid is thrown back into the sea, and the captain listens to his crew's stories instead of telling them his. This story deliberately transgresses fairy-tale norms in that the longed-for transformation does not take place. In the Andersen story, the mermaid first sacrifices her tail to walk on dry land and be with her prince, then refuses to stab him with a dagger and be transformed back into a creature of the sea. In an unexpected reversal, the captain, unable or perhaps unwilling to accept the mermaid's sacrifice, is himself transformed from active storyteller to a passive member of the audience.

"El príncipe y los guerreros" ("The Prince and the Warriors") is about a prince who is drawn to soldiers' camps, from which he returns to draw pictures of men making love. When the story begins, he has never made love to a woman—"Yo nunca he tocado una mujer" ("I have never touched a woman" [11])—but proximity to a chambermaid leads him to experiment; and there is a detailed description, unusual for a fairy tale, of the sexual act. After a while, the prince begins to frequent the soldiers' camps again. At the same time, he hopes the maidservant will give him a son. She sets a condition—that he burn the drawings he has kept locked in a chest. But when he does this, she is surprised. The prince believes that with her love he may never again visit the warriors in their encampment, but the serving maid tells him that she does not love him and leaves the palace. A few years later she marries the majordomo of another palace, but, so it is reported, she already has a babe in arms. This text is unusual in a number of respects. While fairy tales are undoubtedly subject to sexual interpretations, this particular one deals explicitly with heterosexuality and male homosexuality. (Tusquets's *The Same Sea as Every Summer* tackles lesbian relationships.) One explanation for the girl's refusal to marry the prince is not that she disapproves of his sexual orientation but rather that she is jealous of the powerful emotions or urges that drive him first to the soldiers' camp, and then to draw graphic representations of beautiful, entwined male bodies.

Among the themes that run through these brief narratives are isolation and abandonment, rejection or violent punishment for perceived transgressions, the futility of acts of sacrifice, and victimhood (male and female). Membership in the aristocracy or royal family does not confer any special privileges as far as emotional fulfillment is concerned, nor does magic offer any solutions. Characters do not win any rewards; at best they escape with their lives.

CONCLUSION

From even a brief survey, it is clear that Iberian and Latin American women writers have continued to return to the form and content of traditional fairy tales and, within that canon, to a very limited selection of sources, namely, "Sleeping Beauty," "Little Red Riding Hood," "Snow White," "Bluebeard," "Rapunzel," "Cinderella," and "The Little Mermaid." Women authors habitually draw on a fairy tales in order to structure and (re)interpret women's experiences, to explore questions of female identity, social conditioning, gender, and relationships—what Angela Carter designated "the unguessable country of marriage" (*Bloody Chamber* 7). All of the authors mentioned use fairy tales to comment on the human condition from the female perspective. Many use this genre to foreground the incompatibility of authorship or creative art with marriage or emotional commitment.

There is no single method or approach to this kind of revisionist writing by women. In some cases authors appropriate titles, names, or types of characters; they may insert plots, themes, symbols, and settings into their narratives. In others, they take canonical works and rework familiar plots. In yet other instances, writers have adopted conventional fairy-tale structures and language in order to write their own unconventional, authentic, and unique fairy tales. Ironically, a genre frequently blamed for the infantilization of women has now become an important tool in the task of "writing back" against patriarchical social structures. The texts considered here span almost a century, from which it may be concluded that the social attitudes and expectations against which they protest have not greatly changed. No magical transformation has been wrought. Nevertheless, the persistence of the fairy-tale intertext demonstrates that these narratives, especially in their inverted, subversive mode, still have a role to perform and something to say about the construction of gender and woman's identity in Iberian and Latin American culture.

Notes

1. See C. Davies; Galerstein and McNerney; Levine, Marson, and Waldman; McNerney and Enríquez de Salamanca; and Manteiga, Galerstein, and McNerney.

2. See Bassnett, *Knives and Angels;* Guerra-Cunningham; and Agosín, *Landscapes of a New Land, Literatura fantástica,* and *Secret Weavers.*

3. If translations are available, as indicated in the list of works cited, I quote in English from them. Otherwise, translations of quoted passages are my own.

4. See Agosín, "Un cuento"; V. Smith. "La historia de María Griselda" was first published in *Norte* in 1946 and constituted a sequel to *La amortajada.* When Bombal published her own English translation of *La amortajada* in 1948 under the title *The Shrouded Woman,* she incorporated into it a translation of "La historia de María Griselda." Thus Bombal combined two separate but related works in her English translation. "La historia de María Griselda" has also been translated by Celeste Kostopulos-Cooperman as "The Story of María Griselda."

Bibliography of Fairy-Tale Writings by Iberian and Latin American Women

To highlight the wealth of fairy-tale texts by Iberian and Latin American women writers, this bibliography offers a selection of literary works that extends beyond those mentioned in the essay. Critical works cited in this essay are listed in the bibliography at the end of this volume.

Agosín, Marjorie, ed. *Landscapes of a New Land: Fiction by Latin American Women.* 2nd ed. Fredonia, NY: White Pine, 1992.

———, ed. *Secret Weavers: Stories of the Fantastic by Women Writers of Argentina and Chile.* Fredonia, NY: White Pine, 1992.

Blanqué, Andrea. *y no fueron felices.* Montevideo, Uruguay: Uno, 1990.

Bombal, María Luisa. *La amortajada.* Buenos Aires: Sur, 1938.

———. "El árbol." *Sur* 60 (Sept. 1939): 20–30.

———. "Braids." Bombal, *New Islands and Other Stories* 65–74. Trans. of "Trenzas."

———. "The Final Mist." Bombal, *New Islands and Other Stories* 1–47. Trans. of *La última niebla.*

———. "La historia de María Griselda." *Sur* 142 (Aug. 1946): 41–63. Also *Norte* 10 (Aug. 1946): 34–35, 48–54.

———. *House of Mist.* New York: Farrar, 1947. London: Cassell, 1948. Adaptation of *La última niebla.*

———. "Las islas nuevas." *Sur* 53 (Feb. 1939): 13–34.

———. "Mar, cielo y tierra." *Saber vivir* 1.1 (Aug. 1940): 34–35.

———. "New Islands." Bombal, *New Islands and Other Stories* 83–112. Trans. of "Las islas nuevas."

———. *New Islands and Other Stories.* Trans. Richard and Lucía Cunningham. New York: Farrar, 1982.

———. *Obras Completas.* Introd. and comp. Lucía Guerra. Santiago, Chile: Bello, 1996.

———. "Sea, Sky, and Earth." Trans. Celeste Kostopulos-Cooperman. Agosín, *Landscapes of a New Land* 9–12. Trans. of "Mar, cielo y tierra."

———. "Lo secreto." *La última niebla.* 4th ed. Santiago, Chile: Editorial Orbe, 1969. 175–83. Reworking of "Mar, cielo y tierra."

———. *The Shrouded Woman.* Trans. María Luisa Bombal. New York: Farrar, 1948. London: Cassell, 1950. Trans. of *La amortajada* and incorporating a trans. of "La historia de María Griselda."

———. "The Story of María Griselda." Trans. Celeste Kostopulos-Cooperman. Agosín, *Secret Weavers* 60–80. Trans. of "La historia de María Griselda."

———. "The Tree." Bombal, *New Islands and Other Stories* 49–64. Trans. of "El árbol."

———. "Trenzas." *Sabir vivir* 1.2 (Sept. 1940): 36–37.

———. *La última niebla.* Buenos Aires: Colombo, 1935.

———. "The Unknown." Bombal, *New Islands and Other Stories* 75–82. Trans. of "Lo secreto."

Botelho, Fernanda. *Terra sem música.* 2nd ed. Lisbon: Contexto, 1991.

———. *Terra sem música: O livro de Pitch.* Lisbon: Libraria Bertrand, 1969.

Correia, Hélia. *Montedemo.* Lisbon: Ulmeiro, 1983.

Espido Freire, Laura. *Primer amor.* Madrid: Temas de hoy, 2000.

Ferré, Rosario. "La bella durmiente." Ferré, *Papeles de Pandora* 121–54.

———. *Papeles de Pandora.* Mexico City: Joaquín Mortiz, 1976.

———. "Sleeping Beauty." Trans. Diana Vélez. *Reclaiming Medusa: Short Stories by Contemporary Puerto Rican Women.* Ed. Diana Vélez. San Francisco: Spinsters/Aunt Lute, 1988. 34–62. Trans. of "La bella durmiente."

———. *The Youngest Doll.* Trans. Rosario Ferré. Lincoln: U of Nebraska P, 1991. Trans. of *Papeles de Pandora.*

Garro, Elena. *Recollections of Things to Come*. Trans. Ruth L. Simms. Austin: U of Texas P, 1969. Trans. of *Los recuerdos del porvenir*.

———. *Los recuerdos del porvenir*. Mexico City: Joaquín Mortiz, 1963.

Laforet, Carmen. *Andrea*. Trans. Charles Franklin Payen. New York: Vantage, 1964. Trans. of *Nada*.

———. *Nada*. Barcelona: Destino, 1945.

———. *Nada*. Trans. Glafyra Ennis. New York: Lang, 1993. Trans. of *Nada*.

———. *Nada, a Novel . . .* Trans. Inez Muñoz. London: Weidenfeld, 1958. Trans. of *Nada*.

León, María Teresa. *La bella del mal de amor: Cuentos castellanos*. Burgos: Hijos de Santiago Rodríguez, 1930.

———. *Cuentos para soñar*. Burgos: Hijos de Santiago Rodríguez, 1929.

Loynaz, Dulce María. *Jardín*. 1951. Barcelona: Seix Barral, 1992.

Marçal i Serra, Maria-Mercè. *Bruixa de dol (1977–1979)*. Barcelona: Mall, 1979. Barcelona: Edicions 62, 1992.

———. Excerpts from "Fiery Blades" and "Bonfire Joana." Trans. Kathleen McNerney. *Seneca Review* 16.1 (1986): 45–48. Trans. of excerpts from the sections "Foc de pales" and "Foguera Joana" in *Bruixa de dol*.

———. "Witch in Mourning." Trans. Kathleen McNerney. *Catalan Review* 1.2 (1986): 153. Trans. of excerpt from *Bruixa de dol*.

Martín Gaite, Carmen. *The Back Room*. Trans. Helen R. Lane. New York: Columbia UP, 1983. San Francisco: City Lights, 2000. Trans. of *El cuarto de atrás*.

———. *Behind the Curtains*. Trans. Frances M. López-Morillas. New York: Columbia UP, 1990. Trans. of *Entre visillos*.

———. *El cuarto de atrás*. Barcelona: Destino, 1978.

———. *Entre visillos*. Barcelona: Destino, 1958.

———. *The Farewell Angel*. Trans. Margaret Jull Costa. London: Harvill, 1999. Trans. of *La reina de las nieves*.

———. *Nubosidad variable*. Barcelona: Anagrama, 1992.

———. *La reina de las nieves*. Barcelona: Anagrama, 1994.

———. *Variable Cloud*. Trans. by Margaret Jull Costa. London: Harvill, 1995. Trans. of *Nubosidad variable*.

Matute, Ana María. *Awakening*. Trans. James Holman Mason. London: Hutchinson, 1963. Trans. of *Primera memoria*.

———. *Primera memoria*. Barcelona: Destino, 1959.

———. *School of the Sun*. Trans. Elaine Kerrigan. New York: Pantheon, 1963. New York: Columbia UP, 1989. London: Quartet, 1991. Trans. of *Primera memoria*.

Moix, Ana María. *Dangerous Virtues*. Trans. Margaret E. W. Jones. Lincoln: U of Nebraska P, 1997. Trans. of *Las virtudes peligrosas*.

———. *Las virtudes peligrosas*. Barcelona: Plaza, 1985.

Na boca do lobo: Carapuchiña Vermella vista por Carmen Blanco, Quico Cadaval, Carlos Casanova, Manuel Darriba, Daniel Domínguez, Jaureguizar, Aníbal Malvar, Paco Martín, Isidro Novo, Antón Reixa, Mª José González. Pref. Luis Alberto de Cuenca. Lugo: TrisTram, 1998.

Oliver i Cabrer, Maria-Antònia. *El vaixell d'iràs i no tornaràs*. Barcelona: Laia, 1976.

Orfila i Cirach, Dolors. *Petits contes cruels i breus narracions*. Manresa: Bausili, 1981.

Ortiz Sánchez, Lourdes. *Urraca*. Barcelona: Puntual, 1982.

Parra, Teresa de la. *Mamá Blanca's Souvenirs*. Trans. Harriet de Onís. Pittsburgh: U of Pittsburgh P, 1993. Trans. of *Memorias de Mamá Blanca*.

————. *Memorias de Mamá Blanca.* Paris: "Le Livre Libre," 1929.

Pereira, Ana Teresa. *Fairy Tales.* Lisbon: Black Son, 1996.

Pompeia, Núria. *Maternasis.* Barcelona: Kairós, 1967.

————. *Y fueron felices comiendo perdices.* Barcelona: Kairós, 1970.

Solá, Marcela. "Bodas." *Manual de situaciones imposibles.* Buenos Aires: Lohlé, 1990. 11–16.

————. "El lobo feroz." *Los condenados visten de blanco.* Buenos Aires: Lohlé, 1971. 61–69.

Tusquets, Esther. *El mismo mar de todos los veranos.* Barcelona: Editorial Lumen, 1978.

————. *The Same Sea as Every Summer.* Trans. Margaret E. W. Jones. Lincoln: U of Nebraska P, 1990. Trans. of *El mismo mar de todos los veranos.*

Valenzuela, Luisa. "Cuentos de hades." *Simetrías.* Buenos Aires: Sudamericana, 1993. Barcelona: Plaza and Janes, 1997. 83–135.

————. "Firytales." *Symmetries.* Trans. Margaret Jull Costa. London: Serpent's Tail, 1998. 103–51. Trans. of "Cuentos de hades."

8
Babes in the *Bosque:* Fairy Tales in Twentieth-Century Argentine Women's Writing

Fiona Mackintosh

*A*ngela Carter holds a unique position within the English literary tradition, with her exploration of violence and cruelty through the medium of fairy tales and folktales, especially in *The Bloody Chamber and Other Stories,* which contains several rewritings of traditional tales. I begin by mentioning Carter because the space occupied by her work within English literature is comparable to that occupied by the substantial group of women writers in Argentina who engage in the transformation of the same fairy tales as Carter—classic European tales like "Bluebeard" and "Little Red Riding Hood." Parallels between the two literary worlds, like those that Lorna Sage (53) makes between Carter and Italo Calvino, are invited by collections such as *The Oxford Book of Gothic Tales* (Baldick). Here Angela Carter's tale of "The Lady of the House of Love" is anthologized with Argentinian poet Alejandra Pizarnik's study of Countess Erzébet Báthory—*The Bloody Countess* (*La condesa sangrienta*).[1] In addition, the use of fairy tales by these two writers has been explicitly compared by Susan Bassnett: "Like Angela Carter, Pizarnik was fascinated by the darker side of fairy-tales, the wolf with fangs that drip blood, the murderous stepmother, the dolls with hearts of mirrors, that people the landscape of the Central European folklore of her ancestry" ("Blood" 132). This comparison also draws our attention to the important point that the fairy tales Pizarnik reworked are of European traditions. This is true of all the writers to be considered and can surely be explained by the fact that the indigenous element in Argentina is very much a minority, particularly in literary terms. Most tales circulating there have their origin in European tales brought over either by Spanish settlers or by the subsequent vast influxes of immigrants early in the twentieth century.

149

Like Pizarnik's parents, who came from Rovne, large numbers of Italians, Galicians, and Eastern Europeans came to Buenos Aires fleeing war or simply seeking employment.

In this essay I shall look at the use made of fairy-tale material in the work of several Argentine women writers, many of whom—like Carter—twist and rewrite European fairy tales. The most prominent writer to be discussed is Luisa Valenzuela, whose work has also been explicitly compared to Carter's.[2] I shall also refer to other contemporary writers, including Liliana Heker, Marcela Solá, Cristina Piña, and Ana María Shua, and to the earlier writers Victoria and Silvina Ocampo. Although I limit my discussion to Argentine writers, it is worth noting that Stephen M. Hart singles out the fairy tale as a recurrent structural element in Latin American women's writing generally (*White Ink*). This is demonstrated in this volume of essays by Patricia Anne Odber de Baubeta's detailed survey of fairy-tale adaptations in the work of Iberian and Latin American women writers, who in large measure have recourse to the European stories of Perrault, Grimm, and Andersen. What Berta Inés Concha says of the Chilean writer María Luisa Bombal during her time in Paris—that "she was spellbound by the great storytellers like Andersen or the brothers Grimm, who were to have a decisive effect not only on her imagery but also on her subsequent narrative technique"[3]—holds true for the Argentine women authors that I discuss here.

DOES AMERICA NO LONGER BELIEVE IN FAIRY STORIES?

As indicated above, the stalwart Brothers Grimm and Andersen have their following in Latin America, and not only among those Latin Americans who traveled to the cultural mecca, Paris. A glance through the *Index Translationem* for the second half of the twentieth century reveals the popularity of such authors; the 1953 volume registers a huge expansion in translations for Argentina, including both fairy tales and classic children's literature, and in subsequent volumes authors such as Hans Christian Andersen, J. M. Barrie, and Robert Louis Stevenson appear with great regularity. The following year, though listing fewer translations overall, still includes Wilde's *The Happy Prince and Other Tales* together with *A House of Pomegranates*. These reappear in 1958, along with "The Birthday of the Infanta." Among the translations in volume 7 (1956) are Perrault's "Sleeping Beauty" and "Little Red Riding Hood"; meanwhile,

Lewis Carroll's two *Alice* books are reissued almost annually, with a variety of different translators.

These few examples suffice to indicate the popularity of European fairy tales and classic children's literature and a degree of familiarity with them among the Argentinian reading public and writers. Indeed, many of Argentina's most prominent writers at the beginning of the last century were active translators and avid readers of such material. Silvina Ocampo, for example, whose education was biased toward European literature, talks of strong childhood memories of tales by Grimm and Andersen that influenced her own writing (Ulla 56–57); this can be seen in such stories as "El progreso de la ciencia" ("The Progress of Science"). Silvina Ocampo was involved with her sister Victoria's influential magazine and publishing house, *Sur,* as was María Luisa Bombal; this magazine wielded a great deal of cultural power in the long years of its history, running between 1931 and 1970.[4] If its director, Victoria Ocampo, considered fairy tales a worthy subject, this opinion would be widely diffused, if not universally accepted. Victoria Ocampo recalls reading fairy tales in French; as she puts it, "for me, fairies, dwarfs and ogres spoke in French" (*Testimonios: Primera serie* 31).

Victoria Ocampo mentions the subject of fairy tales when discussing the continent of America and its relationship to European culture with Waldo Frank and Drieu La Rochelle—a North American and a European, respectively. She argues: "I thought that if America is young, the world (around) is not, and our continent is like those children whose childhood fades away from living constantly among adults. *America no longer believes in fairy stories. Since it needs to believe in them, it will end up creating them*" (Torres Fierro 18; my emphasis). Ocampo thus willingly—indeed willfully—posits America's "youth" as a positive asset, whose potential is to be guarded against the "adults" of old-world Europe. She apparently feels that America's own vital creative powers are withering, since they are constantly subjected to a process of measuring up against the old world. Her statement about creating fairy stories is open to various interpretations. Is the need to believe in fairy stories a basic craving for an ordered and hermetic world of good rewarded and evil punished? Is she saying that the countries of America will respond to this need by finding their own creative voice, in defiance of the "adults"? Victoria seems to have been ironically prophetic about the writers of her particular nation, who have indeed created fairy stories but have done so predominantly by re-creating, rewriting, and incorporating the fairy stories of Europe, either to critique the "adult" culture or to make thinly veiled criticisms of contemporary Argentine politics and society.[5] The prologue to her *Testimonios: Tercera serie* brings fairy stories into a global vision: "Whether I'm writing about America or Timbuctoo, Valéry or Little Red Riding Hood, what you see in my kaleidoscope . . . will always be a testament" (8). She appears to hold the view that even such "humble" things as fairy stories are valid as grist to the mill of her great American project, her testimony as a vigorously youthful American.

Given Ocampo's forthright stance on America needing to invent its own fairy stories, yet also bearing in mind the Argentinian norm of familiarity with European models, we have a framework within which to read the fairy-tale productions of subsequent Argentinian women writers. Like Ocampo, many of the writers effectively inscribe themselves within a European tradition, either by implicitly alluding to or by actively engaging with different versions of European tales. Perrault's tales in particular provide the source for numerous witty rewritings. Often the perspective of these women writers is a feminist one, and there is a sense in which the critique is felt to be that much stronger than European feminism, coming as it does from a position at once inside and outside Europe. What Octavio Paz observes about the Argentine writer Jorge Luis Borges is appropriate here: "The eccentricity of Latin America can be defined as a European eccentricity: I mean, it is an *other* way of being Western. A non-European way. Both inside and outside the European tradition, the Latin American can see the West as a totality" (qtd. in King, "Borges" 101).

Coming from one particular angle of this "eccentric" perspective, Argentine critic Cecilia Secreto sets fairy tales within a female framework, classifying them as "a space of female heredity, or, more clearly, of transmission from woman to woman" (175). This cozy image of female continuity has nevertheless to take into account the fact that feminist rewritings in the twentieth century are largely based on tales that have been transmitted to this body of female writers through the moralizing versions of Charles Perrault. As does Angela Carter, the Argentine writers to be discussed all view Perrault's "Little Red Riding Hood," to take the most widely reworked figure, as being too naive, sweet, and passive by far; they make her more self-determining, in charge of body, actions, and desires. Secreto maintains that the present historical context is one that loudly proclaims the fall of ideologies, so we should not be surprised that "the discourse of the magical story is mocked or subverted" (196), since the discourse of fairy tales encompasses so many suspect sexist (usually misogynist) ideologies. Secreto concludes by saying that "it is as if these stories, like their characters, were awakening from a long sleep" (197). No longer is the teller simply telling a tale: "this ancestral voice is now embodied in the female narrators who, melancholically, take on and deconstruct this discourse, finding it outmoded, since what might once have been a model for liberation, in these times of emancipation is nothing but another form of subjection and subordination" (202). I would argue with Secreto that the female narrators of today, in Argentina at least, are not so much melancholic in their deconstruction of fairy tales as noticeably ironic and playful. The ancestral voice they adopt is spirited and triumphant—not subordinate to the tales it tells, but cunning and witty. Rather than being like children whose childhood is withering away from the process of being measured against adults, these Argentinian writers are leading the way in infusing European fairy tales with a new and subversive life, setting new standards against which to measure the "adults."

VERSIONS OF VERSIONS

In a self-conscious way, the awareness of countless preexisting versions of fairy tales, and indeed the tales' essentially protean form as versions of versions, is echoed by all of these writers, particularly in those stories based on the most commonly used tale, "Little Red Riding Hood," several versions of which will be compared later. This ironic consciousness informs not only the narratorial stance but also the protagonists' behavior within the retellings. Luisa Valenzuela's *Simetrías* (*Symmetries*) contains a group of six short stories wittily titled "Cuentos de hades" ("Tales from Hades"). The very title subverts the notion of fairy tales, altering the Spanish "Cuentos de hadas," where "hadas" means fairies, to "Cuentos de hades." The translator, Margaret Jull Costa, cleverly renders this as "Firytales," paralleling the essential wordplay of the original Spanish by coining a neologism from the English word "Fairytales" that is suggestive of both the heat of hell and the impact of Valenzuela's words. That Valenzuela is consciously writing from the "eccentric" perspective of a Latin American on these European tales only serves to heighten the subversion. The book draws on "Little Red Riding Hood," "The Frog Prince," "The Princess and the Pea," "Sleeping Beauty," "Diamonds and Toads," "Snow White," "Cinderella," and "Bluebeard"; all are treated as self-consciously as the overall title would suggest.

A similar agenda is at work in Ana María Shua's "Cenicienta I, II, III y IV" ("Cinderella I, II, III and IV") and "Los enanos son mineros" ("The Dwarfs Are Miners") from *Casa de Geishas* (*House of Geishas*), which recall "Cinderella" (note the four versions) and "Snow White and the

Seven Dwarfs," respectively. One section of this book is titled "Versiones" ("Versions"), and in this section Shua rewrites myths, legends, and fairy tales. The word *versions* reminds us that each new version of a fairy tale takes on a life of its own despite its origin in another text, adapting to changing circumstances and new contexts. In Shua's world, Cinderella's ugly sisters have their feet cosmetically altered to fit the glass slipper, Snow White is middle-aged, and the Prince thinks back nostalgically to his first wife, Cinderella.

Obviously, Valenzuela and Shua are not the first to rewrite these stories, nor is rewriting the only use Argentinian authors make of European tales. In their desire to extend the possibilities of fairy tales beyond the very conventional ideology and structures that underlie them, and to write back at the "adults" (in Victoria Ocampo's analogy) by bringing out very knowing and "adult" aspects of these European tales, writers do anything from rewriting whole tales to using single mythemes (to use Propp's terminology from *Morphology of the Folktale*) as points of departure. The mythemes that provide most material for reinterpretation, and that I shall therefore consider in some detail, are the following: orphans and ogres, woods and wolves (particularly with reference to "Little Red Riding Hood"), and weddings.

ORPHANS

Orphans form an important part of the fairy-tale cast of characters: a child audience can empathize with the pathos of their situation; to potential rewriters, perhaps what appeals is the sense of freedom to develop individual codes of behavior as well as this poignant vulnerability. In Victoria Ocampo's child/adult analogy, the figure of the orphan could even in this context of "Argentina rewriting Europe" take on a tone of defiance. Liliana Heker initially develops the main female character in her novel *Zona de clivaje* (*Splitting Zone*) through this character's use of the orphan mytheme (taken from Andersen or the Brothers Grimm) to define herself and present a particular self-image. She fantasizes about becoming an orphan and even ritualizes the act of mourning the loss of her parents: "a perverse little girl who every night acted out the death of her parents and cried over it, really cried, at the desolation of orphanhood and the lack of shelter" (248). When she later fails to conform to her mother's bourgeois ideal of marital bliss, she wonders if the blame is attributable to her fantasies: "who knows, perhaps her consumptive girls, orphans and girls driven mad by love were to blame" (249). What emerges from this example is the deeply seductive power of fairy tales to create fantasy worlds or to shore the self up defiantly against the "real" world; the mythemes of fairy tales, such as orphans, become a kind of semantic shorthand or common currency that have a lasting hold into adulthood through their potent associations. The poet Cristina Piña also appears to view orphanhood as a kind of empowerment in the poem "Ella y sus labores" ("Herself and Her Tasks"), in which she deliberately rejects all other elements of the "Little Red Riding Hood" tale and recasts the female character:

> There's no grandmother nor basket nor precious Little Red Riding Hood all neatly dressed; there's no father nor mother nor memory rising up from the grass. There are no songs nor stories nor lecherous woodcutter.
> Sewing and singing, she plays and cooks and goes about her tasks, she writes with the thread of desire for death the chapter on orphanhood. (*Puesta en escena* [*Mise en scène*] 34)

That this represents a direct challenge to Perrault's moralizing versions is made clear by Piña's ironic citation from Perrault's "Cinderella," which prefaces the section—titled "Ars mutandi"—in which the poem appears. Where Perrault would have Cinderella transformed into a beautiful princess, Piña transforms her persona into a defiant anti-fairy-tale figure, who writes about orphanhood following the thread of thanatic desire—quite the opposite to the desires normally expected of a fairy-tale heroine.

OGRES: BLUEBEARD

The second mytheme these Argentinian writers put to use is that of the ogre, specifically Bluebeard. Conventionally, Bluebeard's successive wives are punished for their curiosity. Silvina Ocampo subverts this theme by swapping the gender roles; Valenzuela subverts it by rewarding—rather than punishing—female curiosity. Both writers give the tale an Argentinian twist, Ocampo by her use of "vos"—the Argentinian familiar form of address—and Valenzuela by her political allusions. Ocampo's "Jardín de infierno" ("Garden of Hell") presents us with an amusingly feminized and naturalized version of Bluebeard (*Cuentos completos* 2: 274–76). The Blue Beard character—in Spanish, *Barba azul*—becomes the female *Bárbara* through a process of elision and shortening. This is not the only role reversal; the narrator is the husband, entirely subordinate to his wife, who combs his hair for him like a child. He is frightened by the loneliness of the castle and trapped within domesticity, seeing knowledge as the key to independence. We shall see later how this perspective taken by Ocampo's narrator is mirrored by Valenzuela's female narrator in "La llave" ("The Key"). Rather than the woman seeking to undermine the existing framework, the framework itself has been reversed, and it is now the man who seeks to subvert it.

One of the most distinctive features of Ocampo's story is the narrative tone. Rather than building up mystery, suspense, and horror, the register is markedly colloquial, tending toward gossip rather than drama. The man's exploration of the castle while his wife is away is motivated not so much by curiosity as by jealousy, as he sees all the photographs of his wife with her previous, good-looking husbands. The ritual of handing over the keys, her departure, his anxiety, her return, and the return of the keys is repeated, emphasizing mundanity rather than heightening dramatic tension. In explaining that the locked room contains treasure amassed for her wonderful husband, Bárbara appears to be turning the tale into a web of clichés about true love, happiness, and a handsome man marred by his material greed. But in the final *volte-face* Ocampo returns us to the original ending; the room does indeed contain bodies of previous spouses. Ocampo's cowardly, henpecked husband finally achieves his liberation from "conjugal life" by preempting his wife's murderous designs and voluntarily joining the other corpses; he leaves a suicide note explaining that he prefers their company. The richness and humor of Ocampo's version lies in its ambiguity of tone. Apparently feminist in its role reversal, the husband's final action nevertheless acts as a kind of antifeminist backlash; it appears to ask, who could reasonably tolerate such a dominant wife? Rather than making self-conscious references in the text to the fairy-tale pre-text, Ocampo prefers to give the tale an air of ordinariness that removes it from the realm of legend and plants it incongruously in colloquial speech. In this tale from the late 1980s, Ocampo is perhaps taking a step back from the first wave of feminist criticism with its focus on "images of women." Instead, she implicitly takes on and deconstructs their methods as much as she deconstructs the discourse of the original tale, as is suggested by Secreto.

Far more provocative and serious is the version of "Bluebeard" published by Luisa Valenzuela in the "Firytales" section of *Symmetries* (145–51). The title, "La llave" ("The Key") makes a shift of emphasis immediately evident. Bluebeard himself is no longer the focus. Instead, our attention is directed toward the key, which symbolizes release through the power of female curiosity. The final dedication to Renée Epelbaum and the Mothers of the Plaza de Mayo puts us firmly into a politicized realm, where the use of fairy tales has a deadly serious message. The Mothers were a strong political voice in calling to account those responsible for the atrocious "disappearances" of their children in Argentina's so-called Dirty War in the late 1970s and early 1980s. Valenzuela mentions Perrault, who—so the narrator informs us—called her curiosity a defect. Now, having escaped alive, the female narrator tells her own story, that of Bluebeard, within the framework of a literary workshop-cum-self-help therapy class she runs for other women. Her aim in retelling the Bluebeard story is to make other women take up the gauntlet, follow their curiosity, and hold the bloodstained key high. In this case it powerfully echoes the Mothers' insistence on knowing the fate of their loved ones. Valenzuela thus retains the original moralizing intent of the tale but puts it to a radically new political use. What emerges from both of these stories, despite their widely differing tones and aims, are strong characters not subordinate to the "original" version or thrust of the tale.

WOMAN AS WOLF

One character that appears to adhere more closely to an "original" folkloric role found in Eastern European folktales—but a role that is intrinsically ambiguous—emerges from Pizarnik's work. This is the image of woman as wolf. Clarissa Pinkola Estés singles out the wolf-woman as a key element in Eastern European fairy tales, tales that Pizarnik (and many other Eastern European immigrant children) may well have heard as a child. Pizarnik's work includes references to this "wolf-woman": "the wolf-woman leaves her offspring on the threshold and flees. . . . The wolf-girl cries" (*Obras* 136). In traditional tales, the wolf-woman collects the bones of wolves and rebuilds the skeleton. She then sings, and the power of her song fleshes out the bones. The wolf opens its eyes, runs away, and is changed into a laughing woman (Pinkola Estés 23). This life-giving and transformatory power is what most compels Pizarnik to the image, since in her poetry she continually strives for language that is inhabited rather than empty, for words that are actions like the wolf-woman's powerful song. By using this image, Pizarnik taps into the quasi-incantatory power and compelling drive of folktale sources.

Pizarnik's most terrible subject, "La condesa sangrienta" ("The Bloody Countess"), is also compared to a wolf. In describing the Bloody

Countess's behavior, she observes that "Crude curses and wolflike howls were her means of expression" (379). In the title poem of the collection, "Los trabajos y las noches" ("Works and Nights"), in which she defines herself as a poet, we see this poetic identity in terms of a wolf:

> I have been wholly an offering
> pure wandering
> like the wolf in the wood
> in the night of the body
>
> trying to speak the innocent word. (99)

Similarly, in "Fragmentos para dominar el silencio" ("Fragments to Dominate Silence"), the poet speaks of another self inside her with a threatening mask: "The reclining woman nests in me with her wolf mask" (123). Pizarnik seems to have lifted this element out of fairy tales and woven it into her poetic identity, along with orphans, babes in the wood, and Little Red Riding Hood, all of whom she incorporates into her poetry. Other key mythemes she uses—the doll and the Lady Death archetype—come from Eastern European folktales (Pinkola Estés 133). In Russian tales—but also in tales from Romania, Yugoslavia, Poland, and the Baltics—there appears the figure of the doll, who is given to Vasalisa (Wassilissa) the Wise by her dying mother (70–71). The doll, which is dressed like Vasalisa herself, acts as a talisman or protective life force (84–86). Dolls in Pizarnik's work, though also linked to surrealist mannikins, have this talisman-like quality. The Lady Death archetype is, of course, embodied in Pizarnik's exploration of the Bloody Countess Bathory and in the many Lewis Carroll–style dialogues she invents between La Muerte, La niña, and La muñeca (Lady Death, the Girl, and the Doll).

Pizarnik's preference for these elements stems from the fact that the poetic and personal identity she painstakingly constructs is obsessed with childhood, and folk or fairy tales carry potent associations of childhood. She tries to create an identity, some sense of roots as defense against the repeated crises of her poetic persona and against more tangible sociocultural feelings of orphanhood. Through Eastern European folktale elements she is reaching out to claim her lost Russian-Polish heritage back in Rovne. When her parents emigrated to Argentina, they lost not only their homeland but also the original version of their surname, Pozharnik.[6] Like so many other second-generation immigrants, Pizarnik was orphaned from her family origins. Fairy tales and their elements thus became something for her to inhabit, and she often expresses in her poetry the desire to find a dwelling place. However, the sinister undercurrents of these tales are never far away.

Woods, Wolves, and Little Red Riding Hoods

"I am drawn to the wood and secretly wish that some time I could be lost in the wood when night falls" (*Cuentos completos* 1: 320). This quotation from Silvina Ocampo's short story "Carta bajo la cama" ("Letter under the Bed") highlights one of the recurrent motivations behind women's versions and adaptations of fairy tales—that is, the inscription of female desire and the attraction toward potentially dangerous and frightening places such as the wood. Whereas in the classical moralizing versions of fairy tales fear was supposed to elicit obedience and moral behavior, these women writers resolutely channel fear into eroticism and boldness. Pizarnik's identification of her voice with dwelling in the wood signals otherness, a resistance to domestication, and a search for a darker identity. In "Extracción de la piedra de locura" ("Extraction of the Stone of Folly"), she defines this voice as a rejection of her human voice: "Not my voice which persists in sounding like a human voice but the other one, which bears witness to the fact that I have never dwelt anywhere except in the wood" (*Obras* 134). Pizarnik also has death and the maiden embracing in the wood (243), making it a place of encounters at once sinister and erotic.

Many rewritings of fairy tales do not only stake a claim on the wood for female exploration and self-discovery, challenging its traditional role as a forbidden and forbidding place; several of the new versions also draw out the female character's positive attraction to the wolf, which is again a point of comparison with Angela Carter. The move from woods to the wolves that lurk in them is made by Pizarnik in her poem succinctly titled "La verdad del bosque" ("The Truth of the Wood"), which features Little Red Riding Hood, the fairy-tale character most associated with wolves:

> [A]nd I crossed my childhood so alone like Little Red Riding Hood crossing the wood before the ferocious encounter. So alone, carrying my basket, so innocent, well behaved and well disposed, but we were all devoured, what are words for if not to state that we were devoured? said the grandmother. . . . But there in my little theatre, the wolf devoured my mother and my grandmother. As for the wolf, I cut him out and stuck him into my school book. (214)

Through the narrating voice of the grandmother, Pizarnik coyly uses a traditional image of Little Red Riding Hood as an innocent, vulnerable figure. The narrative frame is abruptly shattered, however, when everyone is devoured and the emphasis shifts from the tale itself to the function of words in telling the macabre story. The poem becomes increasingly involved with framing: first the devouring wolf is placed in a little theatre, then cut out and stuck in a schoolbook. The effect of this metamorphic poem is to look outward from "Little Red Riding Hood" as a dramatic tale to its reception by the childlike poetic persona. We could also read Pizarnik's rewriting as examining the process of reception as described by Secreto. The tale may have been detrimental to previous female generations, but Pizarnik's generation takes control of the wolf, while simultaneously recognizing that we all are subject to the constraints of language.

Without stepping outside the frame as Pizarnik does, Ana María Shua reexamines the position of Little Red Riding Hood in her prose passage number 21 from *La sueñera* (*The Dreamer*). Poor Little Red Riding Hood exclaims, "But the hours are slipping by and the wolf still hasn't come. What has my grandmother got that I haven't?" (20). Fear has been comically replaced by desire and by questioning the usually unquestioned matrilineal hierarchy of grandmother, mother, and child.

So far we have seen instances of the character Little Red Riding Hood being placed in new contexts. Full story-length rewritings of "Little Red Riding Hood" are found among the stories of both Marcela Solá and Luisa Valenzuela. Here the emphasis is very much on re-creation as play—as recreation. Solá's book of short stories, *Los condenados visten de blanco* (*The Condemned Dress in White*), contains one such rewriting, titled "El lobo feroz" ("The Fierce Wolf"), thus ostensibly putting the wolf at the center of the narrative. In this story, as we shall also see in Valenzuela's, the narrative tone is more self-aware than that of an "original" fairy story. Solá's tale is narrated by a third person, but from the wolf's perspective, and Little Red Riding Hood appears as a very curious little animal. That these two characters, wolf and girl, are repeated from countless versions is clear from the self-parodying style of narratorial pedantry: the wolf lives in his "accustomed habitat," looking for food is his "customary task," and the way he goes about it is "an age-old ancestral custom . . . an acquired right, so to speak" (61). He is cast as somewhat pompous, as if in hunting for food he is exercising some kind of "droit du seigneur," while Little Red Riding Hood comes across as precocious, preferring the wolf's company to "visiting round at granny's house" (note her colloquial tone). Her confidence is indicated in her "wicked giggle" and in the bold action of "tossing her hood back" (62). Hyperbolic rhetorical descriptions of butterflies, wind, leaves, and the checked tablecloth on which Little Red Riding Hood spreads her wares paint a scene like that in a Disney cartoon. This kitsch element is further emphasized when she realizes that between them, she and the wolf have eaten all the food for her grandmother; her distraught tears fall on the earth and produce little flowers. But all this is only to prepare the ground for subversion. Little Red Riding Hood's immediate and ruthlessly pragmatic solution to their problem is for the wolf to eat her grandmother: "So go to my granny's and gobble her up, then I won't get into trouble for eating all the food" (65). Surely this cheeky little madam has overstepped the mark? The wolf takes the shortcut to her grandmother's house, eats the grandmother, and then decides to play a trick on Little Red Riding Hood by dressing up as the grandmother. The trick backfires, since on entering she thinks it really is the grandmother and bursts into tears because she thinks the plan has failed. When she pronounces the familiar ritualistic line, "Grandmother, what big eyes you have!" the wolf takes great offense— large eyes are not a sign of good breeding among wolves, and he prides himself on being well bred. He is no less upset at the second observation ("what a big nose you have"). Here the narrator gives a lewd wink at the reader, since what the child sees is described in suggestive terms as "a promontory rising up amongst the snowy white sheets" (67). She thinks that the wolfish face she sees is a figment of her own imagination and that she has superimposed his face on that of her grandmother. When he finally leaps up to eat her, she realizes who he is and is overjoyed. Little Red Riding Hood is thus something of a wolf in sheep's clothing, and the true wolf is most disappointed that his idyllic impression of her was so far from the truth: "The wolf looked with horror as the tender image he had of his little friend in the wood, that flower born in a brief moment, that sweet creature that offered him buttered toast, was shattered" (68).

The collapse of this hyperbolic, idealized version of Little Red Riding Hood also signals the demise of the sickly, demure stereotype that has been standard fare since Perrault. The feminist fairy tale does not end there, however. Little Red Riding Hood's lack of respect infuriates the wolf, who promptly swallows her up. Enter two woodcutters, who kill the wolf and cut him open to free Little Red Riding Hood. With remarkable self-possession, she displays relief that no one else (referring to her grandmother) was saved from the wolf's stomach, then goes coolly on her way. Solá's Little Red Riding Hood is thus resourceful, single-minded, and pragmatic, whereas the "ferocious wolf" of the title is dragged down by the weight of his traditional role and behavior.

Luisa Valenzuela takes the subversion of Little Red Riding Hood's character one stage further, presenting us with a highly eroticized version titled "Si esto es la vida, yo soy Caperucita Roja" ("If This Is Life, I'm Red Riding Hood").[7] The wolf's obvious metaphorical association with a brutish man (which in Perrault's morally instructive version comes as a warning to naive young girls) and the child's budding sexuality (symbolized by the red hood) provide the framework for Valenzuela's story, which is charged with sexual metaphors. Bruno Bettelheim's reading of the original tale as an initiation ritual with the participation of three generations of women (166–83) certainly has a bearing on Valenzuela's text, though the uniqueness of "If This Is Life" lies in the increasingly willful precocity of the girl, revealed in her knowing and deliberate use of rich erotic metaphors. The open acknowledgment that this tale has already been told and read so many times immediately foregrounds the interaction of narrative levels and invests the protagonist with a sense of urgent anticipation. The wood becomes an erotic metaphor that metamorphoses as Little Red Riding Hood progresses along "the (inevitable) path which leads to my grandmother" (*Symmetries* 107). From "very tall, very erect trees" (103) the scenario gradually evolves to a kind of jungle that "is becoming tropical" (108) and in which "there are tempting fruits. . . . Many are within reach of her hand. There are men who are like fruit. . . . It's a question of tasting them one by one" (108). The narrative voice appears to slip at this point. Is it really Little Red Riding Hood using such an openly erotic simile? It sounds like the voice of experience, the voice of the mother, or even the grandmother, since "the grandmother knows, the grandmother has already trodden that path" (107). Indeed, the symbolic connection between the three female figures in Bettelheim's schema is here made explicit, and the mother and daughter are seen to be one and the same, in a parody of the Holy Trinity (as noted by Boland 234): "In short, I am the mother and I sent my own daughter into the wood. . . . Thus we have made considerable progress. I am Red Riding Hood. I am my own mother, I am walking towards my grandmother, the wolf is stalking me" (111–12).

The tension between the metaphorical or symbolic and the literal events of the story increases as Little Red Riding Hood advances. Her musings as to why generation after generation of women must cross the wood and why each must repeat the clichéd warnings about the fierce wolf question the unthinking transmission from woman to woman (*Secreto* 187) both of classic folkloric tales and of social mores, retold or reiterated without interrogating their underlying ideological biases. The final twist to the scene of Little Red Riding Hood getting into bed with her supposed grandmother is anticipated by the description of her arrival. Little Red Riding Hood's highly suggestive journey through the brambles, during which her hood is ripped, ends in her resting: "I don't want her to see me with my tongue hanging out, red as my cape once was, I don't want her to see me with my teeth bared, and my mouth drooling" (114–15). Her metamorphic journey appears to have turned her not into a woman but into a wolf. In her subsequent encounter with the grandmother, a voice within her gestures ironically toward the ritual words: "And just as I am about to express my surprise, a voice in me speaks as if it were repeating something very old, and it says: What big ears you've got, Grandma. . . . I recognize her, I recognize him, I recognize me" (115). In this phrase the knowing narrator recognizes at once the grandmother figure, the wolf/man, and herself—as both woman and wolf? The narrator's refusal to tie herself down to a definable position seems to be part of her general resistance to fixed patterns of discourse, at any level. However, it is clear that the traditional naive and frightened Little Red Riding Hood has been replaced by an aggressive animalian sexuality, revealed in the evident relish with which the two parties finally consume one another. Little Red Riding Hood's feared, prohibited, yet inevitable encounter with the wolf, made so weighty and inevitable precisely by the countless retellings of this tale, is transformed by her as an all-powerful narrating sexual being into a positive triumph of erotic suggestivity. Valenzuela's rewriting operates for the reader by taking a ritualized and stylized narrative and revitalizing it, ironically drawing to our attention the often sexist assumptions and ideologies around which it is created. Willy O. Muñoz analyzes this function of Valenzuela's writing:

> To underline the limiting effects of fairy stories, Valenzuela rewrites the adventures of Little Red Riding Hood; she recontextualizes this fairy story parodically, with the intention of judging both the written discourse and the context which gave rise to such rigid codification. Valenzuela changes the canonic version by multiplying the narrative voices, including temporal shifts and an ironic tone which transforms the text into a metacommentary of the texts that it parodies. (222)

Metacommentary is the key point here; Valenzuela is playing with discourses. The title, however, links life and fiction: "If this is life, I'm Red Riding Hood." This is an ironic dig at Perrault, whose tales are outdated and inadequate for modern readers—and women in particular.

Weddings

So far we have looked at orphans, ogres, woods, wolves, and Little Red Riding Hood. It only remains to see the Argentinian challenge to that most enduring of fairy-tale clichés, the happy ending in marriage to the prince. The opening story of Marcela Solá's humorous collection *Manual de situaciones imposibles* (*Manual of Impossible Situations*) is titled "Bodas" ("Wedding"). Right from the beginning, this story sets up an ironic relationship to the title of the collection, the implication being that the wedding ceremony—with its excess of flowers, rituals, and symbols—represents an extreme situation that is impossible to deal with. Instead of the bride being overjoyed and that being the happy ending, Solá gives the bride-to-be a will of her own and strong desires, or rather, a crucial absence of desire with respect to the bridegroom. Marina Warner comments that "the happy endings of fairy tales are only the beginning of the larger story" (*From the Beast* xxv). Here the wedding day forms the beginning, not the sugary-sweet ending, of the narrative; yet it is a problematic opening, since the bride-to-be experiences a great lack of desire to marry. "God, please make me want to get married!" ("Bodas" 12). Whereas fairy tales never question that the girl's greatest desire in life is to marry the handsome prince, Solá begins her revisionist tale precisely by questioning this assumption: "Why not just say no, and open the way to more promising horizons?" (12). Only on the second page do we find out the particular fairy tale to which this story refers, when the bride says, "Woe is me, stupid Snow White" (12). Snow White blames her good education, "which has been disastrous at every turn. I don't know how to say no. That's why I'm praying: to save myself from everything I agree to" (13).

As with Valenzuela, we have here an ironic comment on the unthinking transmission of social attitudes, of how a well-brought-up girl should behave. Again, thinking of the "eccentric" perspective, it may also be a jibe at the traditionally acknowledged Argentine zeal for embracing European culture. The mirror on the wall is also treated to a new frame, metaphorically speaking. Rather than having to answer who is the prettiest of them all, the mirror becomes confused by Snow White's asking questions about God. The bride stops short of entering the church and is convinced that her father will throw her into a dungeon because he hates "complicated emotions" (14). Again Solá mocks one of the accepted rules of fairy-tale behavior: a woman's sole desire should be to marry, and whom she should marry is always clear. There is no room for indecision or complex feelings. The bridegroom "was to be the forester who would have saved my life, as it was written, had it not been that what was written differed completely from the text" (15). Like that of Valenzuela, Solá's text has metatextual commentary on the "original" version, involving awareness of the "pre-text" on the part of both protagonist and narrator. Rather than the fairy tale ending in a wedding, Snow White realizes that the only ceremony awaiting her now is one that requires her presence alone. Her life? Or her funeral? From (un)happy endings we move finally to new beginnings.

INVENTION OF NEW FAIRY TALES?

The use of fairy tales in Argentina is not limited to either the reworking of Perrault tales or to the use of mythemes as signifiers within new narratives. New tales are being created, particularly by children's authors such as María Elena Walsh and also by writers normally considered to be adult authors. Luisa Valenzuela further develops her feminist interests in fairy tales in the story titled *Otrariana*. The name of the heroine, Otrariana, could be a contraction of *Otra Ariana* (Another Ariadne) with mythical overtones, but it may also have resonances of *otramente* (otherwise), indicating the contrariness of this story with respect to traditional fairy tales. This Ariadne finds her own way through the wood and is not abandoned. The story bears an interesting dedication to Valenzuela's late mother, the writer known as Lisa Lenson, "who is on the other side of the wood." This use of the wood as metaphor continues the theme of female generations explored in "If This Is Life," and although written for children, it makes for entertaining adult reading too.

Although *Otrariana* includes the traditional mythemes of a castle and a wood, the tale parades its modernity by depicting a wood that has wardens with laser guns, infrared alarms, and an ultrasonic curtain. The heroine's deficiency is not her lack of a potential suitor but her vulnerability, which she had at first thought was timidity and which others considered haughtiness. Like Valenzuela's rewriting of "Little Red Riding Hood," this story centers on an initiatory journey into the wood, which is described as a highly prohibited place: "our Arianna continued into the wood, and since she was enveloped in her recently discovered vulnerability as if it were a cape, the infrared alarms did not go off" (9). The eventual outcome of Otrariana's wanderings among the shapeless monsters in the wood is the loss of her vulnerability (is this a euphemism?) coupled with a joyous sensual awakening: "she felt everything in her body and her body was happy" (27). The fairy tale does have a happy ending, but that ending is not marriage; rather, the couple are "friends for ever," and the desires of both parties are equally expressed. *Otrariana* is a consciously modern fairy tale.

CONCLUSION

In this overview of how a group of Argentine women writers have used and continue to use fairy tales in their writing, we have seen how without exception all adopt a critical stance toward Perrault and his moralizing versions. Their adaptations range from politicized versions to those displaying aggressively sexual images of women, but crucially, with humor. Valenzuela's "La llave" is overtly politicized through her dedication to the Mothers of the Plaza de Mayo. Pizarnik's poetry, which uses isolated fairy-tale elements such as the wolf-woman or Little Red Riding Hood to express facets of her poetic persona, brings out the essential dichotomy between naive and sinister so apparent in fairy tales. All of these writers provoke us into considering the issue of identity, of who we are as determined by the ways in which we react to these traditional tales and to the new versions. To paraphrase Secreto, not only do fairy tales awake from their slumbers— so too do feminist rewritings. Merely revealing underlying sexist biases is *démodé* and has been "done" by European feminists. What the writers considered here achieve is at one stage removed. Their versions are informed by an overview of the whole cultural process whereby meaning is generated through an Argentinian appropriation and subversion of the European heritage of fairy tales and their constituent elements. Although Ocampo, Solá, and Shua all produce rewritings that could rightly be viewed as feminist, the most dominant factor is humor, deriving from their detached point of view on this cultural heritage, which is both theirs and not theirs. Perhaps Victoria Ocampo's statement that America needs to believe in fairy stories and therefore needs to invent them is still applicable some twenty years later; certainly these Argentinian writers believe in the continuing power of fairy stories as a loaded cultural force and springboard for expression. For these writers, the restrictive female roles enshrined by Perrault become the lifeblood of subversive new versions, which have yet to be fully recognized and explored by fairy-tale scholarship.

NOTES

    1. See also María Aline Seabra Ferreira for a specific comparison of the two works. Angela Carter's radio play "Vampirella" draws on similar material: "Among my terrible

forbears, I number the Countess Elizabeth Bathory; they called her the Sanguinary Countess" (101).

2. Roy C. Boland comments, "Like Luisa Valenzuela, Angela Carter . . . and Marina Warner . . . have rewritten fairy tales from novel perspectives. A comparative study of their work is overdue" (237n13).

3. Concha 6. All translations are my own, except where otherwise stated. For discussions of Bombal and fairy tales, see Agosín, "Un cuento" and "María Luisa Bombal"; V. Smith. My thanks to Patricia Odber in Birmingham for all Bombal references and for access to her unpublished paper, "Unhappy Ever After."

4. For an in-depth study of *Sur* and its influence, see King, *Sur.*

5. I am thinking, for instance, of Luisa Valenzuela's "Cuentos de hades" from *Simetrías,* some of which will be discussed later in this essay. "Little Red Riding Hood," "The Princess and the Pea," "The Bad Fairy," and "The Frog Prince" are just some of the fairy tales rewritten with a twist. See Mackintosh, chapter 3. Batato Barea (1961–1991), notorious figure of underground theater in Buenos Aires, used fairy tales to convey political messages. In 1984, for example, he put on a performance titled *Caperucita Rota,* which might translate as *Little Wrecked Riding Hood.* See Dubatti for details.

6. Information from Piña, *Pizarnik* 21.

7. Translations for this story are taken from Margaret Jull Costa's translation (Valenzuela, *Symmetries*).

9
Creolization as Agency in
Woman-Centered Folktales
LEE HARING

The very symbolic and social approaches that appear to set women apart and
to circumscribe their activities may be used by women as a basis for female
solidarity and worth. When men live apart from women, they in fact cannot
control them, and unwittingly they may provide them with the symbols and
social resources on which to build a society of their own.
  Michelle Zimbalist Rosaldo, "Women, Culture, and Society"

*I*n the folk narrative repertoire of the Indian Ocean, a prominent
woman-centered story is the "water-princess" legend of Madagascar, in which a woman from the water—the river or sea—marries a
mortal man. The husband is commanded not to mention his wife's supernatural origin (Motif C31.2 in Thompson). In everyday terms, the motif
means that she tests his ability to refrain from revealing too much information. Such restraint, such careful silence, is a prized ability among at
least one Malagasy group who know this story well (Keenan and Ochs
147–53). Being a male, however, the mortal husband proves incapable of
controlling himself verbally. He breaks her taboo. She immediately returns
to the other world (Motif C952) and becomes sacred. Though she has no
tomb (and thus no family, in the terms of Malagasy patriarchal society),
she is revered. In this legend, as in other folk narratives of Madagascar,
Mauritius, Seychelles, Réunion, and the Comoros, where ethnicities and
languages meet and mix, the woman is central.

Thus I see the creolization that pervades these societies not as something that impersonally happens to languages but as a form of agency. To
that end, I put this term *creolization,* derived from linguistics and then
applied to the convergence of cultures, back into its setting of performance. When I do that, I discover that the performer is often a woman, acting as an agent of mediation. The sex or gender system is a primary

dimension of the history of these islands (Haring, "Prospects" 90–91). In the history of Mauritius it has most often been the woman who was obliged to learn to speak or act across linguistic and ethnic boundaries (M. Carter, *Lakshmi's Legacy* and *Colouring*). In Réunion, Indo-Portuguese (Goan) and Malagasy women became the wives of Europeans when the island was called Ile Bourbon. Creole women married Chinese shopkeepers in nineteenth-century Mauritius (Ng Foong Kwong). Grandmothers are active bearers of tradition in the twentieth-century Comoros. These women's mediating roles persuade me that multilingualism is a set of communicative options. It includes multiple linguistic codes and multiple possibilities for interpreting and performing, which women learn and master. Throughout their history, by adding newer cultural patterns to older ones, Southwest Indian Ocean women have acted as agents of creolization. They have been gatekeepers for the new multiplicity of cultural identities on which survival has depended. For this reason, they furnish empirical substantiation for a historical understanding of creolization.

Moreover, from their position in historical anthropology, Southwest Indian Ocean women offer to speak across disciplinary boundaries. The central place of expressive culture, including folktale and legend, in Indian Ocean history challenges the discipline of folklore to offer aid to feminist theory. Verbal and musical art are the finest evidence for understanding the fashioning and altering of social identities and the social practices that make possible the ways in which cultures describe gender. This, after all, is what a gender scholar wants to know: how social identities are constructed.

The story I began with is an example. The "water princess" is a legendary prototype of woman through the history of Madagascar. Creolization in Madagascar began when African and Indonesian cultures converged in the sixth to ninth centuries. The first settlers were male; their wives came from overseas, if not from undersea. The children the water princess leaves behind, who will engender the clan, are creoles in one classical sense of that term: they have sprung from two radically different cultures. Their mother's distinguishing characteristic is her foreignness. Can I believe that her story is interpretable only as patriarchal ideology? In its many variant African forms, the legend of the water princess illustrates the dangers of marrying a wife from the wrong ethnic group. It affirms patriarchy by condemning intermarriage. Must women in the audience not see this legend differently? Doesn't it proclaim the importance of a clan mother? With further field research, perhaps I shall understand the "folk" interpretation of these tales and the correlation or lack of correlation between the tales and real-life female roles (Dundes, "Metafolklore").

Creolization in female-centered folk narrative is well illustrated in the favorite tale of all Africa and of the Southwest Indian Ocean. The heroine is a defiant young woman who refuses eligible suitors in favor of a murderous, cannibalistic ogre-husband. From him she must escape; often he is punished. The usefulness of this well-known plot to patriarchal ideology is attested by its recurrence throughout West Africa (Biebuyck and Biebuyck). In Sierra Leone, for instance, Donald Cosentino collected so many Mende versions of it that it gave him part of his book's title, *Defiant Maids and Stubborn Farmers*.

Still in West Africa, the defiant girl shows up in many Peul versions from Mali and Burkina Faso. These stories have elicited from Christiane Seydou a magisterial study of two themes: virilocal marriage and the indispensable role of a woman's birth family. What does a woman want? Freud's question is answered by Peul storytellers. As Christiane Seydou reads this girl's obstinacy, she wants "a man without any scar"—a husband who is outside society, untouched by "life"; he has never been circumcised. An animal disguised as a perfect young man presents himself. The fly she employs to inspect her suitors discourages her from this animal; so does her family, but she marries him. After the marriage, the husband resumes his shape. Peul narrators give the tale various endings. In some, she commits suicide. (In my Proppian days, I justifiably called this a Final Lack.) Magic song, a recurrent element in this tale, comes in again. Once the husband retransforms in public, at the marriage festivities, the dishonored wife, isolated and suicidal, causes herself to be buried in earth by magic song (Seydou 90–91). In other endings, equilibrium is restored because she is saved by someone's intervention. In Malian versions, this savior is always a brother (Seydou 89).

A variable element that determines interpretation of the story is whether she stays in her home village, upholding uxorilocal marriage, or goes to her husband's village for virilocal marriage. In two Peul versions she goes to her husband's village, accompanied by a little brother who notifies her family. Consequently, she is sought by one brother after another. All are slain by the python-husband, until a leprous brother (another male of unorthodox appearance) rescues her and decapitates the python. Equilibrium means marrying an ordinary man (Seydou 94).

Versions of this plot, in Africa or beyond, are uncountable (Gutmann 239; Cagnolo 63–66). One scholar collected seventy-eight versions from one West African language group numbering only about fifty-five thousand (Schott). As for Mauritius, so well known was the defiant girl a century ago that Charles Baissac distinguished two variant forms. In one, the wolf-husband is a sorcerer against whom her brother warns her; in the other, the helper is not a relative but a beautiful woman disguised as a mouse (Baissac 146–79). Nelzir Ventre of Poudre d'Or in Mauritius, a gifted veteran singer of *séga* songs, knew the story well, and his performance of it was broadcast on national television in 1983 by the Mauritius Broadcasting Corporation. Previous publications show it to be no less popular in Mauritius than its cognates in Africa and Europe (Aarne and Thompson 101–04, 338).

The widespread popularity of the tale suggests that West and East Africans, Malagasy, and Mauritians are sharing symbols but that they probably differ as to meaning and interpretation. In the European counterpart of this tale there are three sisters, not one, who must be rescued from the ogre's power. Thus the impossible marriage looms less large. African and Indian Ocean versions put the main question: "Who is the rescuer?"

In Seydou's Peul versions the final responsibility for restoring order rests on the males in the family. "It is thanks to the vigilance and perspicacity of a little brother (as opposed to the sister's total lack of awareness), then thanks to the courage of the leprous brother, that the sister escapes the fate of being devoured by her animal partner, with all the ambiguity of meaning hidden in the image of devouring." If the brother can pull his sister out of a bad marriage, Seydou continues, he will have benefited himself and other brothers, for she then will return to the status of a marriageable daughter and be reintegrated into the regular circulation of women (95). Versions in other parts of the world bring the rescuer from outside. Africa consistently makes the rescuer a member of the heroine's party or family, but Malagasy versions make the rescuer a sister rather than a brother (Haring, *Malagasy Tale Index* 363–71). In Ton (Uncle) Nelzir's version, as in the Malian ones, the brother is set apart from the girl by the running sores on his itchy skin. To effect the escape, Malagasy versions include some magical element that aids the fleeing girl(s). Sometimes it is a stretching tree that puts the fugitives out of reach of their pursuer. When Nelzir Ventre tells it, what enables them to travel through the air is the balloon, a uniquely Mauritian essential element. What powers the balloon is song, Nelzir Ventre's special expertise.

How, then, to interpret the tale? No folktale can pose the question of power more emphatically or condemn intermarriage more forcefully. How will this woman married to a beast extricate herself from an impossible marriage? It is a question that many a real-life woman asks. A number of versions present a ready-made, fantasized answer in patriarchal terms: with all his superficial flaws, it is her unpromising brother who defeats the wolf-man and rescues the woman.

If I read the story as a male, thinking of its innumerable West African versions, the real danger, from a brother's point of view, is that his sister's marriage to this alien creature will be consummated. Then his sister will have been removed from the system of the circulation of women (Seydou 117). But if he rescues her, kinship and masculinity will triumph. Another male interpreter writes that both Bantu and Malagasy versions "seem to me to dramatize the dangers of exogamy, which delivers the woman into foreign territory and the goodwill of her husband and his relatives" (Ottino 39–40). If I imagine a woman's interpretation, surely the story looks different. She has undergone an initiation; she has lost her innocence; she has gained a knowledge of the otherness of males, of an alien tribe in an alien environment. That knowledge is both loss and liberation, whether the heroine commits herself to another marriage or decides only to stay with her family of birth.

As a test case for what folklore can offer feminist theory, I now focus on the region's most patriarchal society, the Islamic Republic of the Comoros. Comoran society is strongly stratified. Of all the islands in the Southwest Indian Ocean, the Comoros ought to be the most likely to manifest, in a local remodeling, a phallocentric symbolic order. Here if anywhere we should find what Judith Fetterley calls the "*immasculation* of women by men." We should find folktales that voice an ideology in which "women are taught to think as men, to identify with a male point of view, and to accept as normal and legitimate a male system of values, one of whose central principles is misogyny" (304). "In public you see only men," not women, I was told in Paris in 1982 before going to Ngazidja (Grande Comore). Times must have changed by 1995. In Moroni, the capital, that year, many women could be seen in town, some wearing the blue-jean costume of globalization. History tells us, moreover, that in the nineteenth century, the succession of power in Ngazidja was matrilineal (Gueunier, *La belle* 9). The hegemony of Islam might lead us to imagine that beliefs and practices are monolithic, but in fact the folk Islam of the Comoros offers a promising field for study, as do the religious practices of women. About Mayotte, one authoritative writer says, "Women play a more influential, even conspicuous role in public life . . . than they do in the stricter Koranic paternalism of the other islands" (Allen 33).

What does the Comoran symbolic order show about women's roles? Is Comoran language always masculine, as some feminist critics have charged for Europe? Or as Hélène Cixous asked of French writing in

1975, "Which texts appear to be woman-texts and are recognized as such?" ("Laugh" 324). Folktales have been collected in two of the four islands, Mayotte and Grande Comore (Gueunier, *La belle* and *L'oiseau*; Blanchy and Soilihi; Rombi and Ahmed Chamanga). Power relations between pairs of men are often the subject of tales. To what extent and in what ways, then, are women represented, or how do women represent themselves in the symbolic order of narrative? How is sexuality or gender constructed in Comoran folktales? The answer is that in this repressive social structure, women in folktales are cultural mediators who operate through their manipulation of language.

The most obvious avenue of mediation is performance, not story content. Childbearers—mothers and grandmothers—are the most active bearers of Comoran tradition. Here is one contemporary man's experience:

> As soon as a child is able to understand the language, his grandmother teaches him folktales, taboos, and riddles. Generally tales and riddles are said on nights of the full moon. She recites tales and poses riddles, and the children come around her to listen. They are very attentive to the tales. With riddles, she puts the question and the children try to answer. . . . As for taboos, the grandmother explains what may and may not be eaten. Thus she explains to him what can happen to him if he doesn't respect them, and the origin of these taboos. These sessions reinforce the relation of affection and interdependence between grandmother and grandchildren,

which this writer calls a "very intense relation" (Djoumoi Ali M'madi 19). Noël Gueunier, who has collected extensively in Mayotte, confirms the grandmother's importance (*La belle*). A contemporary Comoran author (Hatubou) titles his collection of tales *Contes de ma grand-mère*.

Comoran women do not wait to become grandmothers, though, before they act as tradition bearers and gatekeepers. One accomplished performer is the storyteller Aïsha Hussein, known as Ma Sula, living in the village of Sada on Mayotte. She was recorded and translated in the 1980s by Sophie Blanchy, who finds the descriptions of gender in Ma Sula's tales to be quite realistic. It is perfectly realistic, she says, to portray a mother-in-law in folktale as hostile, for in real life such a person must be wooed with gifts, patience, and submission by her new daughter-in-law (Blanchy 30). The central document in Blanchy's case for realism is Ma Sula's story "The Mother's House," in which a young woman deprived of her mother's physical presence (here symbolized by a house) wins her place in society through her skill as a performer of song and story. I summarize:

The heroine has been orphaned. Her guardian, a *cadi* (Islamic judge), promises that the contents of her mother's house will be given to her at puberty—that is, that at puberty she will assume her mother's role, indeed her body. Promptly asserting herself, she raids the house from time to time, with other children, for sweets, biscuits, and clothes. Then, responding to the kindness of a new foster mother, the girl transfers her mother's goods to the new house (Motif Q40, Kindness rewarded). The *cadi* discovers the theft and remonstrates with the woman, who reveals herself as an evil stepmother. With her children she drowns the girl (Motif Q467, Punishment by drowning).

In the water the heroine is adopted by a family of *jinn* fish who respect her Islamic faith and food taboos. When she is of marriageable age, they provide her with beds, sheets, plates, and pots and put her on an island. There, a fisherman, who has heard her sing, goes to tell the king, who welcomes her, rewards the fisherman, and marries her to his son (Motif H11.1.3, Recognition by life history sung; Motif T121, Unequal marriage). Soon she tells her husband this story: there was an orphan girl, whose fortune was exhausted and who was then killed. As so often in folklore, the fiction hardly conceals the truth. She takes her husband to the site of her mother's house, removes her brassiere, puts it around a tree trunk (metaphorically claiming it as a body), and sings the song she sang on the island. The next day at sundown, when she takes him back to the site, her mysterious song has caused the *jinns* to begin rebuilding her mother's house (Motif D1781, Magic results from singing). Now taking back her brassiere, she buries an animal skin there; she sings the song again but refuses to explain. As the house is gradually reconstructed on succeeding days, the husband begins to suspect that she is a *jinn,* and the king is angry that someone has built a house without permission.

Against his anger and the husband's refusal to live in the house, the heroine must now recount her whole story to the villagers, first as fiction, then as her life story. The magical reality is that her dead parents have built and furnished the house (Motif Q47, Kindness to orphans repaid by dead parents). The metaphorical reality is that her mature woman's body is the gift of her parents. By telling her life history and thus demonstrating her mastery of language, she is recognized (Motif H11.1). By living, at last, in her mother's house with her husband, she claims her body.

Sophie Blanchy interprets this tale, as popular in the Comoros as the tale of the defiant girl who must escape from an ogre-husband, as what feminists call women's writing. It concerns a woman's life. The relation between mother and daughter, Blanchy says, is the most important relationship of all. It contrasts with the unstable marriage relations that result from negotiations between men. Such tales assimilate the young woman into a continuous existence with her mother; thus the mother's death can be accepted. If the tale is as realistic as Blanchy interprets it, the woman's ability to achieve recognition through song and storytelling is also part of its portrayal of a woman's role.

In many Comoran tales, marriage is the only subject, though represented fantastically in the many versions of the defiant-girl story. On the surface at least, women are invited, indeed required, to identify with the wifely role. Tales seem to function in the way Patrocinio Schweickart describes literature: "The male text draws its power over the female reader from authentic desires, which it rouses and then harnesses to the process of immasculation," of identifying with the male-dominated order (271). In a nation like the Comoros, where one must be multidialectal as well as bilingual, perhaps it is no surprise that the otherness of males and the dangers of marriage are symbolized by the foreignness of language. In some versions of the defiant-girl tale collected by Noël Gueunier, the alien husband (an ogre, *jinn*, or animal) speaks a bizarre language. Yet (says Gueunier, who knows Mahorais storytelling very well) this alien speech is only a slight deformation of the language of a neighboring village. Sometimes the husband manipulates language in another way: he lies about going to cultivate his crops (*La belle* 16). In other versions, only a woman proves capable of understanding a language incomprehensible to everyone else.

Comoran folklore tells us, as does all vernacular culture, that as performers and tradition bearers women maintain their importance. What does it mean, therefore, to ask how big a voice women have in the Indian Ocean or India? The distinguished cultural critic Gayatri Spivak asks, "With what voice-consciousness can the subaltern speak?" ("Can the Subaltern Speak" 27), as if history's first subalterns had not been speaking since the Stone Age. To answer her own question, Spivak cites words of Michel Foucault that neither critic fully understands. Criticism must turn "to a layer of material which had hitherto had no pertinence for history and which had not been recognized as having any moral, aesthetic, political or historical value" (Foucault 50–51). Unbeknownst to elite critics, that layer of material includes storytelling, singing, cookery, costume, belief, custom, and numerous other activities, which in Europe are the purview of ethnology and in the United States are studied under the name of folklore. What a pity Foucault disregarded these things.

Answering Spivak, Benita Parry turns to India and points to these very kinds of expressive culture, "those sites where women inscribed themselves as healers, ascetics, singers of sacred songs, artizans and artists." It is a mistake, Parry goes on, to write off such sites; they are "the evidence of native agency recorded in India's 200 year struggle against British conquest and the Raj" (37). It would be equally a mistake to write them off in nations less well known to the world than India. The challenge today is not to the subaltern to find a voice but for those in dominant positions to develop ears. Margaret Mills transforms Spivak's question accordingly: "How, and under what circumstances, can or does the hegemonic hear?" ("Feminist Theory" 174).

The construction of gender in oral storytelling and the differential interpretations of tales by women and men speak as directly to concerns of feminist philosophers as to critics. Again unbeknownst to them, their concerns are continually being played out in vernacularity. American performance researchers Richard Bauman and Charles Briggs argue that "poetics and politics are one" (239). Though French feminists would agree, they can seldom be bothered to look beyond the horizon of European or American literature for the evidence furnished by vernacular cultures. Hélène Cixous, Monique Wittig, and Luce Irigaray have variously proclaimed that it is difficult for women to express and represent themselves in language. That proclamation would certainly sound strange to a Moroccan market woman (Kapchan) or an African American rapper (Keyes). Feminist philosophers will benefit if they emend a remark of Cixous, who says, "Woman must write her self; must write about women and bring women to writing, from which they have been driven away" (454). In reality, women have been writing themselves ever since they helped to invent fiction and the art of narration at least fifty thousand years ago. Ethnographers and ethnologists can aid the feminist project by a counterproclamation: within and in spite of patriarchal societies, women have developed extraordinary verbal skills. They have mastered multiple linguistic codes, registers, and channels (Scheub; Postma; Keenan, "Norm-Makers"). Folk narratives in particular delineate women's roles and problems, realistically or fantastically. In cultural studies, those who practice feminist theorizing will do well to heed the voices from women's folklore.

10
Genre and Gender in the Cultural Reproduction of India as "Wonder" Tale

Cristina Bacchilega

*T*his essay analyzes three contemporary novels—Salman Rushdie's *Haroun and the Sea of Stories* (1990), Chitra Banerjee Divakaruni's *The Mistress of Spices* (1997), and Arundhati Roy's *The God of Small Things* (1997). It emerges from my teaching Indo-Anglian and South Asian diasporic texts in a variety of courses, as well as from my own interest in tales of magic—or wonder tales, as I prefer to call them—especially since tales from India often blur the line between the fictional and the sacred.[1]

Wonder tales and, more broadly, folktales were seen in early Western folkloristics as having originated in India. As scholars debated whether tales emerged in one place or in many independently, India figured large in their studies either as the cradle of folktale tradition or as the land of plenty, where—enlisted in support of the comparative approach of the historic-geographic school—analogues of European tales abounded.[2] As Edward Said noted, this European fascination with the oral and literary traditions of India represented in various ways a *scholarly* version of the Orientalist association of India with the wondrous, mysterious Other—and thus with the unscientific and the primitive, both the sacred and the fanciful. Presented at folklore studies meetings and in print during recent years, Sadhana Naithani's work has successfully shown how folktale collecting in British India was often the product of administrative colonial enterprise as well as the turns of translation, printing, and authorship according to Western standards.

My focus here is on the present-day popular "idea of India," understood within the broader "idea of the Orient," as the "wonder-ful" land of the imagination. This is not a recent idea. As Hegel wrote in his *Philosophy of History,* "India as a Land of Desire forms an essential element in General History. From the most ancient time downward, all nations have directed their wishes and longings to gaining access to the treasures of this *land of marvels*" (my emphasis); and he was referring not only to its "treasures of Nature" but to those of "wisdom," to its wondrous tales (qtd. in Prashad 1). Naithani too notes the nineteenth-century colonial production of "a folktale about India" by and for the British, a tale that depicts India as a land of marvels while excluding its people from this appreciation ("Prefaced Space" 68). My reason for exploring the dynamics and consequences of this metanarrative—India as wonder tale—and for conceptualizing it as "structure of feeling" (in Raymond Williams's words) is that I believe it continues to play a significant role in the transnational conception and reception of some of the most successful literature of the South Asian diaspora.[3]

"Wonder" is a category that retains a connection with both secular and sacred traditions. It evokes the supernatural as magic or fiction, wisdom or philosophy, and the sacred or religious; while underplaying its threat, it evokes mystery. In Western imagination the racialized figure of woman has centrally represented the mystery and fascination of the Other. How does this apply to "the idea of India" specifically as the land of "wonder tales"? As Sridevi Menon's recent dissertation work develops, "within the Orient . . . colonial discourse staged two distinctive geographical spaces" (15): the Islamic or West Asian one and India. The former—for the historical reasons that Said discusses—represented a "militant," "demonized," Muslim, and "masculine" Orient, the latter a "passive," "domesticated," Hindu, and "feminine" Orient (15–17). I am suggesting that within these "symbolic territories"—which were imagined from the outside and conveniently separated religious groups who, for instance, coexist in India—the tale of wonder is feminized. Even *The Arabian Nights,* which historically within a European archive very much functioned as a peephole view into the mysteries of Islam, privileges the "domestic" and is increasingly read as eroticized/exoticized "wonder" where Sheherazade's feminine (read "nonthreatening") approach overcomes a bloodthirsty masculine drive.[4] In turn, this stereotypically attractive—seductive but safe—construction of the wonder tale has also reinforced a static conception of Indian culture and the place of women within it. Please note that I am not here claiming to interpret *The Arabian Nights* or to discuss the traditions of folk narrative in India, but to foreground "structures of attitude and reference" (Said, *Culture* 52) that may affect our reading of "wonder tales" when they are marketed as India-"related" or "originated" products.

The wonder tale in its "no-suspense" horizon of expectations lends itself easily to reinforcing stereotypes; however, we also know that its very

Title-page illustration by John Batten for *Indian Fairy Tales,* ed.
Joseph Jacobs (London: David Nutt, 1892).

formulaic structure as a genre allows for unpredictable modes of inter-
pellation, both personal and collective, or, put differently, for discovery
and discord in the retelling. I will state now that the point of this essay is
not to confirm the Orientalizing frame within which Rushdie's or
Divakaruni's wonder tales are produced and received; my remarking on
this frame seeks to give it visibility, not more durable substance. As these
novels *negotiate* a stereotypical association of India with the feminized
tale of wonder, I would agree with Arjun Appadurai that "the work of the
imagination . . . is neither purely emancipatory nor entirely disciplined but
is a space of contestation in which individuals and groups seek to annex
the global into their own practices of the modern" (4). These three novels, each in its own way and to varying degrees, contribute to contesting
an exoticized image or fantasy of India; negotiate the gendering of that
association to impact their readers' sexual politics; represent the fragility
of "local" traditions and their transformations; and participate in an unpredictable network of localized politics and globalized marketing. My objec-
tive, therefore, is to discuss the specific dynamics of contestation in these

overtly intercultural novels in ways that foreground gender dynamics as well as notions of intertextuality as interpretations of transnationalism.

HAROUN AND THE SEA OF STORIES

Salman Rushdie's first post-fatwa publication in 1990, *Haroun and the Sea of Stories*, was marketed as a children's book and has often been neglected by critics. Both short and delightful, this book, as another character remarks of its protagonist, Haroun, has more than "meets the blinking eye": a particularly promising mix for classroom use, especially since the unpromising hero's central question is, "What is the use of stories that aren't even true?" Rushdie's answer is playfully serious as, while in hiding, he vicariously reaches out to his then nine-year-old son and, at the same time, with therapeutic lightness, addresses sociopolitical uses of story-telling and advocates freedom of speech. Rushdie's own predicament as a writer is in focus, of course, but through the lens of an astutely global/local metafictionality.

What do I mean? "Metafictionality" is evident in that not only does *Haroun and the Sea of Stories* inscribe storytelling and extol its transfor-mative powers; but as its title previews, it is also a wonder tale about won-der tales. The "global"/"local" qualifying point is, not surprisingly, twofold. First, in a global market, which his writing in English immediately sig-nals, Rushdie foregrounds the metafiction of Oriental tales, and this works wonders to claim "a universalist aesthetics" (Aji 129). Just looking at the image on the book's cover of young Haroun riding the hoopoelike machine named Butt to his all-too-real dream and "Kahani" or "story" world conjures the image—though reversed, but that is the stuff dreams are made on—of Sinbad carried away by a Rukh. To recapitulate what other readers have noted, *The Ocean of Stories* in Rushdie's title, the metaphor on which Haroun reconstructs his life and world, is also the title of a multivolume eleventh-century Sanskrit text, *Katha Sarit Sagara* (Durix 120–21). Together the names of son and father in Rushdie's novel re-present the legendary caliph Haroun el Rashid, who appears in many of the *Arabian Nights* tales, to idealize "the good old times" (historically, 786–809; Gerhardt; Marzolph, "Hārūn ar-Rašīd"; Coppola; Aji). The "silhouetted . . . figure" with "an outsize onion for a head and outsize aubergines for legs" turns out to be a water genie with unusual whiskers, "the palest, most delicate shade of sky blue" (Rushdie, *Haroun* 55). Not unlike the frame tale of *The Arabian Nights* and that collection itself,

Haroun and the Sea of Stories thematizes women's betrayal and represents storytelling as both a liberating and healing practice that deflects violence and rehearses in the shadows slanted ways to face conflict. It is on a house-boat named *Arabian Nights Plus One,* with theme-park furniture, that the many volumes of *The Ocean of the Streams of Stories* are stored (Rushdie, *Haroun* 50–52). Whether readers know of this Kashmiri collection or not, the "idea of the Orient," with its genies and exotic modes of transportation, works—in collagelike fashion or even advertising flashes—as a visual and narrative hook.[5] The fairy-tale motif of "mistaken identity," which Rushdie effectively employs in the novel, could even be seen as operative in the reception of his whole narrative. The "idea of the Orient" becomes metonymically interchangeable with "idea of India"—thanks both to Rushdie's own reputation as an "Indian" writer and to the analogies he builds into *Haroun* between this fictional land of "wonders" and Kashmir. Thus, the "idea" of the Orient/India lures readers—all readers, wherever they belong—into a story world both unfamiliar and familiar.[6]

In this "wonder-ful" Orient or India, where traditionally light and darkness themselves are at issue, Rushdie's young hero pursues his quest for words that will free and enlighten parallel worlds. To do so he must unplug the Common Source of stories from the depths of the ocean. From this Common Source, "the glowing flow of pure, unpolluted stories came bubbling up." And that's when he discovers, as do readers along with him, that "there were so many Streams of Story, in so many different colours, all pouring out of the Source at once," that "it looked like a huge under-water fountain of shining white light" (*Haroun* 167–68). In its phantas-magoria, *Haroun and the Sea of Stories* participates in the reproduction and promotion of a transnational or global fairy-tale genre in which the colors of the Orient sparkle enough to attract but do not leave their mark on a universalizing flow of stories.

However—and this is the second aspect of his global/local metafic-tionality—Rushdie's *Haroun* also cleverly turns the tables on the Orientalist assumption that the West is deciphering the East by unveil-ing it or dressing it up. Having noticed the *Arabian Nights* connections in *Haroun,* most of my students are then quite surprised when they read Rushdie's 1992 statement: "When I first saw *The Wizard of Oz* it made a writer of me. Many years later, I began to devise the yarn that eventually became *Haroun and the Sea of Stories,* and . . . to make it of interest to adults as well as children . . . of all the movies, the one that helped me most as I tried to find the right voice for *Haroun* was *The Wizard of Oz.* The film's traces are there in the text plain to see; in Haroun's companions are clear echoes of the friends who danced with Dorothy down the Yellow Brick Road" (Rushdie, *Oz* 18). The film, Rushdie professes as he begins his analysis of *The Wizard of Oz,* was his "very first literary influence"; but when he watched it as a ten-year-old in Bombay, he "knew a great deal more about the cinema of the fantastic than any Western child of the same age"(11) because of his steady diet of over-the-top Hindi movies. When Rushdie describes *The Wizard of Oz* as dramatizing the "inadequacy" or "weakness" of adults and the need for children to take control (10), *Haroun and the Sea of Stories* clearly fits the bill. Why have we not noticed it if it is "plain to see"? And yet Rushdie offers other playful references to Western mythified "classics," including "Bluebeard," as evoked by the blue-whiskered genie I have mentioned, and "Rapunzel," which with a knowing nod to folklore scholarship is identified as "Princess Rescue Story Number G/1001/RIM/777/M(w)i" (*Haroun* 73). For Rushdie, "the real secret of the ruby slippers is not that 'there is no place like home,' but rather that there is no longer any such place *as* 'home'"— except of course for the "imagined world," "the home we make, or the homes that are made for us, in Oz: which is anywhere, and everywhere, except the place from which we began" (*Oz* 57). Not that I would advocate taking a genie's word at face value, but this *trance*like approach to translation and dislocation not only speaks powerfully to Rushdie's having to lead a "homeless" life in hiding for almost a decade, but—more relevant to my focus—it also ironically points to the transnational makeup of our own "familiar" tales. It is the West that must learn to recognize itself behind the imagined "veil" of the Oriental tale.

While I am arguing that the two-faced metafiction of *Haroun and the Sea of Stories* can be read as anti-Orientalist, I do not see that irony extending to subvert the gendered stereotypes that sustain both Western and Orientalizing "wonder tales." The "ocean of stories" is feminized thematically—the joy of language is lost when Haroun's sweet-singing mother leaves—as well as linguistically. Rashid, Haroun's father, promotes fictional etymology as he decodes the Kashmirian "Valley of K" to be both "Kosh-Mar" and "Kache-Mer," words "from the ancient tongue of the Franj, which is no longer spoken in these parts": one meaning "nightmare" (*cauchemar* in French), the other meaning "what hides the sea" (from the French *cacher* and *mer*), and both aurally evoking *mère*, the mother, the life source from which to regain strength (*Haroun* 40). While Rushdie's tale focuses on the journey of the boy and his father, female figures play well-known, if mocked, supporting roles. Princess Batcheat Chattergy, who, like Haroun's mother, wanders transgressively into enemy territory and, unlike her, sings most horribly, is ultimately no more than the object of the heroic mission of "rescuing the princess." Even Blabbermouth, the talented juggler whose pretense to be a boy is undone when, in fairy-tale fashion, her cap is knocked off and "a great torrent of shiny black hair cascade[s] down over [her] shoulders" (*Haroun* 107), is cast within the structure of the wonder tale as a "helper." In that role she shows Haroun the way to understanding the art of storytelling as a juggling act and serves as an intercultural translator whose function becomes that of a fledgling romantic interest.

The Mistress of Spices

In the contexts of South Asian diasporic and Asian American literatures, Chitra Banerjee Divakaruni's *Mistress of Spices* (1997), like *Haroun and the Sea of Stories*, was dubbed by reviewers and by a number of readers (if one looks at Amazon.com "customer comments") as a "fairy tale" and especially as a story of transformation developing the parallel journeys of protagonist and writer, who both claim: "I too have taken on a new identity in a new land" (Divakaruni, "Dissolving Boundaries"). On the cover, an attractively shaped and "exotically" garbed mystery woman is spicing up the gray-looking Bay Area while either fire spreads from her lower body or she herself emerges out of the flames. Perhaps a postmodern phoenix, the novel's protagonist introduces herself—in the first person—using the simple, paratactical, but imagistically powerful language of wonder: "I am a Mistress of Spices. . . . [T]he spices are my love. . . . At a whisper they yield up to me their hidden properties, their magic powers. . . . But the spices of true power are from my birthland, land of ardent poetry, aquamarine feathers. Sunset skies brilliant as blood" (3). When the narrative focuses retrospectively on her birthland, the events are supernatural: born to a poor village family, the protagonist even as a young child is a powerful seer; then, because she cannot control her own spells, she sails the ocean as the unwilling legendary protector of ruthless pirates; and finally she becomes an apprentice of the "Old One" on an island where women learn the magic of spices and must promise to use it without becoming involved in the world of emotions or pain themselves. Snakes are her friends, and singing "sea serpents" (21) save her from death before she is delivered to the island of her sacred initiation. Suspension of disbelief governs. The heroine literally undergoes trial by water and, in her initiation on the magic island, by fire. When she explains that her "name is Tilo, short for

Tilottama, for I am named after the sun-burnished sesame seed, spice of nourishment" (5), she appears as wonder itself—"Open Sesame"—coming from the land of turmeric and ginger. The "idea of India" as ancient land of wonders lends both credibility and attraction to the tale Tilo tells.[7]

In the "new land" of Oakland, California, Tilo, in wonder-tale fashion, undergoes further transformation, but her adventures are less fanciful and told in a somewhat more realistic register. The everyday problems, small gestures, and intense feelings of South Asian immigrants begin to touch her, and she reaches out herself, thus bending the rule that requires a Mistress of Spices to help "all who come to her in distress or seeking" being "particular to none," "not too far not too near, in calm kindness poised" (96). She becomes partial to Haroun, the wounded Muslim cab driver from Kashmir; Geeta, whose grandfather cannot accept her love for a man not of their caste or country, a Chicano; Jagjit, the angry, marginalized Punjabi boy tempted by the gang world; and Ahuja's wife, raped and beaten by her husband. Eventually she works the spices not only to balance or heal but also to empower those she cares for against violence. She finally accepts the responsibility and risk of love with a Native American tricksterlike figure, Raven. In a predictable recognition of her own human fragility that is presented as a reversal of mythic initiation, Tilo goes from powerful goddess—in her three incarnations of crone, mother, and virgin—to "ordinary" woman. In what appears to be a seamless "happy ending" that meets with the approval of the "old world," the heroine hears "clear, loud, louder now, the sea serpents' song. That shining in the waves is their jewel eyes holding my gaze" (338).

Divakaruni's authorial statements further the novel's metaphoric fantasy of India as the "old world." In Catherine Wald's interview article "Ancient Traditions" we read: "As a child Divakaruni spent every vacation with her grandfather in the village of Gurap, which is located in West Bengal, three hours from Calcutta. 'It was a wonderful place to learn stories and fables and old fairy tales'" (54). But Divakaruni's intervention in the anthology *Mirror, Mirror on the Wall: Women Writers Explore Their Favorite Fairy Tales* (1998) consists of a tale presented through her own experience of role-playing as a child in Calcutta, a retelling that mythically structures *The Mistress of Spices* as well: "All afternoon I would run down the marble staircase to the ground floor, cool and dim as the bottom of the lake, and slowly climb back up, holding the [round glass] paperweight in front of me. I was the princess in the underwater palace of snakes, carrying the jewel that allowed me to rise to the surface of the lake" ("Princess" 97). As in the novel, there are earth and water snakes.

The princess, Divakaruni recounts, has lived happily with the "beautiful, green and yellow and gold" serpents who sing to her and nurture her (97). But, inspired by the prince's stories about his own world above, she takes the earth snake's jewel that allowed her lover to come to her world and goes to explore his. It is this "moment of ascent," Divakaruni says, that caught her fancy as a child (98) and mythically captures for her as a writer the power of "dual vision, the innocence of child-seeing that creates a world newly, the adult consciousness that compares and understands and remembers," the princess being "part of two worlds but wholly of neither" (99). As Divakaruni concludes in her powerful recollection, she lived this "heart-breaking, heart-thrilling moment" herself "when [she] left India to come to America" (99). Both Bengali storytelling and the immigrant experience are thus represented by a singular and mythified retelling in which India is a womblike, story-filled world, but a limited world: "Never again would [the princess] be satisfied by the worldless songs of her serpent companions" (99).

While I am arguing that *The Mistress of Spices* clearly exploits the stereotypical association of India with the feminized tale of wonder, I would also say that Divakaruni's novel draws on Oriental wonder within a notion of transnational intertextuality that is quite different from the one framing *Haroun and the Sea of Stories*.[8] Divakaruni's metafiction is not a naturalized hybridity of the imagination, the bubbling criss-crossing of currents or traditions, where vividly colored streams produce the white overflow of story; rather, her "modern fable," as she calls it, seeks to "dissolve boundaries," the mythic ones of water, earth, fire, and air as well as those between India and the United States. This is a different metaphor of transformation, one that is at the same time more mythified in its singular development *and* more historicizing because "crossing boundaries," the timeless rite of passage, becomes "breaking ethnic barriers" in post-1967 South Asian immigration to the United States. Furthermore, "dissolving boundaries" not only applies to globalization as a whole but also speaks directly to the building of coalitions between different yet equally stereotyped groups—for instance, in the novel, between Asian Indians and American Indians.

That this union is represented in the novel by the utopian love story of Tilo and Raven complicates, or compromises, matters even more. The wonders and stories of their mythic cultures enable them to "emerge transformed" (Divakaruni, "Dissolving Boundaries") and together. But in their romance the two characters also enact the gendered dimensions of their stereotyping: she is his "tropical blossom," his "mysterious Indian beauty"

(309); he is the "lonely American" (70) with whom she will reach an "earthly paradise" of "red-barked sequoia and innocent blue eucalyptus, squirrels with their silk-brown eyes" (308). As Tilo self-consciously articulates, she worries that "each of us [is] loving not the other but the exotic image of the other that we have fashioned out of our own lack" (331). In the end, they both have to give up their "exotic images": Tilo her goddesslike beauty for "ordinary" features (326), Raven his "earthly paradise" for everyday life in conflict-ridden and damaged Oakland. Divakaruni, as I see it, is playing with fire: she presents stereotyping as it informs not only hateful or discriminatory practices but also loving relations. However, in their reproduction, are these stereotypes interrogated or confirmed? I cannot offer a clear-cut answer, though I remain rather skeptical. I do believe that if nothing else, Tilo's new name in the end could signal Divakaruni's own ambivalence. Evocative of both Indian and Native American cultures and translating the life-giving essence of Tilottama into a new world, Maya is a name that "dissolves boundaries" and also transports us into an indeterminate world of dreamlike reality or real-like dream.

Nevertheless, there is one unmistakably clear message that concerns gender politics emerging from this novel, and that is the liberating effect of women's solidarity—in this case not as a mythic "dissolving of boundaries" but specifically as a South Asian women's help line for battered women. Gaining strength from Tilo, whom she addresses as "Mataji," a surrogate mother, Lalita finds her voice and is no longer nameless. When she calls the help line's number in the magazine Tilo has given her, Lalita speaks with a woman who is "Indian like [her]": "she understood a lot without my telling" (288). Lalita's letter to Tilo is a powerful testimonial of her rebirth from shameful victim to a woman who is conflicted but "coming at last into [her] own" (289). Inflecting her "double vision" here is Divakaruni's own activism as a founder of Maitri—which in her words was "the first South Asian service of its kind on the West coast" through which "women in distress . . . talk to trained South Asian volunteers," all women and fluent in a variety of South Asian languages. If Tilo's transformation into Maya is fraught with "misconception" (309), the battered wife's transformation into self-respecting Lalita is not.

THE GOD OF SMALL THINGS

No one has claimed that Arundhati Roy's *The God of Small Things* is a fairy tale, but in 1997, especially after it won the prestigious Booker Prize, "the global media loudly celebrate[d] Arundhati Roy's 'fairy-tale literary debut'" (K. Wilson), thus exploiting the "idea of India" as land of wonder from another angle. There was the unpromising heroine—an architect-actress-aerobics instructor in her mid-thirties, lacking "upper-class British education" and writing in Delhi about village life—who managed to achieve both unprecedented literary recognition in the Western world (she was the first Indian citizen to be awarded the Booker Prize) and riches (newspapers claimed the book earned her over a million U.S. dollars that year).[9] Also paraded in the media, her beauty, in wonder-tale fashion, wordlessly confirmed her "value" as well as her exotic provenance.

But outspoken Arundhati Roy has not acquiesced to the role; rather she has "worked it" to obtain world coverage for her anti–nuclear bomb stand, her denunciation of state corruption in the building of dams, and her antidiscrimination activism. She has been trouble, and so has her much-acclaimed novel. Confirming that to reinforce the "idea of India" is not her project, Roy commented in a 1997 interview that "Rushdie said . . . 'The trouble with Arundhati is that she insists India is an ordinary place.' Well, I ask, 'Why, the hell not?' It is my ordinary life" (Cowley). Interestingly, Ruth Vanita's shrewd review of the novel in *Manushi*, an important women's journal in India, begins: "When I read the first sentence, 'May in Ayemenem is a hot, brooding month,' I thought this was going to be yet another postcolonial novel about the land of heat and dust, incense and spices." But, Vanita continues, "*The God of Small Things* rapidly reveals its disinterest in trying to encapsulate India, and its complete immersion in one community's, one family's universe."

Aijaz Ahmad nevertheless questions whether the novel is actually successful in its countering the myth of India as wonder tale; as he sees it, *The God of Small Things* reproduces "well-known conventions of European fiction" in its representation of sexuality as privatizing "both pleasure and politics" (something I commented on when discussing *The Mistress of Spices*) and privileging the "phallic . . . , with its attendant theme of woman as Sleeping Beauty waiting for Prince Charming to come and awaken her repressed sexuality." The novel was indeed not only a global success but a scandal in India, where Roy faced intellectual charges of political treason from leftist intellectuals like Ahmad as well as legal charges of pornography because of her representation of the sexual relationship between Ammu, an upper-caste Syrian Christian woman, and Velutha, a poor *dalit,* or untouchable. What interests me here is that the controversy exploded over the novel's sexual politics and that the discourse of wonder tales has been invoked both to praise and to discredit Roy.[10]

That others, like Ajay Singh and Arjuna Ranawana, have countered by pointing to Roy's authenticity as "a home-grown Indian who is inspired by local folk idioms, whereas Rushdie is a British citizen who looks to the West for inspiration" hardly works, I believe, to engage the novel's intertextuality in a transnational context. Rather, I find it helpful to take Gayatri Spivak's suggestion in "Diasporas Old and New: Women in the Transnational World" that we rethink "the opposition of diaspora and globality" by focusing on groups "that cannot become diasporic" (246) but that must, along with their stories, be nevertheless understood in their oblique relations to a transnational economy (245).[11] In the case of this novel's world, that means recognizing not only that the river is a polluted yet essential lifeline but also that Roy's story is deliberately about life on the riverbank, as it is affected by the transnational economic flow (of the river) but does not share in its mobility. Rahel's failed story of migration to the United States and her uncle Chacko's Oxford stunt come to mind; given this essay's focus on metafiction, I will dwell on the Kathakali performances of stories from the *Mahabharata* as recounted in Roy's novel so as to foreground her antipatriarchal rescripting of wonder.

The epigraph to Roy's *The God of Small Things,* John Berger's "Never again will a single story be told as though it's the only one," translates into the novel's attention to story—whether it be history or a well-known film like *The Sound of Music*—as multiple and in performance. Specifically, the narrator identifies the *Mahabharata* among the "Great Stories," "the ones you have heard and want to hear again. The ones you can enter anywhere and inhabit comfortably. . . . You know how they end, yet you listen as though you don't" (Roy 218). The incredible success of the *Mahabharata* as a television series in India testifies to its popularity and ordinary, though also religious, standing.[12] For the Kathakali male artist, whose performance of this popular Hindu epic "employs the disciplines of martial art, dance, theater and music" and requires elaborate costuming and makeup, we are told "these stories are his children and his childhood. He has grown up within them" (219). Out of two different performances in the novel, storytellers and audiences produce divergent meanings; the performances affect each other, and their "located" meanings are, as Roy portrays them, inevitably constrained, though not entirely encompassed by transnational dynamics.

In the luxurious hotel called God's Own Country, "truncated Kathakali performances ('Small attention spans,' the Hotel People explained to the dancers)" are staged as "amputated . . . twenty-minute cameos" next to the pool: "While drummers drummed and the dancers danced, hotel guests frolicked with their children in the water. While Kunti revealed her secret to Karna on the riverbank, courting couples rubbed suntan oil on each other. While fathers played sublimated sexual games with their nubile teenage daughters, Poothana suckled young Krishna at her poisoned breast. Bhima disemboweled Dushasana and bathed Draupadi's hair in his blood" (121). The narrator does not dwell on this performance: in excess of "Regional Flavor" for money, there is no exchange between the world of the riverbank and that of the poolside. The Kathakali artist "checks his rage and dances" (220). The performers, we are told explicitly, are "turning to tourism to stave off starvation": they are humiliated and later stop, on an off night, at the Ayemenem temple "to ask pardon of their gods" (218). Here with Rahel and Estha we witness the unraveling of the "same" episodes. The regal Kunti recognizes Karna as the child of her union with the sun god, but she does it only so that Karna will spare her other beloved sons; Karna is made to choose between shedding his own blood and betraying his putative brothers. And Bhima "hunts down," clubs, and rips apart the man who violated Draupadi's honor by attempting to disrobe her in public after Bhima's brother lost her in a game of dice; Draupadi, as Roy notes, "strangely angry only with the men that won her, not the ones that staked her" (223), has sworn to remain disheveled until she washes her hair in the offender's blood.

But Roy's language, when relaying the second performance, tells a different story, actually more than one, each with a limited and differently cathartic effect. On the one hand, Roy's language builds our awareness of the performer's staged agency as "he strives not to *enter* a part but to escape it. But this is what he cannot do. . . . He *is* Karna, whom the world has abandoned. Karna Alone. Condemned goods" (220). It is not simply because he is stoned that the dancer's despair and rage are no performance. His stories, "his children" and "his childhood," are exchanged in the transnational world that excludes him, and he can engage in a staged fight only when the opponent is not the enemy. The story he performs, then, is "a safety net," "all he has to keep him from crashing through the world like a falling stone" (22). Staged murder "cannot quell" his rage (224). When their performance is over, the narrator states, "the Kathakali Men took off their makeup and went home to beat their wives. Even Kunti, the soft one with breasts" (224).

On the other hand, the twins in the audience recognize the performer's despair as the abjection and betrayal they experienced when made to "choose" between the death of their mother and the death of their friend Velutha; they recognize the rage as the frenzy and "fear of powerlessness"

(292) they witnessed in the "savage economy" (224) of Velutha's beating as the police arrested him for the fabricated attempted rape of their mother. If both of the *Mahabharata* stories invoke the "Love Laws"—"the laws that lay down who should be loved, and how. And how much" (33)—they also violate those same laws: a mother is willing to sacrifice a son for another, and a husband loves his wife enough to kill for her but not enough to refrain from wagering her. When Estha and Rahel realize that they too were "tricked into condemnation" (302) and self-condemnation, that the "Great Stories" have multiple (and often violent) incarnations in the ordinary, they begin to reach for a bit of hope by reaching for each other.

In representing the multiple performance and reception of popular tales in Kerala, both at the hotel and in the temple courtyard, Roy provides more than specificity and less than authenticity. The performances dramatize the exploitation of nondiasporic subgroups within a transnational economy, especially what Spivak calls the "ex-orbitant" place of women in this relation, as well as the oppressiveness of caste and gender discrimination. And of course these inscribed performances invite readers to experience and rethink the "great stories" of India in terms of everyday practices and as they apply to the "small things," including living beings on the riverbank. Wonder is thus strongly located in the ordinary and also rescripted on a different scale.

Perhaps this is why the chapter on Kathakali performances is also the one many of my students *at first* consider to be quasi-incomprehensible or simply digressive. This initial reading on their part paradoxically confirms, as I see it, the lasting attraction of India as feminized wonder tale, the features of which—happy ending included—are not readily available in Roy's nevertheless wondrous storytelling. What I have learned from and with my students—since many of them did not declare themselves content with a reading that damned or dismissed the chapter, therefore committing themselves to a self-reflexive process—is that, in the words of folklorists today, the challenge "is not to the subaltern to find a voice but for those in dominant positions to develop ears."[13]

As they negotiate India's stereotypical association with the feminized wonder tale, each of the novels I selected for classroom use and for discussion in this essay participates differently in the intertextual discourse of wonder in relation to transnationalism and engages one of three different associations with the supernatural. *Haroun*, in parodic and defamiliarizing conversation with specific wonder tales from the Eastern and Western traditions, foregrounds wonder as fictional magic. *Mistress of*

Spices evokes the mystery of wonder as it applies to personal initiation and paths of immigration. Here wonder refers to the transformative powers of wisdom and "ancient" philosophy. In the case of *The God of Small Things*, the author's profile, more than the text of the novel itself, has given rise in both the Western and Indian press to talk of wonder and fairy tales. Yet the novel in its own right powerfully rescripts wonder—as the sacred—into multiple and transnationally troubled situations. In my reading, the impact of these novels' antiexoticizing work varies and has no direct correlation with their sexual politics as it applies to unmaking the feminized dimension of India as wonder tale or (Indian) women's sexual stereotypes. I do not wish to suggest that these three novels are representative of specific trends. Instead, I wish to call attention to how the mythification of fairy tales in the Western world has reinforced the idea of India as wonder tale and,[14] most importantly, to encourage recognition of the antimythifying work that Indian fiction in English can accomplish.

NOTES

1. I should clarify from the start that I am not a postcolonial or South Asian literature specialist; rather, my perspective on these texts is the outcome of an ongoing commitment to the study of gender and narrative, an attempt to meet more directly in the classroom and in writing the challenges of studying gender dynamics as inflected by race and ethnicity, and an indirect reflection on my genealogy as an Anglo-Indian Italian.

2. Important collections that reexamine Indian traditions reflexively as sites of contestation are *Folklore in Modern India* (Handoo), which includes Carsten Bregenhøj's essay on "The Indian and Indo-European Theories in Folk Narrative Research: An Update"; and *Gender, Genre, and Power in South Asian Expressive Traditions* (Appadurai, Korom, and Mills).

While I am responsible for any inaccuracies, I am grateful to Ravi Palat for the many exchanges while I was writing this piece and he was working on the conceptualizing of India in dominant spatial imaginaries for his unpublished manuscript "Is India Part of Asia?" I also wish to thank Sridevi Menon, Sanjay Sircar, Sabarimuthu Carlos, Vrinda Dalmyia, Monica Ghosh, and Subramanian Shankar for either responding to my questions or giving me feedback as I drafted the essay.

3. In her important dissertation, "Discursive Realms and Colonial Practices: Contrapuntal Studies of Race in Colonial India and the United States," Sridevi Menon discusses various Orientalist practices as framed by a "structure of feeling," drawing on Raymond Williams's conception of it as a "lived hegemony," a "process" emphasizing "thought as felt and feeling as thought" (Menon 13; qtd. from Williams, *Marxism* 132); she also usefully comments on how Said refers to Williams's term "to observe that 'structures of attitude and reference' appear across cultural texts that do not necessarily appear to be related" (Menon 329; qtd. from Said, *Culture* 52).

4. For recent analyses of gender issues in this classic, see Eva Sallis's *Scheherazade through the Looking Glass* and Fedwa Malti-Douglas's *Woman's Body, Woman's Word*. A

notable study of Western eroticizing and exoticizing of *Arabian Nights,* Rana Kabbani's *Europe's Myths of Orient* discusses both the Burton and the Lane translations. For more general information about oriental fairy tales and *The Arabian Nights,* see Marzolph, "Oriental Fairy Tales," and Goldberg, respectively.

5. In the chapter devoted to "Stories and Motifs from *The Arabian Nights,*" John Stephens and Robyn McCallum make an interesting argument to show how "the idea of the Orient" has played a significant role in contemporary Western children's literature (229–52).

6. Rushdie's "Valley of K"—"with its fields of gold (which really grew saffron) and its silver mountains (which were really covered in glistening, pure, white snow) and its Dull [Dal] Lake (which didn't look dull at all" (*Haroun* 39)—evokes descriptions of Kashmir, a site that localizes the "idea of the Orient" and is consistent with the *Katha Sarit Sagara* being a Kasmiri text. The history of Kashmir, however, also undermines both the Orientalist and the religious fundamentalist "idea of India": Kashmir became part of India after Partition because its Raja was Hindu, and yet the majority of its population was Muslim; it has remained a contested territory between India and Pakistan. Furthermore, another "idea of India" is reinforced, as Suchismita Sen argues, by Rushdie's "use of the South Asian variety of English" as nostalgic of his generation's childhood (655).

7. Even if Divakaruni claims to write for "both Indians and non-Indians," Tilottama, the first-person narrator and protagonist, explicitly addresses a "you" that is different from her. In the "new land" of California, in her Indian spice store, where she leads the double life of Mistress of Spices and ugly crone, Tilo tells readers that "Yes, [spices] all hold magic, even the everyday American spices you toss unthinking into your cooking pot" (3). Her message that "the snakes are everywhere, yes, even in your home, in your favorite room" (20) recalls a similar claim about "ghosts" in Maxine Hong Kingston's *The Woman Warrior: Memoir of a Girlhood among Ghosts* (1976), another story about recognizing race and ethnicity in the western United States.

8. Clearly, Divakaruni's fiction highlights the associations of wonder with wisdom and Eastern philosophy, but I am in no position to be specific about it. For instance, the novel draws on snake worship and Ayurvedic medicine, but it is difficult for me to say how she translates them into the novel. For instance, serpents are a topos of Indian folk-lore, but water serpents are rare to my limited knowledge, and they do not commonly appear as helpers in Bengali tales. Significantly, in Ayurvedic medicine spices have "prop-erties," not magic powers. More work needs to be done on these aspects of the novel by specialists of South Asian traditions.

9. V. P. Naipaul's *In a Free State* (1971), J. G. Farrell's *The Siege of Krishnapur* (1973), Ruth Prawer Jhabvala's *Heat and Dust* (1975), and *Midnight's Children* by Salman Rushdie (1981) were all awarded the Booker Prize. Ajay Singh and Arjuna Ranawana's "Heralding a New Asian Writing" furthers the contrast between Roy and the above books: her win-ning the Booker Prize "was a coup not just for her but for an emerging genre of Indian writing in English that is quite different from the one represented by Rushdie. . . . Roy . . . did not receive formal schooling until she was 10."

10. The novel invokes the Western wonder tale too, as it magnifies the mythic and mystifying power of the film *The Sound of Music* as a romanticized Cinderella story. Estha and Rahel, two dark children who lack a father figure, watch the film in Kerala and would like to identify with the baron's seven children and their "happily ever after" family, but they find themselves rejected, thrown out of the picture as it were, while in their minds they exchange questions about and with the film. "Oh Baron von Trapp, Baron von Trapp, could you love the little fellow with the orange in the smelly auditorium? . . . And his

twin sister? Tilting upward with her fountain in a Love-in-Tokyo? Could you love her too? Baron von Trapp had some questions of his own. (a) *Are they clean white children?*" (101). Though Estha could sing all the songs, this is not their story.

11. Spivak explains that in a "transnational world . . . new and developing states [cannot] escape the orthodox constraints of a 'neo-liberal' world economic system which in the name of Development, and now 'sustainable development,' removes all barriers between itself and fragile national economies, so that any possibility of building for social redistribution is severely damaged" ("Diasporas" 245). Spivak points to the "ex-orbitant" relationship of women to the complex phenomena of diasporas in a transnational world (246) and therefore demands that we rethink "the opposition of diaspora and globality in the name of woman" (258).

12. By focusing on these metafictional episodes in Roy's novel I am not implying that the *Mahabharata* should be read as a wonder tale. This "Great Story of the Bharata Clan" is rather a poem of epic proportions with religious and mythic import. However, the performance and retelling of its episodes may very well elicit "wonder" and continues to involve the rescripting of the sacred within daily-life situations or the ordinary.

13. The quotation is from the conclusion to Lee Haring's essay in the present volume (177) on women as agents of creolization in Madagascar and Mauritius, islands of the Southwest Indian Ocean. Haring is paraphrasing Margaret Mills, who in turn was transforming Gayatri Spivak's famous question "Can the subaltern speak?" into "How, and under what circumstances, can or does the hegemonic hear?" (Mills, "Feminist Theory" 174).

14. See Zipes's discussion of what he calls "mythicization" in *Fairy Tale as Myth* 5–6, and throughout.

11
Disrupting the Boundaries of Genre and Gender: Postmodernism and the Fairy Tale

CATHY LYNN PRESTON

Date: Sun, 19 Sep 1999 21:06:41 EDT
From: Anna XXXXXXXXX
To: humor@listserv.uga.edu
Subject: Once upon a time . . . (offensive to frogs)

Once upon a time in a land far away, a beautiful, independent, self assured princess happened upon a frog as she sat, contemplating ecological issues on the shores of an unpolluted pond in a verdant meadow near her castle. The frog hopped into the princess' lap and said: Elegant Lady, I was once a handsome prince, until an evil witch cast a spell upon me. One kiss from you, however, and I will turn back into the dapper, young prince that I am and then, my sweet, we can marry and set up housekeeping in your castle with my mother, where you can prepare my meals, clean my clothes, bear my children, and forever feel grateful and happy doing so.

That night, as the princess dined sumptuously on a repast of lightly sauteed frog legs seasoned in a white wine and onion cream sauce, she chuckled to herself and thought . . . I don't fucking think so.

GENDERED PERFORMANCE AND AUTHORITATIVE FRAMES

In her essay "Gender and Genre," Amy Shuman explains that "genres are not neutral classification systems but are part of a politics of interpretation in which meaning and the authority to propose and ascribe categories

197

is contested" (71). Noting that "genres exist only in relation to other genres" and that "they are what Bakhtin has termed 'texts bearing upon
texts,'"[1] Shuman analyzes the relationship between a woman's life-history
story and the parable embedded in the telling of that story, explaining that
"parables are a form of reported speech. As Bakhtin warns us, reported
speech can be parodic as easily as it can be referential [*Dialogic Imagination*
342–43]. That is, when we borrow another's words, and traditional phrases
and stories are not only another's words but are the words of the anonymous and sometimes authoritative, traditional 'other,' we negotiate
between the world the authority describes and the world we describe"
(80). In the process of analyzing one woman's appropriation and recon-
textualization of a traditional parable, Shuman raises a series of questions
that are worth exploring further, questions concerning "the ways in which
boundaries [those of genre and those of gender] are maintained, reproduced, transgressed, or shifted" (72). In particular, for feminist studies (and
as she notes, "for feminist studies concerned with the concepts of tradition and change") are questions concerning "what constitutes a rupture in
the status of proposed fixed meanings" and whether "new interpretations"
simply "stand alongside the old ones" or whether "they disturb the status
of the fixed meanings" (80). With these questions in mind, I would like
to return to the joke "Once upon a time . . . (offensive to frogs)."

The joke is, I believe, a good example of a story that references "the
words of the anonymous and . . . authoritative, traditional 'other,'" but it
does so for a parodic purpose. The stylized beginning, "Once upon a time,
in a land far away, a beautiful . . . princess," invokes stereotypical female
gender patterns of the past (enumerated later in the joke by the frog as
marriage, housekeeping, cooking, cleaning, procreation, and child care)
that are associated with the genre of folktale (and specifically with the
subgenre of fairy tale insofar as the specific textual tradition that is referenced is "The Frog King").[2] By means of parody the text then proceeds
to negotiate contestively between the world that the authoritative fairy
tale describes and the world that the narrator of the joke describes: a world
where princesses are independent and self-assured women who own their
own property, cook meals to nurture themselves, use princes to satisfy their
own desires, and contemplate the ecological possibility of a pollution-free
environment. Symbolic inversion becomes a mechanism for breaking the
fairy-tale frame and resituating the tale as a joke, a shift in genre that, I
would argue, "constitutes a rupture in the status of proposed fixed meanings" (Shuman 80), those both of genre and of gender. More difficult to
answer is the question of whether such a rupture "disturb[s] the status of

the fixed meanings" (80) in any permanent way or whether it merely creates a text that stands alongside the older ones, competing for social space but ultimately not displacing their authority.

Part of my difficulty in answering this question stems from the permeability or shape-shifting quality of contemporary genre boundaries. Within folkloristic classification systems, a text, as Amy Shuman explains, "is designated as a this and not a that"; but as she also notes, the "discovery of permeable boundaries" has enabled discussions of dual membership such that a text may be simultaneously both "a this and a that" (76; see also Harris). For example, in the case of "Once upon a time . . . (offensive to frogs)," while one recognizes most readily the slippage between the boundaries of fairy tale and joke, one might also note that the text reads like one of the many literary feminist revisionary folktales of the 1970s, 1980s, and 1990s, in particular the humorous ones (see, for example, Margaret Atwood's "The Little Red Hen Tells All" and "There Was Once" [*Good Bones* 13–15, 20–24]). But most of the revisionary literary texts were formally published, complete with attribution of authorship, whereas "Once upon a time . . . (offensive to frogs)" is informally "published" as an e-mail text and without attribution of authorship. As an e-mail text, it is not told orally (one of the older definitional requirements of a folk performance though now one that is generally questioned), but it is nonetheless "performed" for what might be called the imagined community that is made up by humor@listserv.uga.edu. And while that performance might be understood as being a folk performance, it might just as easily be seen as sharing qualities with the performance of a standup comic. Thus the text exists in a borderland betwixt and between genres, aesthetic registers, and processes of communication. In turn, the breaking and blurring of boundaries problematizes traditionalized notions of real and unreal, of authentic and unauthentic, of authority and lack of authority, and of traditionalized hierarchies associated with the real, the authentic, and the authoritative (Shuman 76–77). To this extent, "Once upon a time . . . (offensive to frogs)" participates in an emergent textual tradition that has indeed disturbed the status of fixed meanings: those of genre and by extension those of gender.

In this time and place, for many people the accumulated web of feminist critique (created through academic discourse, folk performance, and popular media) may function as an emergent and authoritative—though fragmented and still under negotiation—multivocality that cumulatively is competitive with the surface monovocality of the inherited older fairy tale tradition, particularly that tradition as it was mainstreamed into

American culture by means of Perrault's and the Grimm brothers' editions of fairy tales, Disney movie adaptations, senior proms, romance novels, television shows like *The Dating Game,* and so on. The remainder of this essay will explore how three relatively recent media texts—the movie *Ever After,* the American television special *Who Wants to Marry a Millionaire?* and a magazine advertisement for women.com—break or blur genre frame and, in doing so, variously work to maintain, reproduce, transgress, or shift the boundaries of gender associated with the older fairy-tale textual tradition.

EVER AFTER

The movie *Ever After* (1998) is a relatively recent American popular culture production of the Cinderella tale that cleverly blurs the boundaries between folktale and legend in an attempt to retrieve the romantic possibility of "true love" for the generation currently being raised in the aftermath/afterglow of second-wave feminist and post-Marxist critique.[3] The movie opens in the nineteenth century with the arrival of the Brothers Grimm at a magnificent French chateau. Having recently published their collection of folktales, they have been called to court by the chateau's owner so that she might "set the record straight" concerning the ontological status of the Cinderella figure. This she does by producing two material objects, a shoe and a painting, and by reproducing through narrative (which the core of the movie dramatizes) the inherited family story that is linked to and thus legitimatized by the artifacts. The story she tells is set in sixteenth-century France and concerns her great-great-grandmother, Danielle de Barbarac. The narrator begins her story by glancing meaningfully at the Grimm brothers and then at the painting and saying, "Now, what is that phrase you use? Oh yes, once upon a time there was a young girl who," parodically referencing the conventions of the fairy tale in order to highlight the tale's larger framing as legend. Similarly, at the end of the tale per se, Danielle/Cinderella, while playfully chastising the prince, says, "You, sir, are supposed to be charming," to which he replies, "And we, princess, are supposed to live happily ever after." When Danielle asks, "Says who?" the prince responds, "You know? I don't know who," after which the audience is returned to the film's larger frame—that set in the nineteenth-century chateau where Danielle's great-great-grandmother has just finished telling the fairy tale now resituated as family legend. The matronly lineal descendant of Cinderella then concludes her interview with the Grimm brothers by noting that "while Cinderella and her prince did live happily ever after, the point, gentlemen, is that she lived." Thus, while, as the Grimm brothers acknowledge in their interview, there "are many versions of the little ash girl" (they mention, in particular, Perrault's version), thereby seemingly situating the tale firmly within the genre of fairy tale/fiction as well as within the patrilineal line of male collectors and editors, the movie works to negotiate a different status for the tale: familial (and by extension cultural) legend/history that has been transmitted orally and through the gifting of objects through the matrilineal line. Although one might read and dismiss this shift in genre as itself a convention of literature and film (which in part it is), I think the shift in ontological status of the Cinderella figure that accompanies the shift in genre of the tale, as well as the shift in gendered transmission, is significant as an engendering of genre.

I saw the film, when it was first released, with my then thirteen-year-old daughter. When asked to review the film for *Marvels & Tales,* I decided that before writing the review I wanted to hear how the age group that seemed to be the target audience had responded to the PG-13-rated film.[4] Consequently, I turned to my daughter and the young women in the undergraduate Women's Folklore/Folklife course that I was teaching at the time.[5] When asked to talk in general about the fairy tale "Cinderella," my daughter explained to me, first, that "there are many different versions of Cinderella," noting the Disney version and several multicultural versions she had read at school, and then significantly added, "but if a person wants to learn about the real Cinderella, they should see *Ever After.*" Continuing to speak, she fleshed out her definition of "real" by focusing on differences between Disney's 1949 film version and *Ever After,* noting that the one had "cartoon characters" and the other had "real people," that the one was set in "once upon a time," while the other was in a "real" place and at a "real" time, and that the one had overly simple characters, while the other had more complex people ("the way people really are"). Without knowing it, she had given a fairly accurate catalog of the traits normally associated with legend (an incident that is said to have happened in the historical past, that is geographically localized to a specific place, and that happened to real people). To explain further what she meant by complex people, she noted that while Danielle/Cinderella was still "nice," she could also throw an apple at the Prince and hit him with it, that Danielle "punched out" the mean, self-centered, older stepsister (I should note here that my daughter was taking karate at the time and that she, too, has an older sister), and that the younger stepsister wasn't bad but instead turned out to be really "nice" (on the concept of being "nice" in girls' culture, see Hughes). Thus, for my daughter (who is the younger of two sisters, who can throw a punch as well as a ball, and who is coming of age in the late-twentieth and early-twenty-first centuries), the film presented images she could identify with and validated her construction of self by providing a fictionalized historical precedent for that self. As Elliott Oring has explained, "legend often depicts the improbable within the world of the possible" (125).

My daughter also pointed out that the great-great-granddaughter had Danielle's/Cinderella's shoe and the painting of her and that the great-great-granddaughter's ownership of those items proved that the family-based story was true, an assertion that she then qualified by explaining that she knew it was also "just a movie and so not really true, probably." My daughter's waffling over the nature of truth is also consistent with the genre of legend. While folktale is fiction and requires a suspension of disbelief on the part of the audience in order to participate in its world, legend "never asks for the suspension of disbelief." Instead it "is concerned with creating a narrative whose truth is at least worthy of deliberation" (Oring 125). Legends are believed to be true by some and not believed to be true by others, but for many, legends fall within the "maybe/maybe not" category. As Oring notes, the raison d'être for legends is "the creation of a story which requires the audience to examine their world view—their sense of the normal, the boundaries of the natural" (126). Thus, one might argue that the film's overtly self-conscious resituating of folktale as family legend creates a liminal space for the viewer to construct a play-frame for the self in which, through a series of appropriations, the fairy tale/fiction cum family legend/history becomes cultural legend/history and then, in turn, is privatized by the viewer as personal lineage.

Girls older than my daughter (those in high school and the young women in my folklore class) sometimes noted disapprovingly that the point of the film was still focused on Cinderella's getting the prince, and lesbian students in the class similarly noted the implied but unstated injunction of heterosexuality; but just as frequently students pointed to Cinderella's "mastery of language" and "cunning wit," to the moments of gender reversal in the film, and to the fact that "a pretty, but not ravishingly gorgeous, or unhealthily thin" actress played the part of Cinderella as being positive features of the film. And I might add that in the spring following the movie's release more than one girl showed up at her local high school prom wearing wings attached to her dress (wings that were quite similar to the wings worn by the film's Cinderella when she went to the ball). Significantly, though, the girls who attended the prom that year did so often having paid for their own tickets, having bought their own dinners, and having paid their share of the price of renting a limousine for the evening—at least this was the case at our local high school proms.

"To set the record straight" is to call into question and thereby revise a past "record," in terms of both genre and gender. Accompanying the shift in genre from fairy tale to legend was a shift in gender patterns insofar as the movie does attempt to respond to the last thirty years of feminist critique of gender construction in respect to key Western European, popularized versions of the fairy tale (in particular those of Perrault, the Brothers Grimm, and Disney). Feminist critique has ranged from Rosemary Minard's description of fairy-tale heroines as "insipid beauties waiting passively for Prince Charming" (*Womenfolk and Fairy Tales*; qtd. in Yolen, "America's Cinderella" 297) through the catalog of various traits requisite for being chosen for such connubial bliss: gentility, grace, self-lessness (296); beautiful, sweet, patient, submissive, an excellent house-keeper (Stone, "Misuses" 139); and patience, sacrifice, dependency (Rowe, "Feminism" 217). The catalog is by now well rehearsed. As one under-graduate female student (Annie Hurst) in my Women's Folklore/Folklife course in the spring of 1999 noted: "Little girls that are told again and again of princes who come to save a beautiful but foolish princess may be learning that, in order to get a prince, they must be outwardly rich with beauty, but do not need to possess the common sense that is essential in keeping them from needing to be saved in the first place. The fairy tales of the past are permeated with the ideals of the past, and could be updated in a way that would keep the integrity of the story, while relaying behavior that is now socially acceptable."

The latter is what *Ever After* attempts to do. As a review of the film in *People* magazine notes, "a clever movie director [decided to] remake the classic *Cinderella* tale . . . [and has] goosed the story by giving it an unmistakably feminist spin. Out went the pumpkin carriage and the white mice who drew it; in came references to public education and rights of servants" (Rozen). These lectures are delivered to the prince by the populist-minded Cinderella figure, whose most cherished possession is a copy of More's *Utopia*, given to her by her father just before he dies. The screenplay writers kept what Rozen describes as "the bare bones of the *Cinderella* story": "The prince, for example, first meets Cinderella while on the run from an arranged marriage to a Spanish princess. The orphaned Cinderella remains with her stepmother because she keeps hoping the woman will actually express maternal feeling for her. And Cinderella's fairy godmother is—hold on to your paintbrush—Leonardo da Vinci, who is hanging about doing some artwork for the prince's father." To *People* magazine's catalog one might add that not only does this Cinderella use her wit and brawn to save the prince, but she also does likewise for herself, when, toward the end of the story, she is sold off by her stepmother to the local wealthy "scuz-bag" (who is, among other things, old enough to be her father) to use as he sees fit (read *potential rape scene* here). Whether the filmmakers were consciously doing so or not, they have, through a series of displacements, merged tale types 510A and 510B.

In short, the film plays off of what both folklorists and feminists have asked for: an acknowledgment that there have been many versions of "Cinderella" and that there is a need to return, as it were, to a Cinderella figure who is a "shrewd and practical girl persevering and winning a share of the power" (Yolen, "America's Cinderella" 296). That the film negotiates a shift in vision by means of a shift in genre from fairy tale to legend is perhaps a necessity for a generation who still harbor a desire for "happily ever afters" but who are also the product of a revisionary understanding of what that "happily ever after" might be and how it might be attained. In relation to the joke "Once upon a time . . . (offensive to frogs)," many of this generation, when asked to envision themselves as adults, see themselves as independent, self-assured women who will own their own property, nurture themselves, and work for a clean environment but who want to sit down to dinner with the frog rather than have it/him for the main course. This vision of themselves, though, is problematized by the next media text that I now turn to.

WHO WANTS TO MARRY A MILLIONAIRE?

The extent to which *Ever After,* as a single text, did or did not change the "status of fixed meanings" for any extended period of time is perhaps best argued by the number of people who watched the FOX network special *Who Wants to Marry a Millionaire?* that aired 15 February 2000. Described by one newspaper columnist in her editorial titled "Who Wants to Marry a Frog?" as television bringing "the glass slipper to the 21st century" (Estrich) and generally denounced as having set feminist arguments for gender equality back to the Middle Ages, *Who Wants to Marry a Millionaire?* drew a viewing audience that successively grew through the evening from "10 million viewers in its first half hour to 12.3 million in the second half hour to 18.9 million in the third half hour to a huge 22.8

million in the final half hour" (B. Carter). Furthermore, the show's "rat-ings were even bigger among teenage girls and young women," and in "its final half hour, the show pulled in more than a third of all women under age 35 watching television" that night (B. Carter).

With a format reminiscent of the Miss America pageant, *The Dating Game,* and ABC's *Who Wants to Be a Millionaire?* the show, as many peo-ple noted at the time, some with disgust, offered women (the one thou-sand who applied to be on the show and from which were chosen fifty, a number that was then paired down to ten semifinalists, five finalists, and then ultimately one "winner") the "chance to be Cinderella" (Estrich), and the numbers of applicants and viewers would seem to suggest, as Estrich pointed out, that the "pre-feminist ideal is alive and well." Not only does the "perfect couple" remain "a beautiful woman and a rich man," but the man did the choosing. As Estrich continues to explain in her editorial, the women who put "themselves on the auction block" knew nothing about the man (Rick Rockwell, age forty-two) except that he was supposed to be a multimillionaire. The man was kept in shadow during the show while the women went through a series of interviews and paraded for him and the viewing audience in evening gowns and beachwear. The show con-cluded with the contestants appearing in wedding gowns, Rockwell kneel-ing to propose to the winning contestant, and a legal wedding. Beyond a husband and what was described as a "standard prenuptial agreement," the bride, Darva Conger (a "34-year-old emergency-room nurse from Santa Monica, Calif., who also served in the Gulf War"), received "a two week vacation (the honeymoon), an Isuzu Trooper and a $35,000 dia-mond ring" (B. Carter).

Ironically, while the television special (an example of what is now ubiquitous and being termed "real-life programming," or "reality TV") turned fiction into one kind of reality (at least for Darva Conger and Rick Rockwell), almost overnight both Conger and the viewing audience were faced with another form of reality: questions were raised concerning the real-life nature of the "prince," in terms of both his economic status and his previous treatment of women: "Rick Rockwell may or may not have a million dollars to his name. Sorry Darva, but I wouldn't bet on it. What he does have is a record of abusing the woman with whom he was involved, to the point that she had to get a restraining order. Real princes don't have to go on television to find a mate. Rick Rockwell is no prince" (Estrich). In other words, Rick Rockwell turned out to be "a wannabe with a record" (Estrich). In Estrich's words, "Fantasy meets reality. The prince turns out to be a frog. What else is new?"

Two days after it aired, I discussed the show with students in the
various classes I was teaching that semester. Many had watched the show
or some piece of it, all but a couple of students had heard about the show,
and most students readily identified the show as a contemporary literal-
ization of a Cinderella script, one that disclosed, openly reproduced, and
sanctioned the gendered economic relations of the older tale. While the
students situated themselves along various ideological lines in response to
the show and why they had or had not watched it, the one comment that
repeatedly surfaced had to do with its real-life format, a format that is not
only increasingly being used in television programming but one that is
also increasingly drawing in large viewing audiences ranging in age from
adolescents through young adults (more recent examples of real-life programming would be the limited serial show *Survivor* and its sequels).

While the viewers of these "real life" shows seem generally aware
that the programs have been shaped by a film editor and thus, through
that shaping, are in some way fictions, the viewers continue to cite the
shows' nonfiction status as the reason they are drawn to them. As several
students have explained, it is the difference between watching a fictional
train/car wreck and watching a real train/car wreck, or watching fictional
comedy and watching real people make fools of themselves, or watching
a fictional soap opera and watching the soap opera of real people's lives
(spring 2001). This slippage between fiction and reality is analogous to
the crossing and blurring of the boundaries between fairy tale and legend
in the film *Ever After*. But while *Ever After* blurred genre boundaries in
order to negotiate a space in which to redefine gender boundaries, *Who
Wants to Marry a Millionaire?* blurred genre boundaries in order to reproduce and thereby maintain traditional gender boundaries.

Although blurred boundaries do not always disturb the status of
fixed gender meanings, they do seem to provide a liminal space in which
the artifice of storytelling itself is disclosed. As Donald Haase notes earlier in this volume when discussing Cristina Bacchilega's work on post-
modernist fairy tales, the magic mirror (which Bacchilega understands to
be the "controlling metaphor" of the fairy tale and of its revisions) is "something more subtle than a static image that could be simply shattered—or
replaced with a truer mirror—to reveal women's 'real' or 'natural' identity,"
because "mirrors . . . are neither natural objects nor unmediated reflections
of what is natural" (24). Thus, "As with all mirrors, . . . refraction and the
shaping presence of a frame mediate the fairy tale's reflection. As it images
our potential for transformation, the fairy tale refracts what we wish or
fear to become. Human—and thus changeable—ideas, desires, and prac-

tices frame the tale's images" (Bacchilega, *Postmodern Fairy Tales* 28). Drawing on the idea of the tale's refracting "what we wish or fear to become" might enable us to see the ways in which both wishes and fears were at work in the audience's viewing of *Who Wants to Marry a Millionaire?* For example, it might help to explain the desire to watch Cinderella be played out as real life (wish fulfillment) but also to watch for the same reason that people are attracted to a car wreck or are willing to see other people make fools of themselves (fear of what might actually happen to themselves). It is this interplay between fantasy and reality and between wish fulfillment and fear that I will address by means of the next text, an advertisement.

WOMEN.COM

Lying before me on my desk is a page (dated 1999) torn from a magazine.[6] The page is light blue with a small strip of yellow running down the right-hand side. In the center of the page is a small but dominating cartoon caricature of a young woman (blushing white, with long blond hair and blue eyes) dressed in a ball gown that is a slightly lighter shade of blue than that of the surrounding page. The figure holds the edges of the gown's skirt delicately in her hands, lifting them as if in dance, showing a hint of white petticoat and one small foot in a blue slipper pointed in a dance step. Her head is slightly tilted down as if watching her step or avoiding her imaginary partner's eyes. Around her swirls an effervescent, white gyroscope of stars.

Underneath the figure is printed the following message: "A website for princesses [in white letters]. Also: women who get really annoyed with women who act like princesses; actual princesses; descendants of princesses; anyone who dressed like a princess for Halloween; women who believe in fairy godmothers; women who wear crowns; women with gold-crowned teeth; every woman who ever lost a slipper; and any woman who wore a puffy gown to the prom [in black letters]." Horizontally, across the bottom of the page are printed the words "money, career, shopping, family, health, relationships, food, fitness," followed by the comment "the smart way to get things done" and a Web site address: women.com.

The figure in the women.com ad is clearly a Disneylike cartoon caricature of Cinderella; in fact, the color of the page and the figure bear a remarkable resemblance to that on the jacket of the video version of Disney's 1949 *Cinderella*. In the advertisement, the dainty and demure female figure appears to be caught in the timeless swirl of "once upon a time" and "ever after" magic. She is, as I have argued elsewhere concerning Disney's *Cinderella,* a representation of Mikhail Bakhtin's classical body: a "smooth" and "impenetrable surface" that situates itself as "a separate and completed phenomenon" in terms of both image and the story that is intertextually invoked by the image (Bakhtin, *Rabelais* 318; qtd. in Preston, "Cinderella" 29). This fantasy image, if taken alone, is referential (both in terms of genre and a specific textual tradition within that genre) and invokes the authoritative voice of tradition as interpreted and reinscribed specifically by the Disney movie and more generally as a fixed figure in media representations of "princess."

The verbal text below the image is participatory in what the visual image invokes insofar as it situates all women (those who are real princesses, those who want to be or ever wanted to be princesses, and those who "get really annoyed with women who act like princesses") in relation to the word "princess," suggesting the extent to which authoritative discourse successfully "strives . . . to determine the very bases of our ideological interrelations with the world, the very basis of our behavior" (Bakhtin, *Dialogic Imagination* 342). Simultaneously, though, the verbal text is contestive of that authority and seeks to resist its historically privileged status. The tone of the verbal text is ironic, disclosing discrepancies between idealized representations of "women who wear crowns" and the everyday-life realities of "women with gold-crowned teeth," between fictional lost slippers and real lost slippers, and between fantasy balls and ball gowns and the realities of "puffy gown[s]" and high school "prom[s]." Finally, the mapping of "money, career, shopping, family, health, relationships, food, fitness" at the bottom of the page foregrounds what might be called "real-life" concerns of women as opposed to fantasy "happy ever afters."

In the advertisement, the phrase used to describe the Web site—the "smart way to get things done"—seems at once to be a reference to the performance of tasks required of the Cinderella figure and a continuation of parodic critique: real tasks and problems require real information and action for resolution. Having acknowledged all of this ("this" being the latter part of the verbal text's seeming disruption of the dreamy passivity of the visual image), one nonetheless cannot help but notice that there is also a way in which that same piece of text returns us to the world of fairy tale (or perhaps, as Linda Dégh argues, resituates fairy tale as legend) by displacing the magic of the "old" fairy-tale tradition with that of the "new" world of the Internet: subliminally, women.com is situated as a magical agent, as fairy godmother (or perhaps the Internet itself is the fairy godmother), and the words women.com are the "bibbidi, bobbidi, boo" that calls forth that agent's transformative power.

Quoting Theodor Adorno's assertion that "mass media consists of various layers of meanings superimposed on one another, all of which contribute to the effect" (Adorno 601; qtd. in Dégh, *American Folklore* 51), Dégh has analyzed television commercials and mail-order advertisements in relationship to a two-part layering of meaning. The top, or surface, layer, she argues, is märchenlike:

> The top layer [of the märchenlike commercial] is the manifest tale, which we have already ascertained is functionally no more than figurative expression, dramatized metaphor: an ingredient of the advertisement but not the whole of it. In a story, a witch is shown in a characteristic outfit. Her magic wand, which she waves over a lady's hairdo, splits in two. As it turns out, there is no need for the wand because Hidden Magic hair spray does the trick. The idea behind this story is not that there was once a witch whose magic wand broke, but rather that whoever applies the hair spray in question will have no need for any other help. (51)

The second, or obscured, layer, Dégh argues, is legendlike:

> A genre like the Märchen, which is fiction and by definition cannot be believed, is unfit for the conveyance of belief. The symbol must be understood and the figurative expression decoded in order to reach the second layer, in which the suggested to-be-believed statement is expressed. . . .
>
> What is being stated in the commercial (and what we have to call the "story," for lack of a better term) is, at least formally, nonfiction: something that is believed by some, doubted by others, but, after all, might also be true. This description fits the legend best. (51)

What is unstated here is that at the center of many legends, particularly contemporary legends, is everyday fear, whether the fear is that of not having perfect hair or a more general fear of simply not being in control of everyday life. As "something that is believed by some, doubted by others, but, after all, might also be true," legend mediates between the wish for control and the fear of lack of control; but unlike the fairy tale, both its wishes and its fears are located in historical rather than fictional time and space. The blurring of the boundaries between fairy tale and legend, like the blurring of the boundaries between fiction and nonfiction, creates a site of cultural production in which social transformation has both imaginative and material possibility.

The women.com ad is multivocal, with respect to both genre and the ad's gendered voices. It is perhaps best described as a postmodern text: a "tentative grouping of ideas, stylistic traits, and thematic preoccupations" that in the arts include "pastiche, the incorporation of different textual genres, and contradictory 'voices,'" as well as "fragmented or 'open' forms that give the audience the power to assemble the work and determine its meaning" (Geyh, Leebron, and Levy x). As such, it is at once complicit with and resistant to the reproduction of the genre and gender expectations associated with the older fairy-tale tradition.

Conclusion

In postmodernity the "stuff" of fairy tales exists as fragments (princess, frog, slipper, commodity relations in a marriage market) in the nebulous realm that we might most simply identify as cultural knowledge. From an etic positioning the scholar may delineate among forms of transmission and impose genre classification on individual performances of the "stuff" for the purposes of analysis, but from an emic positioning it is free-floating cultural data that can be invoked conversationally, narratively, dramatically, or graphically as an e-mail message sent to an individual or a self-defined group, as a movie or a television special, or as a magazine advertisement, not to mention the many other forms it may take: a bedtime story told to a child, an edited text in a published collection, an authored short story or poem, a text in or of an academic article, a comic strip or cartoon, a television commercial, an item in the news or an item rumored to have been in the news, or a ritual enactment. The performer's and the audience's fragmented cultural knowledge may have been acquired through any or all of the above forms of cultural production. As Trudier Harris has noted, when "technology expands, so does the possibility for broadening categories of folklore genre" (518).

As textual strategies that adopt "a playful irony as a stance that seems to prove itself endlessly useful" (Geyh, Leebron, and Levy x), "Once upon a time … (offensive to frogs)," *Ever After, Who Wants to Marry a Millionaire?* and women.com problematize older dichotomies between the real and the unreal, between the authentic and the unauthentic, and between the authoritative and the nonauthoritative as they blur genre boundaries:

fairytalejokefairytalelegendmoviefairytalejokeTVspecialfairytalejokelegen
dadvertisement.

Doing so, they disclose "the constructedness of meaning, truth, and history," while reflecting and refracting "the complexities of subjectivity and identity" (Geyh, Leebron, and Levy x). One might think here of that moment in the movie *Ever After* when the prince, looking at the portrait of Danielle/Cinderella, turns to da Vinci and says, "I must say, Leonardo, for a man of your talents, it doesn't look anything like her." This is the painting that Danielle's great-great-granddaughter uses to authenticate her own family-based storytelling, a performance that in turn contests that of the Grimm brothers and of Perrault. The moment is metatextual: artistic performance, art, and audience reception are self-consciously brought to the foreground, disclosing not only the painting's artifice but that of Perrault's and the Grimm brothers' edited texts, that of the great-great-granddaughter's oral narrative, and that of the movie itself. In such a moment one should ask, as has Bacchilega, "Who is holding the mirror and whose desires does it represent and contain?" and "How is the fairy tale's magic produced narratively?" (*Postmodern Fairy Tales* 28); or as Shuman has asked, what "kinds of authority does the [performance] appeal to: to the authority of male tradition or to gendered genres" (76)? In the case of *Ever After* the appeal to authority is multivocal. The film invokes the historical authority of male tradition (Perrault, Brothers Grimm, da Vinci), which it then contests through a performance of gendered genre: the great-great-granddaughter's appropriation of the painting and resituating of the fairy tale as legend such that male authority, both as storytellers and as those who historically have defined genre boundaries, is called into question. By disrupting genre boundaries, she is able to tell a different story, one that played to the competing authority of a popularized 1990s feminism.

Similarly, when "Once upon a time . . . (offensive to frogs)," *Who Wants to Marry a Millionaire?* and women.com are brought into the same frame, they too disclose their respective appeals to the authority of male tradition or to gendered genres as they variously work to maintain, reproduce, transgress, or shift the boundaries of genre and gender. As Bacchilega has explained, "the tale of magic's controlling metaphor is the *magic mirror* because it conflates mimesis (reflection), refraction (varying desires), and framing (artifice)" (*Postmodern Fairy Tales* 10). In turn, the blurred genre boundaries of the texts that I have been examining in this chapter "hold mirrors to the magic mirror of the fairy tale [and to each other], playing with its [and their] framed images out of a desire to multiply its [and their] refractions and to expose its [and their] artifices" (23). In this way, although no performance has displaced the authority associated with the older fairy-tale genre, contemporary texts have cumulatively achieved a competitive authority, one that is fragmented, multivocal, fraught with contestation, and continually emergent.

NOTES

1. Shuman 83. She quotes the phrase "texts bearing upon texts" from Todorov 22–23.

2. For a discussion of domestic duties, particularly the politics of tactical incompetence, and the fairy tale, see Lanser.

3. For an overview of feminist scholarship on the genre of the fairy tale, see Haase's survey in this volume.

4. My discussion of *Ever After* is largely based on my earlier review of the movie (Preston, review).

5. Student commentary is from undergraduate students at the University of Colorado, Boulder.

6. I have the page because a female student in one of my women's literature classes gave it to me following a class discussion of the Cinderella figure as it is manifested textually and culturally in American society. The student had handwritten on the top left-hand corner of the page, "Thought you might enjoy this! I did!"

Bibliography

The fairy tales of eighteenth- and nineteenth-century German women cited by Jeannine Blackwell and the fairy-tale texts of Iberian and Latin American women cited by Patricia Anne Odber de Baubeta are listed separately in dedicated bibliographies at the end of those essays. Otherwise, the following bibliography includes all works cited throughout this volume. In addition, this bibliography contains an extensive selection of feminist and gender-based research on folktales and fairy tales. It offers the most extensive listing available of woman-centered fairy-tale scholarship published since 1970.

Aarne, Antti, and Stith Thompson. *The Types of the Folktale: A Classification and Bibliography.* 2nd revision. Helsinki: Suomalainen Tiedeakatemia, 1961.

Abel, Elizabeth, Marianne Hirsch, and Elizabeth Langland, eds. *The Voyage In: Fictions of Female Development.* Hanover, NH: UP of New England, 1983.

Adam, Antoine. *Histoire de la littérature française du XVIIe siècle.* 5 vols. Paris: del Duca, 1968.

Adorno, Theodor W. "Television and the Patterns of Mass Culture." 1960. *Mass Communications.* Ed. Wilbur Schramm. Urbana: U of Illinois P, 1972. 594–612.

Agosín, Marjorie. "Un cuento de hadas a la inversa: *La historia de María Griselda* o la belleza aniquilada." *Hispanic Journal* 5 (1983): 141–49.

———, ed. *Landscapes of a New Land: Fiction by Latin American Women.* 2nd ed. Fredonia, NY: White Pine, 1992.

———, ed. *Literatura fantástica del Cono Sur: Las mujeres.* San José: EDUCA, 1992.

———. "María Luisa Bombal: Biography of a Story-Telling Woman." Bassnett, *Knives and Angels* 26–35.

———, ed. *Secret Weavers: Stories of the Fantastic by Women Writers of Argentina and Chile.* Fredonia, NY: White Pine, 1992.

Ahmad, Aijaz. "Reading Arundhati Roy Politically." *Frontline* 8 (Aug. 1997): 103–06.

Aji, Aron R. "'All Names Mean Something': Salman Rushdie's *Haroun* and the Legacy of Islam." *Contemporary Literature* 36.1 (1995): 103–31.

Allen, Philip M. *Security and Nationalism in the Indian Ocean: Lessons from Latin Quarter Islands.* Boulder, CO: Westview, 1987.

Altmann, Anna E. "Parody and Poesis in Feminist Fairy Tales." *Canadian Children's Literature* 73 (1994): 22–31.

Andersen, Hans Christian. *The Complete Fairy Tales and Stories.* Trans. Erik Christian Haugaard. New York: Anchor-Doubleday, 1974.

Anderson, Celia Catlett. "Spindle, Shuttle, and Scissors: Ambiguous Power in the Grimm Brothers' Tales." *Children's Literature in Education* 17 (1986): 226–32.

Anievas Gamallo, Isabel C. "Subversive Storytelling: The Construction of Lesbian Girlhood through Fantasy and Fairy Tale in Jeanette Winterson's *Oranges Are Not the Only Fruit*." *The Girl: Construction of the Girl in Contemporary Fiction by Women.* Ed. Ruth O. Saxton. New York: St. Martin's, 1998. 119–34.

Apo, Satu. *The Narrative World of Finnish Fairy Tales: Structure, Agency, and Evaluation in Southwest Finnish Folktales.* Helsinki: Academia Scientiarum Fennica, 1995.

Apo, Satu, Aili Nenola, and Laura Stark-Arola, eds. *Gender and Folklore: Perspectives on Finnish and Karelian Culture.* Helsinki: Finnish Literature Society, 1998.

Appadurai, Arjun. *Modernity at Large: Cultural Dimensions of Globalization.* Minneapolis: U of Minnesota P, 1996.

Appadurai, Arjun, Frank J. Korom, and Margaret A. Mills, eds. *Gender, Genre, and Power in South Asian Expressive Traditions.* Philadelphia: U of Pennsylvania P, 1991.

Arditi, Jorge. *A Genealogy of Manners: Transformations of Social Relations in France and England from the Fourteenth to the Eighteenth Century.* Chicago: U of Chicago P, 1998.

Ariès, Philippe. "Love in Married Life." Ariès and Béjin, 130–39.

Ariès, Philippe, and André Béjin, eds. *Western Sexuality: Practice and Precept in Past and Present Times.* Trans. Anthony Forster. Oxford: Blackwell, 1985.

Ariès, Philippe, and Georges Duby, eds. *A History of Private Life: Passions of the Renaissance.* Trans. Arthur Goldhammer. Cambridge, MA: Harvard UP, 1989.

Arrizabalaga, Jon, John Henderson, and Roger French. *The Great Pox: The French Disease in Renaissance Europe.* New Haven, CT: Yale UP, 1997.

Ashliman, D. L. "Symbolic Sex-Role Reversals in the Grimms' Fairy Tales." *Forms of the Fantastic: Selected Essays from the Third International Conference on the Fantastic in Film and Literature.* Ed. Jan Hokenson and Howard Pearce. New York: Greenwood, 1986. 192–98.

Attwood, Feona. "Who's Afraid of Little Red Riding Hood? Male Desire, Phantasy and Impersonation in the Telling of a Fairytale." *Thamyris* 6.1 (1999): 95–105.

Atwood, Margaret. *Good Bones and Simple Murders.* New York: Talese-Doubleday, 1994.

———. "Grimms' Remembered." Haase, *Reception of Grimms' Fairy Tales* 290–92.

———. *Surfacing.* 1972. New York: Ballantine, 1987.

Auerbach, Nina, and U. C. Knoepflmacher, eds. *Forbidden Journeys: Fairy Tales and Fantasies by Victorian Women Writers.* Chicago: U of Chicago P, 1992.

Aulnoy, Marie-Catherine Le Jumel de Barneville, baronne [aka comtesse] d'. *Contes.* Ed. Jacques Barchilon and Philippe Hourcarde. 2 vols. Paris: Société des Textes Français Modernes, 1997–1998.

———. *Contes de Madame d'Aulnoy.* Ed. Elizabeth Lemirre. Arles: Picquier, 1994.

Auneuil, Louise de Bossigny, comtesse d'. *La tyrannie des fées détruite.* Pref. Alice Colanis. Paris: côté-femmes, 1990.

Bacchilega, Cristina. "The Framing of 'Snow White': Narrative and Gender (Re)Production." Bacchilega, *Postmodern Fairy Tales* 27–48, 151–55. Rpt. of "Cracking the Mirror: Three Re-Visions of 'Snow White.'" *boundary 2* 15.3–16.1 (Spring/Fall 1988): 1–25.

———. "The Fruit of the Womb: Creative Uses of a Naturalizing Tradition in Folktales." *Creativity and Tradition in Folklore.* Ed. Simon Bronner. Logan: Utah State UP, 1992. 153–66.

———. "Palimpsest Readings: The Märchen and Contemporary Fiction." Diss. State U of New York, Binghamton, 1983.

———. *Postmodern Fairy Tales: Gender and Narrative Strategies*. Philadelphia: U of Pennsylvania P, 1997.

———. "'Writing' and 'Voice': The Articulations of Gender in Folklore and Literature." *Folklore, Literature, and Cultural Theory: Collected Essays*. Ed. Cathy Lynn Preston. New York: Garland, 1995. 83–101.

Bacchilega, Cristina, and Steven Swann Jones, eds. *Perspectives on the Innocent Persecuted Heroine in Fairy Tales*. Special issue of *Western Folklore* 52.1 (1993).

Bachorski, Hans-Jürgen. "Das aggressive Geschlecht: Verlachte Männlichkeit in Mären aus dem 15. Jahrhundert." *Zeitschrift für Germanistik* 8 (1998): 263–81.

Baissac, Charles. *Folklore de l'île Maurice*. 1947. Paris: G. P. Maisonneuve et Larose, 1967.

Bakhtin, M. M. *The Dialogic Imagination*. Ed. Michael Holquist. Trans. Caryl Emerson and Michael Holquist. Austin: U of Texas P, 1981.

———. *Rabelais and His World*. Trans. Helene Iswolsky. Bloomington: Indiana UP, 1984.

Baldick, Chris, ed. *The Oxford Book of Gothic Tales*. Oxford: Oxford UP, 1992.

Barchers, Suzanne. "In Search of Female Heroes." *Merveilles et contes* 1 (1987): 116–18.

———. *Wise Women: Folk and Fairy Tales from Around the World*. Englewood, CO: Libraries Unlimited, 1990.

Barchilon, Jacques. *Le conte merveilleux français de 1690 à 1790: Cent ans de féerie et de poésie ignorés de l'histoire littéraire*. Paris: Champion, 1975.

Barz, Helmut. *Blaubart: Wenn einer vernichtet, was er liebt*. Zürich: Kreuz, 1987.

Barzilai, Shuli. "Reading 'Snow White': The Mother's Story." *Signs* 50 (1990): 515–34.

Basile, Giambattista. *Lo cunto de li cunti, overo lo trattenemiento de peccerille*. Ed. and trans. Michele Rak. Milan: Garzanti, 1986.

———. *The Pentamerone of Giambattista Basile*. Trans. Benedetto Croce. Ed. N. M. Penzer. 1932. 2 vols. Westport, CT: Greenwood, 1979.

Bassnett, Susan. "Blood and Mirrors: Imagery of Violence in the Writings of Alejandra Pizarnik." *Latin American Women's Writing: Feminist Readings in Theory and Crisis*. Ed. Anny Brooksbank Jones and Catherine Davies. Oxford: Clarendon, 1996. 127–47.

———, ed. *Knives and Angels: Women Writers in Latin America*. London: Zed, 1990.

Bassoff, Evelyn. *Cherishing Our Daughters: How Parents Can Raise Girls to Become Confident Women*. 1998. New York: Plume, 1999.

Bauman, Richard. *Verbal Art as Performance*. Prospect Heights, IL: Waveland, 1977.

Bauman, Richard, and Charles L. Briggs. "Poetics and Performance as Critical Perspectives on Language and Social Life." *Annual Review of Anthropology* 19 (1990): 59–88.

Beauvoir, Simone de. *Le deuxième sexe*. 2 vols. 1949. Paris: Gallimard, 1961.

———. *The Second Sex*. Trans. H. M. Parshley. New York: Knopf, 1953.

Bechtolsheim, Barbara von. "Die Brüder Grimm neu schreiben: Zeitgenössische Märchengedichte amerikanischer Autorinnen." Diss. Stanford U, 1987.

Beese, Henriette, ed. *Von Nixen und Brunnenfrauen*. Berlin: Ullstein, 1972.

Bell, Elizabeth. "Somatexts at the Disney Shop: Constructing the Pentimentos of Women's Animated Bodies." Bell, Haas, and Sells 107–24.

Bell, Elizabeth, Lynda Haas, and Laura Sells, eds. *From Mouse to Mermaid: The Politics of Film, Gender, and Culture*. Bloomington: Indiana UP, 1995.

Benjamin, Walter. *Selected Writings: Volume 1, 1913–1926*. Ed. Marcus Bullock and Michael Jennings. Cambridge, MA: Harvard UP, 1996.

Bennett, Judith M. *Ale, Beer, and Brewsters in England: Women's Work in a Changing World, 1300–1600.* New York: Oxford UP, 1996.

———. "Medieval Women, Modern Women: Across the Great Divide." *Culture and History, 1350–1600: Essays on English Communities, Identities, and Writing.* Ed. David Aers. Detroit: Wayne State UP, 1992. 147–75.

Bennett, Judith M., and Maryanne Kowaleski. "Crafts, Guilds, and Women in the Middle Ages: Fifty Years after Marian K. Dale." *Sisters and Workers in the Middle Ages.* Ed. Bennett et al. Chicago: U of Chicago P, 1989. 11–38.

Benson, Stephen. "Craftiness and Cruelty: A Reading of the Fairy Tale and Its Place in Recent Feminist Fictions." *Cycles of Influence: Fiction, Folktale, Theory.* Detroit: Wayne State UP, 2003. 167–246.

———. "Stories of Love and Death: Reading and Writing the Fairy Tale Romance." *Image and Power: Women in Fiction in the Twentieth Century.* Ed. Sarah Sceats and Gail Cunningham. New York: Longman, 1996. 103–13.

Bernheimer, Kate, ed. *Mirror, Mirror on the Wall: Women Writers Explore Their Favorite Fairy Tales.* New York: Anchor-Doubleday, 1998.

———, ed. *Mirror, Mirror on the Wall: Women Writers Explore Their Favorite Fairy Tales.* 2nd ed. New York: Anchor-Random, 2002.

Bernikow, Louise. "Cinderella: Saturday Afternoon at the Movies." *Among Women.* New York: Harmony, 1980. 17–38, 271–72.

Bettelheim, Bruno. *The Uses of Enchantment: The Meaning and Importance of Fairy Tales.* New York: Knopf, 1976.

Beyer, Jürgen. *Schwank und Moral: Untersuchungen zum altfranzösischen Fabliau und verwandten Formen.* Heidelberg: Winter, 1969.

Biebuyck, Daniel P., and Brunhilde Biebuyck. *"We Test Those Whom We Marry": An Analysis of Thirty-Six Nyanga Tales.* Budapest: African Research Program, Department of Regional Geography, Lorand Eötvös University, 1987.

Birkhäuser-Oeri, Sibylle. *The Mother: Archetypal Images in Fairy Tales.* Trans. Michael Mitchell. Toronto: Inner City, 1988. Trans. of *Die Mutter im Märchen: Deutung der Problematik des Mütterlichen und des Mutterkomplexes am Beispiel bekannter Märchen.* Ed. Marie-Luise von Franz. 1976. Stuttgart: Bonz, 1979.

Blackwell, Jeannine. "Fractured Fairy Tales: German Women Authors and the Grimm Tradition." *Germanic Review* 62 (1987): 162–74.

———. "Laying the Rod to Rest: Narrative Strategies in Gisela and Bettina von Arnim's Fairy-Tale Novel *Gritta*." *Marvels & Tales* 11 (1997): 24–47.

———. "The Many Names of Rumpelstiltskin: Recent Research on the Grimms' *Kinder- und Haus-Märchen*." *German Quarterly* 63 (1990): 107–12.

———. "Die verlorene Lehre der Benedikte Naubert: Die Verbindung zwischen Fantasie und Geschichtsschreibung." *Untersuchungen zum Roman von Frauen um 1800.* Ed. Helga Gallas and Magdalene Heuser. Tübingen: Niemeyer, 1990. 148–59.

Blackwell, Jeannine, and Susanne Zantop, eds. *Bitter Healing: German Women Writers, 1700–1830. An Anthology.* Lincoln: U of Nebraska P, 1990.

Blanchy, Sophie. *Lignée féminine et valeurs islamiques à travers quelques contes de Mayotte (Comores).* MA thesis. Saint-Denis (La Réunion), 1986.

Blanchy, Sophie, and Zaharia Soilihi. *Furukombe et autres contes de Mayotte = Furukombe na hadisi za hale zangina za Maore.* Paris: Editions Caribéennes, 1991.

Blinderman, Barry, and Timorthy Porges, eds. *pixerinaWITCHERINA.* Normal: University Galleries of Illinois State U, 2002.

Bly, Robert. *Iron John: A Book about Men.* Reading, MA: Addison-Wesley, 1990.

Boccaccio, Giovanni. *Decameron*. Trans. John Payne. Revised by Charles S. Singleton. 3 vols. Berkeley: U of California P, 1982.

Bohde, Rebecca Sue. "The German Märchen from 1970 to 1985: Versions of a Literary Genre in Areas of Topical Interest." Diss. U of Iowa, 1991.

Boland, Roy C. "Luisa Valenzuela and *Simetrías*: Tales of a Subversive Mother Goose." *Antípodas* 6–7 (1994–1995): 229–37.

Bottigheimer, Ruth B. "Cupid and Psyche vs. Beauty and the Beast: The Milesian and the Modern." *Merveilles et contes* 3 (1989): 4–14.

———. "Fairy Tale Illustrations: Children's Drawings and the Male Imagination." *Papers of the 4th Congress of the Société Internationale d'Ethnologie et de Folklore*. Ed. Bente Gullveig Alver and Torunn Selberg. Vol. 2. Bergen: Société Internationale d'Ethnologie et de Folklore, 1991. 55–62.

———. "Fairy Tales and Children's Literature: A Feminist Perspective." *Options for the Teaching of Children's Literature*. Ed. Glenn Edward Sadler. New York: MLA, 1992. 101–08.

———, ed. *Fairy Tales and Society: Illusion, Allusion, and Paradigm*. Philadelphia: U of Pennsylvania P, 1986.

———. "From Gold to Guilt: The Forces Which Reshaped *Grimms' Tales*." McGlathery, *Brothers Grimm and Folktale* 192–204.

———. *Grimms' Bad Girls and Bold Boys: The Moral and Social Vision of the Tales*. New Haven, CT: Yale UP, 1987.

———. "Iconographic Continuity in Illustrations of 'The Goose Girl.'" *Children's Literature* 13 (1985): 49–71.

———. "Marienkind (KHM 3): A Computer-Based Study of Editorial Change and Stylistic Development within Grimms' Tales from 1808 to 1864." *ARV: Scandinavian Yearbook of Folklore* 46 (1990): 7–31.

———. "Silenced Women in the Grimms' Tales: The 'Fit' Between Fairy Tales and Society in Their Historical Context." Bottigheimer, *Fairy Tales and Society* 115–31. Rev. and trans. as "'Still, Gretel!': Verstummte Frauen in Grimms' 'Kinder- und Hausmärchen.'" *Frauensprache, Frauenliteratur? Für und wider einer Psychoanalyse literarischer Werke*. Ed. Inge Stephan and Carl Pietzcker. Vol. 6 of *Kontroversen, alte und neue: Akten des VII. Internationalen Germanisten-Kongresses, Göttingen 1985*. Ed. Albrecht Schöne. Tübingen: Niemeyer, 1986. 43–53. Rpt. in *Beiträge zur Kinder- und Jugendliteratur* 91 (1989): 28–41.

———. "Straparola's *Piacevoli notti*: Rags-to-Riches Fairy Tales as Urban Creations." *Merveilles et Contes* 8 (1994): 281–96.

———. "Tale Spinners: Submerged Voices in Grimms' Fairy Tales." *New German Critique* 27 (1982): 141–50.

———. "The Transformed Queen: A Search for the Origins of Negative Female Archetypes in Grimms' Fairy Tales." *Amsterdamer Beiträge zur neueren Germanistik* 10 (1980): 1–12.

Bourdieu, Pierre. *Les règles de l'art*. Paris: Seuil, 1992.

Bregenhøj, Carsten. "The Indian and Indo-European Theories in Folk Narrative Research: An Update." Handoo 23–35.

Briggs, Robin. *Communities of Belief: Cultural and Social Tension in Early Modern France*. Oxford: Clarendon, 1989.

Brodzki, Bella. "Mothers, Displacement, and Language in the Autobiographies of Nathalie Sarraute and Christa Wolf." Brodzki and Schenck 243–59.

Brodzki, Bella, and Celeste Schenck, eds. *Life/Lines: Theorizing Women's Autobiography*. Ithaca, NY: Cornell UP, 1988.

Bronfen, Elisabeth. "Bodies on Display." *Over Her Dead Body: Death, Femininity, and the Aesthetic.* New York: Routledge, 1992. 95–109.

Brown, Rosellen. "It Is You the Fable Is About." Bernheimer (1998) 50–63.

Brownmiller, Susan. *Against Our Will: Men, Women, and Rape.* New York: Simon, 1975.

Bryant, Sylvia. "Re-Constructing Oedipus through 'Beauty and the Beast.'" *Criticism* 31 (1989): 439–53.

Bürger, Christa. "Das Märchen und die Entwicklung normativer Strukturen." *Tradition und Subjektivität.* Frankfurt a.M.: Suhrkamp, 1980. 97–118, 186–90.

———. "Märchen und Sage." *Kritische Stichwörter zum Deutschunterricht.* Ed. E. Dingeldey and J. Vogt. Munich: Fink, 1974. 245–53.

———. "Die soziale Funktion volkstümlicher Erzählformen—Sage und Märchen." *Kritisches Lesen: Märchen, Sage, Fabel, Volksbuch.* Vol. 1 of *Projekt Deutschunterricht.* Ed. Heinz Ide. Stuttgart: Metzler, 1971. 26–56.

Burkhart, Dagmar. "Heldenjungfrau." *Enzyklopädie des Märchens* 6: 745–53.

Burns, E. Jane. *Bodytalk: When Women Speak in Old French Literature.* Philadelphia: U of Pennsylvania P, 1993.

Byatt, A. S. "Ice, Snow, Glass." Bernheimer (1998) 64–84.

Cagnolo, Fr. C. "Kikuyu Tales, Part 4." *African Studies* (June 1953): 63–66.

Calame-Griaule, Geneviève, and Ioana Andreesco, eds. *Le pouvoir de la femme.* Special issue of *Cahiers de littérature orale* 34 (1993).

Canepa, Nancy L., ed. *Out of the Woods: The Origins of the Literary Fairy Tale in Italy and France.* Detroit: Wayne State UP, 1997.

Cardigos, Isabel. *In and Out of Enchantment: Blood Symbolism and Gender in Portuguese Fairy Tales.* Helsinki: Academia Scientiarum Fennica, 1996.

Carter, Angela. *The Bloody Chamber and Other Stories.* Harmondsworth: Penguin, 1979.

———. "The Lady of the House of Love." Baldick 482–97.

———, ed. *The Old Wives' Fairy Tale Book.* New York: Pantheon, 1990. Rpt. of *The Virago Book of Fairy Tales.* London: Virago, 1990.

———, ed. *Strange Things Sometimes Still Happen: Fairy Tales from Around the World.* 1993. Boston: Faber, 1994. Rpt. of *The Second Virago Book of Fairy Tales.* London: Virago, 1992.

———. "Vampirella." *Come unto These Yellow Sands.* Newcastle: Bloodaxe, 1985. 83–118.

Carter, Bill. "Newest 'Millionaire' Ratings Bliss for Fox." *Denver Post* 17 Feb. 2000: 1A.

Carter, Marina, ed. *Colouring the Rainbow: Mauritian Society in the Making.* Port Louis (Mauritius): Centre for Research in Indian Ocean Societies, 1998.

———. *Lakshmi's Legacy: The Testimonies of Indian Women in Nineteenth-Century Mauritius.* Stanley, Rose-Hill (Mauritius): Editions de l'Océan Indien, 1994.

Cavallo, Sandra, and Simona Cerutti. "Female Honor and the Social Control of Reproduction in Piedmont between 1600 and 1800." Muir and Ruggiero 73–109.

Chainani, Soman. "Sadeian Tragedy: The Politics of Content Revision in Angela Carter's 'Snow Child.'" *Marvels & Tales* 17 (2003): 212–35.

Chartrand, Claudine Denise. "Fairyland Revisited: A Gynocentric Reading of Selected English, French, and German Folk and Fairy Tales." Diss. Pennsylvania State U, 1990.

Chervin, Ronda, and Mary Neill. *The Woman's Tale: A Journal of Inner Exploration.* Minneapolis: Seabury/Winston, 1980.

Chinen, A. B. *Waking the World: Classic Tales of Women and the Heroic Feminine.* New York: Tarcher-Putnam, 1996.

Christensen, Peter G. "Farewell to the Femme Fatale: Angela Carter's Rewritings of Frank Wedekind's Lulu Plays." *Marvels & Tales* 12 (1998): 319–36.

Cinderella. Directed by Clyde Geronimi, Wilfred Jackson, and Hamilton Luske. Written by Ken Anderson et al. Based on the story "Cendrillon" by Charles Perrault. Produced by Walt Disney. Walt Disney Home Video, 1950.

Cixous, Hélène. "The Laugh of the Medusa." *The Critical Tradition: Classic Texts and Contemporary Trends.* Ed. David H. Richter. 2nd ed. Boston: Bedford, 1998. 1453–66.

———. "The School of Dreams." *Three Steps on the Ladder of Writing.* Trans. Sarah Cornell and Susan Sellers. New York: Cornell UP, 1993. 55–108.

———. "Sorties: Out and Out: Attacks/Ways Out/Forays." *The Newly Born Woman.* By Hélène Cixous and Cathérine Clément. Trans. Betsy Wing. Minneapolis: U of Minnesota P, 1986. 63–132.

Claffey, Anne, Linda Kavanaugh, and Sue Russell, eds. *Rapunzel's Revenge: Fairytales for Feminists.* Dublin: Attic, 1985.

Clark, Alice. *The Working Life of Women in the Seventeenth Century.* 1919. New York: Routledge, 1992.

Clements, Robert J., and Joseph Gibaldi. *The Novella: The European Tale Collection from Boccaccio and Chaucer to Cervantes.* New York: New York UP, 1977.

Comtois, Rita J. "A Qualitative Study of the Perceived Impact of Fairy Tales on a Group of Women." Diss. Boston College, 1995.

Concha, Berta Inés. "María Luisa Bombal, la abeja de fuego." *Quimera* 123 (1994): 6.

Condé, L. P., and S. M. Hart, eds. *Feminist Readings on Spanish and Latin American Literature.* Lewiston: Mellen, 1991.

Conger, Bill. "What Big Teeth." Blinderman and Porges 4–15.

Connell, Eileen. "Playing House: Frances Hodgson Burnett's Victorian Fairy Tale." *Keeping the Victorian House: A Collection of Essays.* Ed. Vanessa D. Dickerson. New York: Garland, 1995. 149–71.

Conrad, JoAnn. "Docile Bodies of (Im)Material Girls: The Fairy-Tale Construction of JonBenet Ramsey and Princess Diana." *Marvels & Tales* 13 (1999): 125–69.

Cooks, Leda M., Mark P. Orbe, and Carol S. Bruess. "The Fairy Tale Theme in Popular Culture: A Semiotic Analysis of *Pretty Woman.*" *Women's Studies in Communication* 16.2 (1993): 86–104.

Cooper, Barbara Rosmarie Latotsky. "Madame de Villeneuve: The Author of 'La belle et la bête' and Her Literary Legacy." Diss. U of Georgia, 1985.

Coppola, Carlo. "Salman Rushdie's *Haroun and the Sea of Stories*: Fighting the Good Fight or Knuckling Under." *Journal of South Asian Literature* 26.1–2 (1991): 229–37.

Cortez, Maria Teresa. "Die Emanzipation der Frau und Grimms Märchen: Portugiesische Fassungen des 19. Jahrhunderts." *A germanística portuguesa em tempo de debate.* Special issue of *Runa: Revista portuguese de estudos Germanísticos* 25.2 (1996): 603–12.

Cosentino, Donald. *Defiant Maids and Stubborn Farmers: Tradition and Invention in Mende Story Performance.* Cambridge: Cambridge UP, 1982.

Cowley, Jason. "Why We Chose Arundhati." *India Today* 27 Oct. 1997: 28. Available at http://www.indiatoday.com/itoday/27101997/cov3.html (accessed 11 Mar. 2002).

Daly, Mary. *Gyn/Ecology: The Metaethics of Radical Feminism.* Boston: Beacon, 1978.

Dan, Ilana. "The Innocent Persecuted Heroine: An Attempt at a Model for the Surface Level of the Narrative Structure in the Female Fairy Tale." *Patterns in Oral Literature.* Ed. Heda Jason and Dimitri Segal. The Hague: Mouton, 1977. 13–30.

Davies, Bronwyn. *Frogs and Snails and Feminist Tales: Preschool Children and Gender.* St. Leonards, New South Wales: Allen and Unwin, 1989.

Davies, Catherine. *Spanish Women's Writing, 1849–1996.* London: Athlone, 1998.

Davis, Natalie Zemon. "Women in the Crafts in Sixteenth-Century Lyon." *Women and Work in Preindustrial Europe.* Ed. Barbara A. Hanawalt. Bloomington: Indiana UP, 1986. 167–97.

Davis, Russell H. *Freud's Concept of Passivity.* Madison, CT: International UP, 1993.

Dawson, Ruth P. "The Search for Women's Experience of Pregnancy and Birth." *Anthropology and the German Enlightenment: Perspectives on Humanity.* Ed. Katherine M. Faull. Special issue of *Bucknell Review* 38.2. Lewisburg, PA: Bucknell UP, 1995. 101–25.

Defrance, Anne. *Les contes de fées et les nouvelles de Madame d'Aulnoy (1690–1698).* Geneva: Droz, 1998.

Dégh, Linda. *American Folklore and the Mass Media.* Bloomington: Indiana UP, 1994.

———. "Beauty, Wealth and Power: Career Choices for Women in Folktales, Fairy Tales, and Modern Media." *Fabula* 30 (1989): 43–62.

———. "Frauenmärchen." *Enzyklopädie des Märchens* 5: 211–20.

———. *Hungarian Folktales: The Art of Zsuzsanna Palkó.* Jackson: U of Mississippi P, 1995.

———. *Narratives in Society: A Performer-Centered Study of Narration.* Helsinki: Suomalainen Tiedeakatemia, 1995.

DeGraff, Amy. "The Fairy Tale and Women's Studies: An Annotated Bibliography." *Merveilles et contes* 1 (1987): 76–82.

———. "From Glass Slipper to Glass Ceiling: 'Cinderella' and the Endurance of a Fairy Tale." *Marvels & Tales* 10 (1996): 69–85.

Dersch-Lawson, Ursula. "The Image of the Female in Grimm's Fairy Tales." *Selected Proceedings of the Pennsylvania Foreign Language Conference.* Ed. Gregorio C. Martin. Pittsburgh: Duquesne University, Dept. of Modern Languages, 1988. 128–32.

Derungs, Kurt. *Der psychologische Mythos: Frauen, Märchen und Sexismus: Manipulation und Indoktrination durch populärpsychologische Märcheninterpretation: Freud, Jung und Co.* Bern: edition amalia, 1996.

Dewald, Jonathan. *Aristocratic Experience and the Origins of Modern Culture: France, 1570–1715.* Berkeley: U of California P, 1993.

Dika, Vera. "A Feminist Fairy Tale?" *Art in America* 75 (Apr. 1987): 31–33.

Divakaruni, Chitra Banerjee. "Dissolving Boundaries." *Bold Type* May 1997. Available at http://www.randomhouse.com/ boldtype/0597/divakaruni/essay.html (accessed 23 Feb. 2004).

———. *The Mistress of Spices.* New York: Anchor, 1997.

———. "The Princess in the Palace of Snakes." Bernheimer (1998) 96–99.

Djoumoi Ali M'madi. "Transmission traditionnelle des savoirs et des savoir-faire à Ndzaoudze, M'Vouni." MA thesis. Ecole Nationale d'Enseignement Supérieur, M'Vouni, 1989.

Dollerup, Cay, Iven Reventlow, and Carsten Rosenberg Hansen. "A Case Study of Editorial Filters in Folktales: A Discussion of the *Allerleirauh* Tales in Grimm." *Fabula* 27 (1986): 12–30.

Donoghue, Emma. *Kissing the Witch: Old Tales in New Skins.* New York: HarperCollins, 1997.

Dorsch, Nikolaus. *"Sich rettend aus der kalten Würklichkeit": Die Briefe Benedikte Nauberts: Edition, Kritik, Kommentar.* Frankfurt a.M.: Lang, 1986.

Dowling, Colette. *The Cinderella Complex: Women's Hidden Fear of Independence.* New York: Simon, 1981.

Downing, Christine. "Fairy-Tale Sisters." *Psyche's Sisters: Re-Imagining the Meaning of Sisterhood.* San Francisco: Harper, 1988. 21–40.

Dross, Annemarie. "Blaubarts Schloß steht im Wald." *Weiblich-Männlich: Kulturgeschichtliche Spuren einer verdrängten Weiblichkeit.* Ed. Brigitte Wartmann. Berlin: Ästhetik und Kommunikation, 1980. 134–49.

Dubatti, Jorge. *Batato Barea y el nuevo teatro argentino.* Buenos Aires: Planeta, 1995.

Duggan, Anne E. "Feminine Genealogy, Matriarchy, and Utopia in the Fairy Tale of Marie-Catherine D'Aulnoy." *Neophilologus* 82 (1998): 199–208.

———. "Nature and Culture in the Fairy Tale of Marie-Catherine d'Aulnoy." *Marvels & Tales* 15 (2001): 149–67.

Duncker, Patricia. "Re-Imagining the Fairy Tale: Angela Carter's Bloody Chambers." *Literature and History* 10 (1984): 3–14.

Dundes, Alan. "Interpreting Little Red Riding Hood Psychoanalytically." McGlathery, *Brothers Grimm and Folktale* 16–51.

———. "Metafolklore and Oral Literary Criticism." *The Monist* 50.4 (1966): 505–16.

Durix, Jean-Pierre. "'The Gardener of Stories': Salman Rushdie's *Haroun and the Sea of Stories." Journal of Commonwealth Literature* 28.1 (1993): 114–22.

D'Uva, Michele. "Barthelme's *Snow White,* Calvino's *The Castle of Crossed Destinies,* and Contemporary Discourse on the Fairy Tale: Feminist and Foucauldian Approaches." Diss. State U of New York, Binghamton, 1992.

Dworkin, Andrea. "The Fairy Tales." *Woman Hating.* New York: Dutton, 1974. 29–49, 205.

Elias, Norbert. *The Court Society.* Trans. Edmund Jephcott. Cambridge, MA: Blackwell, 1993.

El-Shamy, Hasan, ed. and trans. *Tales Arab Women Tell and the Behavioral Patterns They Portray.* Bloomington: Indiana UP, 1999.

Enzyklopädie des Märchens: Handwörterbuch zur historischen und vergleichenden Erzählforschung. Ed. Rolf Wilhelm Brednich et al. 9 vols. to date. Berlin: De Gruyter, 1975–.

Erler, Mary, and Maryanne Kowaleski, eds. *Women and Power in the Middle Ages.* Athens: U of Georgia P, 1988.

Estrich, Susan. "Who Wants to Marry a Frog? *Denver Post* 25 Feb. 2000: 7B.

Even-Zohar, Basmat. "The Female Role in Fairy Tales: 300 Years of *Little Red Riding Hood." Kinderliteratur im interkulterellen Prozeß: Studien zur allgemeinen und vergleichenden Kinderliteraturwissenschaft.* Ed. Hans-Heino Ewers, Gertrud Lehnert, and Emer O'Sullivan. Stuttgart: Metzler, 1994. 181–90.

Ever After. Directed by Andy Tenant. Written by Charles Perrault (1729). Screenplay by Susannah Grant. Twentieth Century Fox, 1998.

Ewald, Johann Ludwig. *Der gute Jüngling, gute Gatte und Vater, oder Mittel, um es zu werden: Ein Gegenstück zu der Kunst, ein gutes Mädchen zu werden.* 2 vols. Frankfurt a.M.: Friedrich Wilmanns, 1804.

Fabre, Nicole. "Les frères et les soeurs: Identité sexuelle et rêves de bisexualité." *Europe: Revue littéraire mensuelle* 787–88 (1994): 126–34.

Fairy Tale Liberation—Thirty Years Later. Special issue of *Marvels & Tales* 14.1 (2000): 1–209.

Farrell, J. G. *The Siege of Krishnapur.* London: Weidenfeld, 1973.

Farrell, Michèle L. "Celebration and Repression of Desire in Mme d'Aulnoy's Fairy Tale: *La Chatte Blanche." L'Esprit Créateur* 29.3 (1989): 52–64.

————. "*Griselidis*: Issues of Gender, Genre, and Authority." *PFSCL* [*Papers on French Seventeenth-Century Literature*] 30 (1987): 97–120.

Fernández Rodríguez, Carolina. *La bella durmiente a través de la historia.* Oviedo: U de Oviedo, 1998.

————. "The Deconstruction of the Male-Rescuer Archetype in Contemporary Feminist Revisions of 'The Sleeping Beauty.'" *Marvels & Tales* 16 (2002): 51–70.

Ferrante, Lucia. "Honor Regained: Women in the Casa del Soccorso di San Paolo in Sixteenth-Century Bologna." Muir and Ruggiero 46–72.

Fetterley, Judith. "The Resisting Reader." *Feminist Literary Theory: A Reader.* Ed. Mary Eagleton. 2nd ed. Oxford: Blackwell, 1996. 303–06.

Feyl, Renate. *Sein ist das Weib. Denken der Mann: Ansichten und Äusserungen für und wider die gelehrten Frauen.* Cologne: Kiepenheuer, 1991.

Flandrin, Jean-Louis. "Sex in Married Life in the Early Middle Ages: The Church's Teaching and Behavioural Reality." Ariès and Béjin 114–29.

Foa, Anna. "The New and the Old: The Spread of Syphilis (1494–1530)." Muir and Ruggiero 26–45.

Foucault, Michel. "Prison Talk." Interviewer J.-J. Brochier. *Power/Knowledge: Selected Interviews and Other Writings, 1972–1977.* Ed. Colin Gordon. Trans. Colin Gordon et al. New York: Pantheon, 1980. 37–54.

Franz, Marie-Louise von. *Problems of the Feminine in Fairy Tales.* Dallas: Spring, 1972.

Friday, Nancy. *The Power of Beauty.* New York: HarperCollins, 1996.

Friedan, Betty. *The Feminine Mystique.* New York: Norton, 1963.

Friedl, Erika, Lois Beck, and Nikki Keddie. "Women in Contemporary Persian Folktales." *Women in the Muslim World.* Ed. Lois Beck and Nikki Keddie. Cambridge, MA: Harvard UP, 1978. 629–50.

Früh, Sigrid, ed. *Europäische Frauenmärchen.* Frankfurt a.M.: Fischer, 1996. Exp. ed. of *Die Frau, die auszog, ihren Mann zu erlösen.* Frankfurt a.M.: Fischer, 1985.

Früh, Sigrid, and Rainer Wehse, eds. *Die Frau im Märchen.* Kassel: Röth, 1985.

Fuller, Margaret. *Woman in the Nineteenth Century.* New York: Greely and McElrath, 1845. *American Transcendentalism Web.* Ed. Ann Woodlief et al. 1999. English Dept., Virginia Commonwealth U. Available at http://www.vcu.edu/engweb/transcendentalism/authors/fuller/woman1.html (accessed 23 Feb. 2004).

Fullerton, Romayne Chaloner Smith. "Sexing the Fairy Tale: Borrowed Monsters and Postmodern Fantasies." Diss. U of Western Ontario, 1996.

Funcke, Eberhard W. "Die Hexe im Märchen: Entstehung und Existenz des Hexenbildes im Volksmärchen und in unserer Zeit." *Acta Germanica* 10 (1977): 265–318.

Galerstein, Carolyn L., and Kathleen McNerney, eds. *Women Writers of Spain: An Annotated Bio-Bibliographical Guide.* New York: Greenwood, 1986.

Ganas, Monica Carroll. "'Queen for a Day,' the Cinderella Show: Broadcasting Women's True Stories." Diss. U of Kentucky, 1995.

Garton, Janet. "Little Red Riding Hood Comes of Age: Or, When the Fantastic Becomes the Feminist." *Essays in Memory of Michael Parkinson and Janine Dakyns.* Ed. Christopher Smith. Norwich: School of Modern Languages and European Studies, U of East Anglia, 1996. 289–94.

Gaunt, Simon. *Troubadours and Irony.* Cambridge: Cambridge UP, 1989.

Geoffroy-Menoux, Sophie. "Angela Carter's *The Bloody Chamber*: Twice Harnessed Folk-Tales." *Paradoxa* 2 (1996): 249–62.

Gerhardt, Mia I. *The Art of Story-Telling: A Literary Study of the Thousand and One Nights.* Leiden: Brill, 1963.

Geyh, Paula, Fred G. Leebron, and Andrew Levy, eds. *Postmodern American Fiction: A Norton Anthology*. New York: Norton, 1998.

Gilbert, Sandra. "Life's Empty Pack: Notes Towards a Literary Daughteronomy." *Critical Inquiry* 11 (1985): 355–84.

Gilbert, Sandra M., and Susan Gubar. *The Madwoman in the Attic: The Woman Writer and the Nineteenth-Century Literary Image*. New Haven, CT: Yale UP, 1979.

Glazer, Mark. "Women Personages as Helpers in Turkish Folktales." *Studies in Turkish Folklore in Honor of Pertev N. Boratav*. Ed. Ilhan Basgoz and Mark Glazer. Bloomington: Maccallum, 1978. 98–109.

Gmelin, Otto. *Böses aus Kinderbüchern und ein roter Elefant*. Frankfurt a.M.: Haag und Herchen, 1977. 2nd rev. and exp. ed. of *Böses kommt aus Kinderbüchern: Die verpaßten Möglichkeiten kindlicher Bewußtseinsbildung*. Munich: Kindler, 1972.

Gobrecht, Barbara. "Die Frau im russischen Märchen." Früh and Wehse 89–110, 222–23.

Goldberg, Christine. "The Forgotten Bride (AaTh 313 C)." *Fabula* 33 (1992): 39–54.

Goldberg, Harriet. "The Arabian Nights." Zipes, *Oxford Companion to Fairy Tales* 22–25.

Golden, Stephanie. "Mythmaking." *The Women Outside: Meanings and Myths of Homelessness*. Berkeley: U of California P, 1992. 73–94, 272–74.

Gordon, Susan. "The Powers of the Handless Maiden." Radner 252–88.

Gornick, Vivian. "Taking a Long Hard Look at 'The Princess and the Pea.'" Bernheimer (1998) 158–67.

Göttner-Abendroth, Heide. *Die Göttin und ihr Heros: Die matriarchalen Religionen in Mythos, Märchen und Dichtung*. 1980. Munich: Frauenoffensive, 1988.

———. "Matriarchale Mythologie: Ausgewählte Beispiele aus Mythos, Märchen, Dichtung." *Weiblich-Männlich: Kulturgeschichtliche Spuren einer verdrängten Weiblichkeit*. Ed. Brigitte Wartmann. Berlin: Ästhetik und Kommunikation, 1980. 202–40.

Grabinska, Kornelia. "Women Who Refused to Marry: A Jungian Interpretation of Selected Inuit Folktales." Diss. Union Institute, 1994.

Graham, Merika Sonia. "Psychological Aspects of the Feminine in Ukrainian Folk Tales: A Jungian Analysis with Implications for Psychotherapy." Diss. Union for Experimenting Colleges/University without Walls and Union Graduate School, 1985.

Grätz, Manfred. *Das Märchen in der deutschen Aufklärung: Vom Feenmärchen zum Volksmärchen*. Stuttgart: Metzler, 1988.

Green, Jeanette Evelyn. "Literary Revisions of Traditional Folktales: Bowen, Carter, Hong Kingston, Morrison, Oates, Sexton, Welty, and Capote." Diss. U of Texas, Austin, 1989.

Grimm, Jacob, and Wilhelm Grimm. *The Complete Fairy Tales of the Brothers Grimm*. Trans. Jack Zipes. New York: Bantam, 1988.

Gubar, Susan. "What Ails Feminist Criticism?" *Critical Inquiry* 24.4 (1998): 878–902.

Guerra-Cunningham, Lucía, ed. *Splintering Darkness: Latin American Women Writers in Search of Themselves*. Pittsburgh: Latin American Literary Review Press, 1990.

Gueunier, Noël J. *La belle ne se marie point: Contes comoriens en dialecte malgache de l'île de Mayotte*. Collected by Noël J. Gueunier et al. Paris: Peeters, 1990.

———. *L'oiseau chagrin: Contes comoriens en dialecte malgache de l'île de Mayotte*. Paris: Peeters, 1994.

Gutmann, Bruno. "Die Fabelwesen in den Märchen der Wadschagga." *Globus* 91 (1907): 239–43.

Haase, Donald. "German Fairy Tales and America's Culture Wars: From Grimms'

Kinder- und Hausmärchen to William Bennett's *Book of Virtues.*" *German Politics and Society* 13.3 (1995): 17–25.

———. "Gold into Straw: Fairy Tale Movies for Children and the Culture Industry." *Lion and the Unicorn* 12.2 (1988): 193–207.

———, ed. *The Reception of Grimms' Fairy Tales: Responses, Reactions, Revisions.* Detroit: Wayne State UP, 1993.

———. "Response and Responsibility in Reading Grimms' Fairy Tales." Haase, *Reception of Grimms' Fairy Tales* 230–49.

———. "Re-Viewing the Grimm Corpus: Grimm Scholarship in an Era of Celebrations." *Monatshefte* 91 (1999): 121–31.

———. "Television and Fairy Tales." Zipes, *Oxford Companion to Fairy Tales* 513–18.

Habermas, Jürgen. *Strukturwandel der Öffentlichkeit: Untersuchungen zu einer Kategorie der bürgerlichen Gesellschaft.* Berlin: Luchterhand, 1962.

Haboucha, Reginetta. "Misogyny or Philogyny: The Case of a Judeo-Spanish Folktale." *New Horizons in Sephardic Studies.* Ed. Yedida K. Stillman and George K. Zucker. Albany: State U of New York P, 1993. 239–51.

Hamilton, Virginia. *Her Stories: African American Folktales, Fairy Tales, and True Tales.* New York: Blue Sky/Scholastic, 1995.

Handoo, Jawaharlal, ed. *Folklore in Modern India.* Mysore: Central Institute of Indian Languages, 1998.

Handoo, Lalita, and Ruth B. Bottigheimer, eds. *Folklore and Gender.* Mysore: Zooni, 1999.

Hannon, Patricia. *Fabulous Identities: Women's Fairy Tales in Seventeenth-Century France.* Amsterdam: Rodopi, 1998.

———. "Feminine Voice and the Motivated Text: Madame d'Aulnoy and the Chevalier de Mailly." *Merveilles et contes* 2 (1988): 13–24.

Haring, Lee. *Malagasy Tale Index.* Helsinki: Suomalainen Tiedeakatemia, 1982.

———. "Prospects for Folklore in Mauritius." *International Folklore Review* 8 (1991): 83–95.

Harries, Elizabeth Wanning. "Fairy Tales about Fairy Tales: Notes on Canon Formation." Canepa 152–75.

———. Review of *Myth and Fairy Tale in Contemporary Women's Fiction,* by Susan Sellers. *Marvels & Tales* 17 (2003): 164–66.

———. *Twice upon a Time: Women Writers and the History of the Fairy Tale.* Princeton, NJ: Princeton UP, 2001.

Harris, Trudier. "Genre." *Journal of American Folklore* 108 (1995): 509–27.

Hart, Stephen M. "On the Threshold: Cixous, Lispector, Tusquets." Condé and Hart 91–105.

———. *White Ink: Essays on Twentieth-Century Feminine Fiction in Spain and Latin America.* London: Támesis, 1993.

Hatubou, Salim. *Contes de ma grand-mère (contes comoriens).* Paris: L'Harmattan, 1994.

Hawes, Jane Harris. "Psychosexual Contrasts in the Grimm's Fairy Tales: The Youth Who Feared Nothing versus the Girl Who Lost It All." Diss. U of Michigan, 1978.

Hawkins, Harriett. "Maidens and Monsters in Modern Popular Culture: *The Silence of the Lambs* and *Beauty and the Beast.*" *Textual Practice* 7 (1993): 258–66.

Heker, Liliana. *Zona de clivaje.* 1987. Buenos Aires: Alfaguara, 1997.

Heidebrecht, Brigitte, ed. *Dornröschen nimmt die Heckenschere: Märchenhaftes von 30 Autorinnen.* Bonn: kleine schritte, 1985.

Heilbrun, Carolyn G. *Reinventing Womanhood.* 1979. New York: Norton, 1993.

Helms, Cynthia. "Storytelling, Gender and Language in Folk/Fairy Tales: A Selected Annotated Bibliography." *Women and Language* 10.2 (1987): 3–11.

Henein, Eglal. "Male and Female Ugliness through the Ages." *Merveilles et contes* 3 (1989): 45–56.

Herlihy, David. *Women and Work in Medieval Europe*. Philadelphia: Temple UP, 1990.

Herman, Judith Lewis. "Introduction: Cinderella as Saint Dympna." *Father-Daughter Incest*. Cambridge, MA: Harvard UP, 1981. 1–4, 261.

Hermansson, Casie. *Reading Feminist Intertextuality through Bluebeard Stories*. Lewiston, NY: Mellen, 2001.

Herrmann, Claudine. *Les voleuses de langue*. Paris: Des Femmes, 1979.

Hilgar, Marie-France, ed. *Actes de Las Vegas: Théorie dramatique, Théophile de Viau, les contes de fées*. Paris: Papers on French Seventeenth Century Literature, 1991.

Hines, John. *The Fabliau in English*. London: Longman, 1993.

Hirsch, Marianne. "Ideology, Form, and 'Allerleirauh': Reflections on *Reading for the Plot*." *Children's Literature* 14 (1986): 163–68.

Hoffmann, Kathryn A. "Matriarchal Desires and Labyrinths of the Marvelous: Fairy Tales by Old Regime Women." *Women Writers in Pre-Revolutionary France: Strategies of Emancipation*. Ed. Colette H. Winn and Donna Kuizenga. New York: Garland, 1997. 281–97.

Hofius, Annegret. "Sneewittchen oder die Schöne und das Böse." *Das selbstverständliche Wunder: Beiträge germanistischer Märchenforschung*. Ed. Wilhelm Solms and Charlotte Oberfeld. Marburg: Hitzeroth, 1986. 63–81.

Hollis, Susan Tower, Linda Pershing, and M. Jane Young, eds. *Feminist Theory and the Study of Folklore*. Urbana: U of Illinois P, 1993.

Hoogland, Cornelia. "Real 'Wolves in Those Bushes': Readers Take Dangerous Journeys with *Little Red Riding Hood*." *Canadian Children's Literature* 73 (1994): 7–21.

Hooker, Jessica. "The Hen Who Sang: Swordbearing Women in Eastern European Fairytales." *Folklore* 101 (1990): 178–84.

Horn, Katalin. "Held, Heldin." *Enzyklopädie des Märchens* 6: 721–45.

Hruschka, John. "Anne Sexton and Anima Transformations: *Transformations* as a Critique of the Psychology of Love in Grimm's Fairy Tales." *Mythlore* 20.1 (1994): 45–47.

Huang Mei. *Transforming the Cinderella Dream: From Frances Burney to Charlotte Brontë*. New Brunswick, NJ: Rutgers UP, 1990.

Hudson, Glenda. *Sibling Love and Incest in Jane Austen's Fiction*. New York: St. Martin's 1992.

Hughes, Linda A. "'You Have to Do It with Style': Girls' Games and Girls' Gaming." Hollis, Pershing, and Young 130–48.

Hunt, Margaret, trans. *The Complete Grimm's Fairy Tales*. Rev. James Stern. 1944. New York: Pantheon, 1972.

Huston-Findley, Shirley Annette. "Subverting the Dramatic Text: Folklore, Feminism, and the Images of Women in Three Canonical American Plays." Diss. U of Missouri, Columbia, 1998.

Hyams, Barbara. "Is the Apolitical Woman at Peace? A Reading of the Fairy Tale in *Germany, Pale Mother*." *Wide Angle* 10.3 (1988): 40–51. Rpt. in *Perspectives on German Cinema*. Ed. Terri Ginsberg and Kirsten Moana Thompson. New York: Hall, 1996. 346–60.

Hyman, Trina Schart. "Cut It Down, and You Will Find Something at the Roots." Haase, *Reception of Grimms' Fairy Tales* 293–300.

Ikeda, Kayoko. ["Die Entstehung KHM 65 Allerleirauh: Eine progressive Annäherung an den Cinderella-Stoff."] *Doitsu Bungaku* 86 (1991): 114–25. [Japanese with German abstract.]

Immel, Andrea, and Jan Susina, eds. *Considering the Kunstmärchen: The History and Development of Literary Fairy Tales.* Special issue of *Marvels & Tales* 17.1 (2003): 1–187.

Jacobsen, Grethe. "Nordic Women and the Reformation." Marshall 47–67.

Jarvis, Shawn C. "Feminism and Fairy Tales." Zipes, *Oxford Companion to Fairy Tales* 155–59.

———, ed. *Das Leben der Hochgräfin Gritta von Rattenzuhausbeiuns.* By Gisela and Bettine von Arnim. Frankfurt a.M.: Insel, 1986.

———. "Literary Legerdemain and the *Märchen* Tradition of Nineteenth-Century German Women Writers." Diss. U of Minnesota, 1990.

———, ed. *Märchenbriefe an Achim.* By Gisela von Arnim. Frankfurt a.M.: Insel; Leipzig: Edition Leipzig, 1991.

———, trans. "The Rose Cloud." By Gisela von Arnim. *Marvels & Tales* 11 (1997): 134–59.

———. "Spare the Rod and Spoil the Child? Bettine's *Das Leben der Hochgräfin von Rattenzuhausbeiuns.*" *Women in German Yearbook* 3 (1986): 77–89.

———. "Trivial Pursuit? Women Deconstructing the Grimmian Model in the *Kaffeterkreis.*" Haase, *Reception of Grimms' Fairy Tales* 102–26.

———. "The Vanished Woman of Great Influence: Benedikte Naubert's Legacy and German Women's Fairy Tales." *In the Shadow of Olympus: German Women Writers from 1790–1810.* Ed. Katherine R. Goodman and Edith Waldstein. Albany: State U of New York P, 1991. 189–209.

———, trans. "The Wicked Sisters and the Good One: A Fairy Tale." By Caroline Stahl. *Fairy Tale Liberation* 159–64.

Jarvis, Shawn C., and Jeannine Blackwell, eds. and trans. *The Queen's Mirror: Fairy Tales by German Women, 1780–1900.* Lincoln: U of Nebraska P, 2001.

Jasmin, Nadine. *Naissance du conte féminin. Mots et merveilles: Les contes de fées de Madame d'Aulnoy (1690–1698).* Paris: Champion, 2002.

Jason, Heda. "The Fairy Tale of the Active Heroine: An Outline for Discussion." *Le Conte, pourquoi? comment? Folktales, Why and How?* Ed. Geneviève Calame-Griaule, Veronika Görög-Karady, and Michèle Chiche. Paris: Editions du Centre de la Recherche Scientifique, 1984. 79–97.

Jeffords, Susan. "The Curse of Masculinity: Disney's *Beauty and the Beast.*" Bell, Haas, and Sells 161–72.

Jenkins, Henry. "'It's Not a Fairy Tale Anymore': Gender, Genre, and *Beauty and the Beast.*" *Journal of Film and Video* 43 (1991): 90–110.

Jeter, Kris. "Cinderella: Her Multi-Layered Puissant Messages over Millennia." *Women and the Family: Two Decades of Change.* Ed. Beth B. Hess and Marvin B. Sussman. Special issue of *Marriage and Family Review* 7 (1984): 233–45.

Jhabvala, Ruth Prawer. *Heat and Dust.* London: Murray, 1975.

Jones, Christine. "The Poetics of Enchantment (1690–1715)." Immel and Susina 55–74.

Jungblut, Gertrud. "Märchen der Brüder Grimm—feministisch gelesen." *Diskussion Deutsch* 17 (1986): 497–510.

Kabbani, Rana. *Europe's Myths of Orient: Devise and Rule.* London: MacMillan, 1986.

Kamenetsky, Christa. *The Brothers Grimm and Their Critics: Folktales and the Quest for Meaning.* Athens: Ohio State UP, 1992.

Kapchan, Deborah A. *Gender on the Market: Revoicing Tradition in Beni Mellal, Morocco.* Philadelphia: U of Pennsylvania P, 1993.

Karant-Nunn, Susan C. "The Women of the Saxon Silver Mines." Marshall 29–46.

Kavablum, Lea. *Cinderella: Radical Feminist, Alchemist.* N.p.: privately printed, 1973.

Keenan, Edward Louis, and Elinor Ochs. "Becoming a Competent Speaker of Malagasy." *Languages and Their Speakers.* Ed. Timothy Shopen. Cambridge: Winthrop, 1979. 113–58.

Keenan, Elinor Ochs. "Norm-Makers, Norm-Breakers: Uses of Speech by Men and Women in a Malagasy Community." *Explorations in the Ethnography of Speaking.* Ed. Richard Bauman and Joel Sherzer. 2nd ed. Cambridge: Cambridge UP, 1989. 125–43.

Keiser, Elizabeth B. *Courtly Desire and Medieval Homophobia: The Legitimization of Sexual Pleasure in Cleanness and Its Contexts.* New Haven, CT: Yale UP, 1997.

Kellenter, Sigrid. "Geertje Suhrs Märchengedichte: Grimms Heldin mündig?" *German Studies Review* 18 (1995): 393–418.

Kelly, Joan G. "Did Women Have a Renaissance?" *Women, History and Theory: The Essays of Joan Kelly.* Chicago: U of Chicago P, 1984. 19–50.

Kermode, Frank. *The Sense of an Ending: Studies in the Theory of Fiction.* New York: Oxford UP, 1967.

Kestenbaum, Clarice J. "Fathers and Daughters: The Father's Contribution to Feminine Identification in Girls as Depicted in Fairy Tales and Myths." *American Journal of Psychoanalysis* 43 (1983): 119–27.

Keyes, Cheryl L. "Empowering Self, Making Choices, Creating Spaces: Black Female Identity via Rap Music Performance." *Journal of American Folklore* 113 (2000): 255–69.

King, John. "Jorge Luis Borges: A View from the Periphery." *Modern Latin American Fiction: A Survey.* Ed. John King. London: Faber, 1987. 101–16.

———. *Sur: A Study of the Argentine Literary Journal and its Role in the Development of a Culture, 1931–1970.* Cambridge: Cambridge UP, 1986.

Kingston, Maxine Hong. *The Woman Warrior: Memoir of a Girlhood among Ghosts.* New York: Knopf, 1976.

Knoepflmacher, U. C. "Introduction: Literary Fairy Tales and the Value of Impurity." Immel and Susina 15–36.

———. *Ventures into Childland: Victorians, Fairy Tales, and Femininity.* Chicago: U of Chicago P, 1998.

Köhler-Zülch, Ines, and Christine Shojaei Kawan, eds. *Schneewittchen hat viele Schwestern: Frauengestalten in europäischen Märchen. Beispiele und Kommentare.* Gütersloh: Mohn, 1988.

Köhler-Zülch, Ines, and Isabel Cardigos, eds. *Gender.* Special issue of *Estudos de literatura oral* 5 (1999): 1–238.

Kolbenschlag, Madonna. *Kiss Sleeping Beauty Good-Bye: Breaking the Spell of Feminine Myths and Models.* 1979. Toronto: Bantam, 1981.

Kuckuck, Anke, and Heide Wohlers, eds. *Vaters Tochter: Von der Notwendigkeit, den Frosch an die Wand zu Werfen.* Reinbek bei Hamburg: Rowohlt, 1988.

Lang, Andrew, ed. *The Pink Fairy Book.* 1897. New York: Dover, 1967.

Lanser, Susan S. "Burning Dinners: Feminist Subversions of Domesticity." Radner 36–53.

Lappas, Catherine. "Rewriting Fairy Tales: Transformation as Feminist Practice in the Nineteenth and Twentieth Centuries." Diss. St. Louis U, 1995.

Leapley, Margaret J. *Women's Dependence and Independence during the Late Ante-partum to Post-partum Period.* 1987. Ann Arbor: UMI Research Press, 1989.

Leavy, Barbara Fass. *In Search of the Swan Maiden: A Narrative on Folklore and Gender.* New York: New York UP, 1994.

Leblans, Anne. *"Kinder- und Hausmärchen*: The Creation of Male Wombs as a Means of Protection against the Fear of Engulfment." *Subversive Sublimities: Undercurrents of the German Enlightenment.* Ed. Eitel Timm. Columbia, SC: Camden House, 1992. 86–97.

Lee, Tanith. *Red as Blood or Tales from the Sisters Grimmer.* New York: Daws, 1983.

Le Grand, Léon. "Les béguines de Paris." Paris, 1893. Rpt. from *Mémoires de la Société de l'histoire de Paris et de l'Ile de France* 20 (1892).

Lehnert, Nicole. *Brave Prinzessin oder freie Hexe? Zum bürgerlichen Frauenbild in den Grimmschen Märchen.* Münster: Professur für Frauenforschung, FB. 06 der WWU-Münster, 1996.

Lemirre, Elizabeth, ed. *Le cabinet des fées.* 4 vols. Arles: Picquier, 1994.

Leupin, Alexandre. *Barbaralexis: Medieval Writing and Sexuality.* Cambridge, MA: Harvard UP, 1989.

Leventen, Carol. *"Transformations's* Silencings." *Critical Essays on Anne Sexton.* Ed. Linda Wagner-Martin. Boston: Hall, 1989. 136–49.

Levine, Linda Gould, Ellen Engelson Marson, and Gloria Feiman Waldman, eds. *Spanish Women Writers: A Bio-Bibliographical Source Book.* Westport, CT: Greenwood, 1993.

Levorato, Alessandra. *Language and Gender in the Fairy Tale Tradition: A Linguistic Analysis of Old and New Story-Telling.* London: Palgrave Macmillan, 2003.

Lewallen, Avis. "Wayward Girls But Wicked Women? Female Sexuality in Angela Carter's *The Bloody Chamber.*" *Perspectives on Pornography: Sexuality in Film and Literature.* Ed. Gary Day and Clive Bloom. New York: St. Martin's, 1988. 144–57.

Lichtenberger, Sigrid. "Die Rolle der Frau im deutschen und russischen Volksmärchen." *Festschrift für Wolfgang Gesemann, II: Beiträge zur slawischen Literaturwissenschaft.* Ed. Hans-Bernd Harder, Gert Hummel, and Helmut Schaller. München: Hieronymus, 1986. 137–59.

Lieberman, Marcia. "'Some Day My Prince Will Come': Female Acculturation through the Fairy Tale." *College English* 34 (1972): 383–95. Rpt. in Zipes, *Don't Bet on the Prince* 185–200.

Liebs, Elke. "'Spieglein Spieglein an der Wand': Mutter-Mythen/Märchen-Mutter/Tochter-Märchen. Brüder Grimm: *Marienkind, Frau Trude, Schneewittchen, Die Gänsemagd, Frau Holle, Schneeweißchen und Rosenrot.*" *Mütter—Töchter—Frauen: Weiblichkeit in der Literatur.* Ed. Helga Kraft and Elke Liebs. Stuttgart: Metzler, 1993. 115–47.

Link, Hannelore. *Rezeptionsforschung: Eine Einführung in Methoden und Probleme.* 2nd ed. Stuttgart: Kohlhammer, 1980.

Lovell-Smith, Rose. "Dundes' Allomotifs and Female Audiences: A Reading of Perrault's *Les Fées.*" *Fabula* 37 (1996): 241–47.

Lundell, Torborg. *Fairy Tale Mothers.* New York: Lang, 1990.

———. "Gender-Related Biases in the Type and Motif Indexes of Aarne and Thompson." Bottigheimer, *Fairy Tales and Society* 150–63. Rev. exp. rpt. of "Folktale Heroines and the Type and Motif Indexes." *Folklore* 94 (1983): 240–46.

Lurie, Alison, ed. *Clever Gretchen and Other Forgotten Folktales.* New York: Crowell, 1980.

———. *Don't Tell the Grown-Ups: Why Kids Love the Books They Do.* 1990. New York: Avon, 1991.

———. "Fairy Tale Fiction: Fitzgerald to Updike." Lurie, *Don't Tell the Grown-Ups* 29–40. Rev. rpt. of "Witches and Fairies."

———. "Fairy Tale Liberation." *New York Review of Books* 17 Dec. 1970: 42–44.

———. "Folktale Liberation." Lurie, *Don't Tell the Grown-Ups* 16–28. Rev. rpt. of "Fairy Tale Liberation."

———. "Witches and Fairies: Fitzgerald to Updike." *New York Review of Books* 2 Dec. 1971: 6–11.

Lüthi, Max. *The European Folktale: Form and Nature.* Trans. Jon Erickson. Bloomington: Indiana UP, 1984.

Lyons, Heather. "Some Second Thoughts on Sexism in Fairy Tales." *Literature and Learning.* Ed. Elizabeth Grugeon and Peter Walden. London: Open UP, 1978. 42–59.

Mabee, Barbara. "Reception of Fairy Tale Motifs in Texts by Twentieth-Century German Women Writers." *Femspec* 1.2 (2000): 16–29.

MacDonald, Ruth. "The Tale Retold: Feminist Fairy Tales." *Children's Literature Association Quarterly* 7.2 (1982): 18–20.

Mackintosh, Fiona. "The Flesh Made Word: Metaphor and Literality in Selected Novels and Short Fiction of Luisa Valenzuela." MPhil diss. U of Oxford, 1995.

Madison, D. Soyini. "*Pretty Woman* through the Triple Lens of Black Feminist Spectatorship." Bell, Haas, and Sells 224–35.

Märchen aus deutschen Landschaften: Unveröffentlichte Quellen. Ed. Karl Schulte-Kemminghausen. Vol 2. Aschendorff: Aschendorffer Buchdruckerei, 1976.

Mainil, Jean. *Madame d'Aulnoy et le rire des fées: Essai sur la subversion féerique et le merveilleux comique sous l'Ancien Régime.* Paris: Kimé, 2001.

Maldonado, Fátima. "A égua da noite." *Expresso* 24 Jan. 1998. Available at http://www.instituto-camoes.pt/arquivos/literatura/eguanoite.htm (accessed 31 Mar. 2003).

Malti-Douglas, Fedwa. *Woman's Body, Woman's Word: Gender and Discourse in Arabo-Islamic Writing.* Princeton, NJ: Princeton UP, 1991.

Manley, Kathleen E. B. "Atwood's Reconstruction of Folktales: *The Handmaid's Tale* and 'Bluebeard's Egg.'" *Approaches to Teaching Atwood's* The Handmaid's Tale *and Other Works.* Ed. Sharon R. Wilson, Thomas B. Friedman, and Shannon Hengen. New York: MLA, 1996. 135–39.

Manteiga, Roberto, Carolyn L. Galerstein, and Kathleen McNerney, eds. *Feminine Concerns in Contemporary Spanish Fiction by Women.* Potomac, MD: Scripta Humanistica, 1988.

Marin, Catherine C. "Pouvoir et subversion féminine: Les contes de fées à l'époque classique." Diss. U of Wisconsin, 1991.

———. "Silence ou éloquence: Les heroïnes des contes de fées de l'époque classique." *Merveilles et contes* 10 (1996): 273–84.

Marshall, Sherrin, ed. *Women in Reformation and Counter-Reformation Europe: Public and Private Worlds.* Bloomington: Indiana UP, 1989.

Martin, Biddy. "Success and Its Failures." *Feminist Consequences: Theory for the New Century.* Ed. Elisabeth Bronfen and Misha Kavka. New York: Columbia UP, 2001. 353–80.

Martin, Laura. "The Rübezahl Legend in Benedikte Naubert and Johann Karl August Musäus." *Marvels & Tales* 17 (2003): 197–211.

Marzolph, Ulrich. "Hārūn ar-Rašīd." *Enzyklopädie des Märchens: Handwörterbuch zur vergleichenden und historischen Erzählforschung.* Ed. Rolf Wilhelm Brednich et al. Vol. 6. Berlin: De Gruyter, 1990. 534–37.

———. "Oriental Fairy Tales." Zipes, *Oxford Companion to Fairy Tales* 370–73.

McCracken, Peggy. "The Body Politic and the Queen's Adulterous Body in French

Romance." *Feminist Approaches to the Body in Medieval Literature.* Ed. Linda Lomperis and Sarah Stanbury. Philadelphia: U of Pennsylvania P, 1993. 38–64.

McDonnell, Ernest W. *The Beguines and Beghards in Medieval Culture and with Special Emphasis on the Belgian Scene.* New York: Octagon, 1969.

McGillis, Roderick. "'A Fairytale Is Just a Fairytale': George MacDonald and the Queering of Fairy." Immel and Susina 86–99.

McGlathery, James M., ed. *The Brothers Grimm and Folktale.* Urbana: U of Illinois P, 1988.

———. *Grimms' Fairy Tales: A History of Criticism on a Popular Classic.* Columbia, SC: Camden House, 1993.

McMaster, Juliet. "Bluebeard: A Tale of Matrimony." *A Room of One's Own* 2 (1976): 10–19.

McNerney, Kathleen, and Cristina Enríquez de Salamanca, eds. *Double Minorities of Spain: A Bio-Bibliographical Guide to Women Writers of the Catalan, Galician, and Basque Countries.* New York: MLA, 1994.

Méchoulan, Eric. "The Embodiment of Culture: Fairy Tales of the Body in the 17th and 18th Centuries." *Romanic Review* 83 (1992): 427–36.

Melamed, Elissa. *Mirror, Mirror: The Terror of Not Being Young.* New York: Linden/Simon, 1983.

Mendelson, M. "Forever Acting Alone: The Absence of Female Collaboration in Grimms' Fairy Tales." *Children's Literature in Education* 28.3 (1997): 111–25.

Menon, Sridevi. "Discursive Realms and Colonial Practice: Contrapuntal Studies of Race in Colonial India and the United States." Diss. U of Hawai'i-Mānoa, 2000.

Mettam, Roger. *Power and Faction in Louis XIV's France.* Oxford: Blackwell, 1988.

Metzger, Erika A. "Zu Beispielen von Depersonalisation im Grimmschen Märchen." *Fairy Tales as Ways of Knowing: Essays on Märchen in Psychology, Society, and Literature.* Ed. Michael M. Metzger and Katharina Mommsen. Bern: Lang, 1981. 99–116.

Mieder, Wolfgang, ed. *Disenchantments: An Anthology of Modern Fairy Tale Poetry.* Hanover, NH: UP of New England, 1985.

———. *Mädchen, pfeif auf den Prinzen! Märchengedichte von Günter Grass bis Sarah Kirsch.* 1983. Cologne: Diederichs, 1984.

Miller, Nancy K. "Men's Reading, Women's Writing: Gender and the Rise of the Novel." *Yale French Studies* 75 (1988): 40–55.

Miller, Sara. "Evil and Fairy Tales: The Witch as Symbol of Evil in Fairy Tales." Diss. California Institute of Integral Studies, 1983.

Mills, Margaret. "A Cinderella Variant in the Context of Muslim Women's Ritual." *Cinderella: A Casebook.* Ed. Alan Dundes. 1982. New York: Wildman, 1983. 180–99.

———. "Feminist Theory and the Study of Folklore: A Twenty-Year Trajectory toward Theory." *Western Folklore* 52.2–4 (1993): 173–92.

Minard, Rosemary, ed. *Womenfolk and Fairy Tales.* Boston: Houghton, 1975.

Montaiglon, Anatole de, and Gaston Reynaud, eds. *Recueil général et complet des fabliaux des XIIIe et XIVe siècles.* 1872. New York: Franklin, 1966.

Moog, Hanna, ed. *Die Wasserfrau: Von geheimen Kräften, Sehnsüchten und Ungeheuern mit Namen Hans.* Cologne: Diederichs, 1987.

Mooijman, Anna. "Mata Masu Dubara Da Asiri Suke Daga: The Roles of Women and Gender Complementarity in Hausa Folktales." Diss. Temple U, 1998.

Moore, Robert. "From Rags to Witches: Stereotypes, Distortions and Anti-Humanism in Fairy Tales." *Interracial Books for Children* 6.7 (1975): 1–3.

Morris-Keitel, Helen G. "The Audience Should Be King: Bettina Brentano-von Arnim's 'Tale of the Lucky Purse.'" *Marvels & Tales* 11 (1997): 48–60.

———, trans. "Tale of the Lucky Purse." By Bettina Brentano-von Arnim. *Marvels & Tales* 11 (1997): 127–33.

Mortimer, Armine Kotin. *La clôture narrative.* Paris: Corti, 1985.

Moser-Rath, Elfriede. "Frau." *Enzyklopädie des Märchens* 5: 100–37.

Moss, Anita. "Mothers, Monsters, and Morals in Victorian Fairy Tales." *Lion and the Unicorn* 12.2 (1988): 47–60.

Motley, Mark. *Becoming a French Aristocrat: The Education of the Court Nobility, 1580–1715.* Princeton, NJ: Princeton UP, 1990.

Muir, Edward, and Guido Ruggiero, eds. *Sex and Gender in Historical Perspective.* Trans. Margaret A. Gallucci with Mary M. Gallucci and Carole C. Gallucci. Baltimore: Johns Hopkins UP, 1990.

Müller, Elisabeth. *Das Bild der Frau im Märchen: Analysen und erzieherische Betrachtungen.* Munich: Profil, 1986.

Muñoz, Willy O. "Luisa Valenzuela y la subversión normativa en los cuentos de hadas: 'Si esto es la vida, yo soy Caperucita Roja.'" *La palabra en vilo: Narrativa de Luisa Valenzuela.* Ed. Gwendolyn Díaz and María Inés Lagos. Chile: Santiago, 1996. 221–46.

Murphy, Patrick D. "'The Whole Wide World Was Scrubbed Clean': The Androcentric Animation of Denatured Disney." Bell, Haas, and Sells 125–36.

Muscatine, Charles. *The Old French Fabliaux.* New Haven, CT: Yale UP, 1986.

Naipaul, V. P. *In a Free State.* New York: Knopf, 1971.

Naithani, Sadhana. "The Colonizer-Folklorist." *Journal of Folklore Research* 34 (1997): 1–14.

———. "Prefaced Space." *Imagined States: Nationalism, Utopia, and Longing in Oral Cultures.* Ed. Luisa Del Giudice and Gerald Porter. Logan: Utah State UP, 2001. 64–79.

Neumann, Erich. *Amor and Psyche: The Psychic Development of the Feminine.* Trans. Ralph Manheim. Princeton, NJ: Princeton UP, 1956.

Ng Foong Kwong, James. "The Role of Creoles in Chinese Settlement." *Colouring the Rainbow: Mauritian Society in the Making.* Ed. Marina Carter. Port Louis (Mauritius): Centre for Research in Indian Ocean Societies, 1998. 97–118.

Nicolaisen, W. F. H. "Why Tell Stories about Innocent, Persecuted Heroines?" Bacchilega and Jones 61–71.

Nitschke, August. "Aschenputtel aus der Sicht der historischen Verhaltensforschung." *Und wenn sie nicht gestorben sind . . . : Perspektiven auf das Märchen.* Ed. Helmut Brackert. Frankfurt a.M.: Suhrkamp, 1980. 71–88.

———. *Soziale Ordnungen im Spiegel der Märchen.* 2 vols. Stuttgart: Fromann-Holzboog, 1976–1977.

Noomen, Willem, and Nico van den Boogaard, eds. *Nouveau Recueil complet des fabliaux.* 6 vols. Assen: Van Goocum, 1983.

Nouveau cabinet des fées. 18 vols. Geneva: Slatkine, 1978.

Nussbaum, Felicity A. *The Autobiographical Subject: Gender and Ideology in Eighteenth-Century England.* Baltimore: Johns Hopkins UP, 1989.

Nykrog, Per. *Les fabliaux.* 1957. Geneva: Droz, 1973.

Oates, Joyce Carol. "In Olden Times, When Wishing Was Having: Classic and Contemporary Fairy Tales." Bernheimer (1998) 247–72.

Ocampo, Silvina. *Cuentos completos.* 2 vols. Buenos Aires: Emecé, 1999.

Ocampo, Victoria. *Testimonios: Primera serie.* Madrid: Revista de Occidente, 1935.

———. *Testimonios: Tercera serie.* Buenos Aires: Sudamericana, 1946.

Odber de Baubeta, Patricia Anne. "Unhappy Ever After: 'Tan triste como ella' and the Disconsolate Heroine(s) of María Luisa Bombal." Unpublished essay.

Olivieri, Achillo. "Eroticism and Social Groups in Sixteenth-Century Venice: The Courtesan." Ariès and Béjin 76–102.

Opitz, Claudia. "Lieber Grimm und Verstand als Mythen und Märchen oder: Was Frauen über Märchen denken." *Der Grimm auf Märchen: Motive Grimmscher Volksmärchen und Märchenhaftes in den aktuellen Künsten.* Ed. W. P. Fahrenberg and Armin Klein. Marburg: Kulturamt der Stadt Marburg, 1985. 37–49.

Oring, Elliott. "Folk Narratives." *Folk Groups and Folklore Genres: An Introduction.* Ed. Elliott Oring. Logan: Utah State UP, 1986. 121–45.

Ostrem, Francine. "Maternal Inscriptions: Jelinek, Kafka, Sacher-Masoch." Diss. U of California, Berkeley, 1991.

Ostriker, Alicia. "The Thieves of Language: Women Poets and Revisionist Mythmaking." *Signs* 8 (1982): 68–90.

Ottino, Paul. "Les aventures de Petit Jean: Les aspects bantous et malgaches." *Notre Librairie* 72 (Oct.–Dec. 1983): 33–41.

Owen, Hilary. "Fairies and Witches in Hélia Correia." *Women, Literature, and Culture in the Portuguese-Speaking World.* Ed. Cláudia Pazos Alonso. Lewiston: Mellen, 1996. 85–103.

Pancritius, Marie. "Aus mutterrechtlicher Zeit: Rotkäppchen." *Anthropos* 27 (1932): 743–78.

Panttaja, Elisabeth. "Going Up in the World: Class in 'Cinderella.'" Bacchilega and Jones 85–104.

———. "Making Reality Evident: Feminine Disempowerment and Reempowerment in Two Grimm's Fairy Tales." *Folklore Forum* 21 (1988): 166–80.

———. "The Poor Girl and the Bad Man: Fairytales of Feminine Power." *Kentucky Review* 12.1–2 (1993): 29–37.

Parry, Benita. "Problems in Current Theories of Colonial Discourse." *The Post-Colonial Studies Reader.* Ed. Bill Ashcroft, Gareth Griffiths, and Helen Tiffin. London: Routledge, 1995. 36–44.

Paz, Octavio. "El arquero, la flecha y el blanco." *Vuelta* 117 (1986): 26–29.

Pendleton, Edith Kay. "Cinderella Imagery in the Fiction of Kurt Vonnegut." Diss. U of South Florida, 1993.

Perco, Daniella. "Female Initiation in North Italian Versions of 'Cinderella.'" Trans. Cristina Bacchilega. Bacchilega and Jones 73–84.

Perera, Sylvia Brinton. *Descent of the Goddess.* Toronto: Inner City, 1981.

Pérez, Janet. "Once upon a Time: Post-war Spanish Women Writers and the Fairy-Tale." *Hers Ancient and Modern: Women's Writing in Spain and Brazil.* Ed. Catherine Davies and Jane Whetnall. Manchester: U of Manchester, Department of Spanish and Portuguese, 1997. 57–71.

Perrault, Charles. *Contes.* Ed. Jean-Pierre Collinet. Paris: Folio, 1981.

———. *Contes.* Ed. François Flahaut. Paris: Le Livre de Poche, 1987.

———. *Contes.* Ed. Gilbert Rouger. Paris: Garnier, 1967.

———. *Contes.* Ed. Marc Soriano. Paris: Garnier-Flammarion, 1989.

Perrot, Jean, ed. *Tricentenaire Charles Perrault: Les grands contes du XVIIe siècle et leur fortune littéraire.* Paris: In-Press Editions, 1998.

Peters, Pearlie Mae Fisher. *The Assertive Woman in Zora Neale Hurston's Fiction, Folklore, and Drama.* New York: Garland, 1998.

Peterson, Nancy J. "'Bluebeard's Egg': Not Entirely a 'Grimm' Tale." *Margaret Atwood:*

Reflection and Reality. Ed. Beatrice Mendez-Egle. Edinburg, TX: Pan American UP, 1987. 131–38.

Petrie, Duncan. "But What If Beauty Is a Beast? Doubles, Transformations, and Fairy Tale Motifs in *Batman Returns.*" *Cinema and the Realms of Enchantment: Lectures, Seminars, and Essays by Marina Warner and Others.* Ed. Duncan Petrie. London: British Film Institute, 1993. 98–110.

Phelps, Ethel Johnston, ed. *The Maid of the North: Feminist Folk Tales from Around the World.* New York: Holt, 1981.

———, ed. *Tatterhood and Other Tales.* Old Westbury, NY: Feminist, 1978.

Piña, Cristina. *Alejandra Pizarnik.* Buenos Aires: Planeta, 1991.

———. *Puesta en escena.* Buenos Aires: Grupo Editor Latinoamericano, 1993.

Pinkola Estés, Clarissa. *Women Who Run with the Wolves: Myths and Stories of the Wild Woman Archetype.* 1992. London: Rider, 1993.

Pizarnik, Alejandra. "The Bloody Countess." Trans. Alberto Manguel. Baldick, 466–77.

———. "Extraction of the Stone of Folly." *Alejandra Pizarnik: A Profile.* Ed. Frank Graziano. Trans. Maria Rosa Fort and Frank Graziano with additional translations by Suzanne Jill Levine. Durango, CO: Logbridge-Rhodes, 1987. 57–63.

———. *Obras completas: Poesía Completa y prosa selecta.* Ed. Cristina Piña. Buenos Aires: Corregidor, 1994.

Pohl, Marie Elizabeth. "Cold-Blooded Tales of Women with Tails in the Works of Johannes Praetorius (1630–1680)." Diss. U of Pennsylvania, 1996.

Postma, Minnie. *Tales from the Basotho.* Trans. Susie McDermid. Notes by John M. Vlach. Austin: U of Texas P, 1974.

Prashad, Vijay. *The Karma of Brown Folk.* Minneapolis: U of Minnesota P, 2000.

Preston, Cathy Lynn. "'Cinderella' as a Dirty Joke: Gender, Multivocality, and the Polysemic Text." *Western Folklore* 53 (1994): 27–49.

———. Review of *Ever After. Marvels & Tales* 14 (2000): 175–78.

Probyn, Elspeth. *Sexing the Self: Gendered Positions in Cultural Studies.* London: Routledge, 1993.

Propp, Vladimir. *Morphology of the Folktale.* Trans. Laurence Scott. Rev. and ed. Louis A. Wagner. 2nd ed. Austin: U of Texas P, 1968.

Radner, Joan Newlon, ed. *Feminist Messages: Coding in Women's Folk Culture.* Urbana: U of Illinois P, 1993.

Ragan, Kathleen, ed. *Fearless Girls, Wise Women, and Beloved Sisters: Heroines in Folktales from Around the World.* New York: Norton, 1998.

Ralph, Phyllis C. "Transformations: Fairy Tales, Adolescence, and the Novel of Female Development in Victorian Fiction." Diss. U of Kansas, 1985.

Rappoport, Philippa Ellen. "Doll Folktales of the East Slavs: Invocations of Women from the Boundary of Space and Time." Diss. U of Virginia, 1998.

Raynard, Sophie. *La seconde préciosité: Floraison des conteuses de 1690 à 1756.* Tübingen: Narr, 2002.

Riddle, John M. *Eve's Herbs: A History of Contraception and Abortion in the West.* Cambridge, MA: Harvard UP, 1997.

Riedel, Ingrid. *Die weise Frau in uralt-neuen Erfahrungen: Der Archetyp der alten Weisen im Märchen und seinem religionsgeschichtlichen Hintergrund.* Olten: Walter, 1989.

Rifelj, Carol de Dobay. "Cendrillon and the Ogre: Women in Fairy Tales and Sade." *Romanic Review* 81 (1990): 11–24.

Rirodan, James, ed. *The Woman in the Moon and Other Tales of Forgotten Heroines.* New York: Dial, 1985.

Robert, Raymonde. *Le conte de fées littéraire en France de la fin du XVIIe à la fin du XVIIIe siècle.* Nancy: PU de Nancy, 1982.

Robinson, William Andrew. "The End of Happily Ever After: Variations on the Cinderella Theme in Musicals, 1960–1987." Diss. Bowling Green State U, 1991.

Rockey, Denyse. "Three Faces of the Great Goddess: Shulamite, Cinderella, Black Virgin." *Annual Review of Women in World Religions* 1 (1991): 31–70.

Roemer, Danielle M., and Cristina Bacchilega, eds. *Angela Carter and the Fairy Tale.* Detroit: Wayne State UP, 2001.

Röhrich, Lutz. "Das Bild der Frau im Märchen und im Volkslied." *Das selbstverständliche Wunder: Beiträge germanistischer Märchenforschung.* Ed. Wilhelm Solms and Charlotte Oberfeld. Marburg: Hitzeroth, 1986. 83–108.

Rölleke, Heinz, ed. *Die älteste Märchensammlung der Brüder Grimm: Synopse der handschriftlichen Urfassung von 1810 und der Erstdrucke von 1812.* Cologny-Genève: Fondation Martin Bodmer, 1975.

———. "Die Frau in den Märchen der Brüder Grimm." Früh and Wehse 72–88. Rpt. in Rölleke, *"Wo das Wünschen noch geholfen hat"* 220–35.

———, ed. *Kinder- und Hausmärchen: Ausgabe letzter Hand mit den Originalanmerkungen der Brüder Grimm: Mit einem Anhang sämtlicher, nicht in allen Auflagen veröffentlichter Märchen und Herkunftsnachweisen.* 3 vols. Stuttgart: Reclam, 1980.

———. *"Nebeninschriften": Brüder Grimm, Arnim und Brentano, Droste-Hülshoff: Literarhistorische Studien.* Bonn: Bouvier, 1980.

———. "The 'Utterly Hessian' Fairy Tales by 'Old Marie': The End of a Myth." Trans. Ruth B. Bottigheimer. Bottigheimer, *Fairy Tales and Society* 287–300. Trans. of "Die 'stockhessischen' Märchen der 'Alten Marie': Das Ende eines Mythos um die frühesten KHM-Aufzeichnungen der Brüder Grimm." *Germanisch-Romanische Monatsschrift* ns 25 (1975): 74–86. Rpt. in Rölleke, *"Wo das Wünschen noch geholfen hat"* 39–54.

———. *"Wo das Wünschen noch geholfen hat": Gesammelte Aufsätze zu den "Kinder- und Hausmärchen" der Brüder Grimm.* Bonn: Bouvier, 1985.

Rombi, Marie Françoise, and Mohamed Ahmed Chamanga. *Contes Comoriens.* Illus. Gérard Bois. Paris: EDICEF, 1980.

Rosaldo, Michelle Zimbalist. "Women, Culture, and Society: A Theoretical Overview." *Women, Culture, and Society.* Ed. Louise Lamphere and Michelle Zimbalist Rosaldo. Stanford, CA: Stanford UP, 1974. 17–42.

Rose, Ellen Cronan. "Through the Looking Glass: When Women Tell Fairy Tales." Abel, Hirsch, and Langland 209–27.

Rosenberg, S. L. Millard. "Two Sixteenth-Century Doctors on Syphilis and Guaiacum— Frascatoro and Ferri." *California and Western Medicine* 35.5 (1931): 367–72.

Rossiaud, Jacques. "Prostitution, Sex, and Society in French Towns in the Fifteenth Century". Ariès and Béjin 76–94.

Rowe, Karen E. "'Fairy-born and human-bred': Jane Eyre's Education in Romance." Abel, Hirsch, and Langland 69–89.

———. "Feminism and Fairy Tales." *Women's Studies* 6 (1979): 237–57. Rpt. in Zipes, *Don't Bet on the Prince* 209–26.

———. "To Spin a Yarn: The Female Voice in Folklore and Fairy Tale." Bottigheimer, *Fairy Tales and Society* 53–74.

Rowen, Norma. "Reinscribing Cinderella: Jane Austen and the Fairy Tale." *Functions of the Fantastic: Selected Essays from the Thirteenth International Conference on the Fantastic in the Arts.* Ed. Joe Sanders. Westport, CT: Greenwood, 1995. 29–36.

Roy, Arundhati. *The God of Small Things.* New York: Random House, 1997.

Royer, Berit C. R. "Sophie Albrecht (1757–1840) im Kreis der Schriftstellerinnen um 1800: Eine literatur- und kulturwissenschaftliche Werk-Monographie." Diss. U of California, Davis, 1999.

Rozen, Leah. "Ever After." *People* 10 Aug. 1998: 31.

Runge, Anita. *Literarische Praxis von Frauen um 1800: Briefroman, Autobiographie, Märchen.* Hildesheim: Olms-Weidmann, 1997.

Rusch-Feja, Diann. *The Portrayal of the Maturation Process of Girl Figures in Selected Tales of the Brothers Grimm.* Frankfurt a.M.: Lang, 1995.

Rushdie, Salman. *Haroun and the Sea of Stories.* London: Granta, 1990.

———. *Midnight's Children.* New York: Knopf, 1981.

———. *The Wizard of Oz.* London: British Film Institute, 1992.

Rüttner-Cova, Sonja. *Frau Holle: Die gestürzte Göttin: Märchen, Mythen, Matriarchat.* Basel: Sphinx, 1986.

Sage, Lorna. "Angela Carter: The Fairy Tale." *Marvels & Tales* 12 (1998): 52–68.

Said, Edward. *Culture and Imperialism.* New York: Knopf, 1993.

———. *Orientalism.* New York: Vintage, 1978.

Sallis, Eva. *Sheherazade through the Looking Glass: The Metamorphosis of the Thousand and One Nights.* Richmond, Surrey: Curzon, 1999.

Schechtman, Jacqueline. "Hansel and Gretel." *The Stepmother in Fairy Tales: Bereavement and the Feminine Shadow.* Boston: Sigo, 1991.

Scheub, Harold. *The Tongue Is Fire: South African Storytellers and Apartheid.* Madison: U of Wisconsin P, 1996.

Schmitt, Jean-Claude. *Mort d'une hérésie: L'église et les clercs face aux béguines et aux béghards du Rhin supérieur du XIVe au XVe siècle.* Hague: Mouton, 1978.

Schmölders, Claudia, ed. *Die wilde Frau: Mythische Geschichten zum Staunen, Fürchten und Begehren.* Cologne: Diederichs, 1983.

Schott, Rüdiger. "The Rebellious Girl Who Wants the Perfect Man: Role Assignments in Folktales of the Bulsa in Northern Ghana." Köhler-Zülch and Cardigos 121–36.

Schreinert, Kurt. *Benedikte Naubert: Ein Beitrag zur Entstehungsgeschichte des historischen Romans in Deutschland.* 1941. Berlin: Kraus, 1969.

Schweickart, Patrocinio. "Reading Ourselves: Toward a Feminist Theory of Reading." *Falling Into Theory: Conflicting Views on Reading Literature.* Ed. David H. Richter. Boston: Bedford, 1994. 269–78.

Seabra Ferreira, María Aline. "Alejandra Pizarnik's *Acerca de la condesa sangrienta* and Angela Carter's 'The Lady of the House of Love': Transgression and the Politics of Victimization." *New Comparison* 22 (1997): 27–57.

Secreto, Cecilia. "Herencias femeninas: nominalización del malestar." *Mujeres que escriben sobre mujeres (que escriben).* Ed. Cristina Piña. Buenos Aires: Biblos, 1998. 149–202.

Seifert, Lewis C. "Disguising the Storyteller's 'Voice': Perrault's Recuperation of the Fairy Tale." *Cincinnati Romance Review* 8 (1989): 13–23.

———. *Fairy Tales, Sexuality, and Gender in France, 1690–1715: Nostalgic Utopias.* Cambridge: Cambridge UP, 1996.

———. "*Les fées modernes:* Women, Fairy Tales, and the Literary Field in Late Seventeenth-Century France." *Going Public: Women and Publishing in Early Modern France.* Ed. Elizabeth Goldsmith and Dena Goodman. Ithaca, NY: Cornell UP, 1995. 129–45.

———. "Female Empowerment and Its Limits: The *Conteuses'* Active Heroines." *Cahiers du dix-septième* 3.1 (1989): 121–39.

———. "Marvelous Realities: Reading the *Merveilleux* in the Seventh-Century French Fairy Tale." Canepa 131–51.

———. "Tales of Difference." Hilgar 179–94.

———. "The Time That (N)ever Was: Women's Fairy Tales in Seventeenth-Century France." Diss. U of Michigan, 1989.

Sellers, Susan. *Myth and Fairy Tale in Contemporary Women's Fiction.* New York: Palgrave, 2001.

Sells, Laura. "'Where Do the Mermaids Stand?' Voice and Body in *The Little Mermaid.*" Bell, Haas, and Sells 175–92.

Sen, Suchismita. "Memory, Language, and Society in Salman Rushdie's *Haroun and the Sea of Stories. Contemporary Literature* 36.4 (1995): 654–75.

Sexton, Anne. *Transformations.* Boston: Houghton Mifflin, 1971.

Seydou, Christiane. "Du mariage sauvage au mariage héroïque." *Le mariage dans les contes africains.* Ed. Veronika Görög-Karady. Paris: Karthala, 1994. 85–134.

Shaw, David Gary. *The Creation of a Community: The City of Wells in the Middle Ages.* Oxford: Clarendon, 1993.

Shealy, Daniel, ed. *Louisa May Alcott's Fairy Tales and Fantasy Stories.* Knoxville: U of Tennessee P, 1992.

Sheets, Robin Ann. "Pornography, Fairy Tales, and Feminism: Angela Carter's 'The Bloody Chamber.'" *Journal of the History of Sexuality* 1 (1991): 633–57.

Shojaei Kawan, Christine. "A Masochism Promising Supreme Conquests: Simone de Beauvoir's Reflections on Fairy Tales and Children's Literature." *Marvels & Tales* 16 (2002): 29–48.

Shua, Ana María. *Casa de Geishas.* Buenos Aires: Sudamericana, 1992.

———. *La sueñera.* Buenos Aires: Minotauro, 1984.

Shuman, Amy. "Gender and Genre." Hollis, Pershing, and Young 71–85.

Simpson, Janice C. "Fanny Price as Cinderella: Folk and Fairy-Tale in *Mansfield Park.*" *Persuasions* 16.9 (1987): 25–30.

Simpson, Robin Smith. "Fairy-Tale Representations of Social Realities: Madame d'Aulnoy's *Contes des fées* (1697–98)." Diss. Duke U, 1996.

Singh, Ajay, and Arjuna Ranawana. "Heralding a New Asian Writing." *Asiaweek* 26 Dec. 1997. Available at http://www.asiaweek.com/asiaweek/97/1226/ye6.html (accessed 24 Feb. 2004).

Smith, Jay M. *The Culture of Merit: Nobility, Royal Service, and the Making of the Absolute Monarchy in France, 1600–1789.* Ann Arbor: U of Michigan P, 1996.

Smith, Sidonie. "Autobiographical Manifestoes." *Women, Autobiography, Theory: A Reader.* Ed. Sidonie Smith and Julia Watson. Madison: U of Wisconsin P, 1998. 433–40.

Smith, Verity. "Dwarfed by Snow White: Feminist Revisions of Fairy Tale Discourse in the Narrative of Maria Luisa Bombal and Dulce Maria Loynaz." Condé and Hart 137–49.

Solá, Marcela. "Bodas." *Manual de situaciones imposibles.* Buenos Aires: Lohlé, 1990. 11–16.

———. "El lobo feroz." *Los condenados visten de blanco.* Buenos Aires: Lohlé, 1971. 61–69.

Soriano, Marc. *Les Contes de Perrault: Culture savante et traditions populaires.* Paris: Gallimard, 1968.

Spaeth, Janet. "The Grimms' Housekeepers: Women in Transition Tales." *Children's Literature Association Quarterly* 7.2 (1982): 20–22.

Spivak, Gayatri Chakravorty. "Can the Subaltern Speak?" *The Post-Colonial Studies*

Reader. Ed. Bill Ashcroft, Gareth Griffiths, and Helen Tiffin. London: Routledge, 1995. 24–28.

———. "Diasporas Old and New: Women in the Transnational World." *Textual Practice* 10.2 (1996): 245–69.

Spörk, Ingrid. "Das Bild der Frau im Märchen." *Über Frauenleben, Männerwelt und Wissenschaft: Österreichische Texte zur Frauenforschung.* Ed. Beate Frakele, Elisabeth List, and Gertrude Pauritsch. Vienna: Verlag für Gesellschaftskritik, 1987. 121–42.

———. *Studien zu ausgewählten Märchen der Brüder Grimm: Frauenproblematik—Struktur—Rollentheorie—Psychoanalyse—Überlieferung—Rezeption.* Königstein/Ts.: Hain, 1985.

Steedman, Carolyn Kay. *Landscape for a Good Woman: A Story of Two Lives.* 1986. New Brunswick, NJ: Rutgers UP, 1997.

Steinchen, Renate. "Märchenerzählerin und Sneewittchen—Zwei Frauenbilder in einer deutschen Märchensammlung: Zur Rekonstruktion der Entstehungsgeschichte Grimmscher Märchenfiguren im Kontext sozial- und kulturhistorischer Entwicklung." *Mythos Frau: Projektionen und Inszenierungen im Patriarchat.* Ed. Barbara Schaeffer-Hegel and Brigitte Wartmann. Berlin: Publica, 1984. 280–308.

Steinisch, Sabine. "Subversive Fabulations: The Twofold Pull in Sunti Namjoshi's Feminist Fables." *Engendering Realism and Postmodernism.* Ed. Beate Neumeier. Amsterdam: Rodopi, 2001. 265–77.

Stephens, John, and Robyn McCallum. *Retelling Stories, Framing Culture: Traditional Story and Metanarratives in Children's Literature.* New York: Garland, 1998.

Stewart, Susan. *On Longing: Narratives of the Miniature, the Gigantic, the Souvenir, the Collection.* Baltimore: Johns Hopkins UP, 1984.

Stone, Kay F. "And She Lived Happily Ever After?" *Women and Language* 19.1 (1996): 14–18.

———. "Burning Brightly: New Light from an Old Tale." Radner 289–305.

———. *Burning Brightly: New Light on Old Tales Told Today.* Peterborough, Ontario: Broadview, 1998.

———. "The Curious Girl." *Next Teller: A Book of Canadian Storytelling.* Ed. Dan Yashinsky. Charlottetown, Prince Edward Island: Ragweed, 1994. 8–14.

———. "Difficult Women in Folktales: Two Women, Two Stories." *Undisciplined Women: Tradition and Culture in Canada.* Ed. Pauline Greenhile and Diane Tye. Kingston, Ontario: McGill-Queen's UP, 1997. 250–65.

———. "Fairy Tales for Adults: Walt Disney's Americanization of the Märchen." *Folklore on Two Continents: Essays in Honor of Linda Dégh.* Ed. Nikolai Burlakoff and Carl Lindahl. Bloomington, IN: Trickster, 1980. 40–48.

———. "Feminist Approaches to the Interpretation of Fairy Tales." Bottigheimer, *Fairy Tales and Society* 229–36.

———. "'Macht mit mir, was Ihr wollt': Frauen und Erzählen heute." Früh and Wehse 164–73.

———. "Mißbrauchte Verzauberung: Aschenputtel als Weiblichkeitsideal in Nordamerika." *Über Märchen für Kinder von heute: Essays zu ihrem Wandel und ihrer Funktion.* Ed. Klaus Doderer. Weinheim: Beltz, 1983. 78–93. Trans. of "The Misuses of Enchantment."

———. "The Misuses of Enchantment: Controversies on the Significance of Fairy Tales." *Women's Folklore, Women's Culture.* Ed. Rosan A. Jordan and Susan J. Kalcik. Philadelphia: U of Pennsylvania P, 1985. 125–45.

————. "Romantic Heroines in Anglo-American Folk and Popular Literature." Diss. Indiana U, 1975.

————. "Things Walt Disney Never Told Us." *Journal of American Folklore* 88 (1975): 42–50. Rpt. in *Women and Folklore*. Ed. Claire R. Farrer. Austin: U of Texas P, 1975. 42–50.

Storer, Mary Elizabeth. *Un épisode littéraire de la fin du XVIIe siècle: La mode des contes de fées (1685–1700)*. 1928. Geneva: Slatkine, 1972.

Straparola, Giovanfrancesco. *The Facetious Nights of Giovanni Francesco Straparola da Caravaggio*. Trans. W. G. Waters. Illus. Jules Garnier and E. R. Hughes. 4 vols. London: Society of Bibliophiles, 1898.

————. *Le piacevoli notti*. Ed. Giuseppe Rua. 2 vols. Bologna: Presso Romagholi-dall'Acqua, 1908.

Susina, Jan. "Straw into Gold: The Transforming Nature of Fairy Tales and Fairy Art." Blinderman and Porges 38–49.

Sweet, Denis. Introd. "The Cloak." By Benedikte Naubert. Blackwell and Zantop 203–06.

Tatar, Maria. "Beauties vs. Beasts in the Grimms' *Nursery and Household Tales*." McGlathery, *Brothers Grimm and Folktale* 133–45.

————. "Born Yesterday: The Spear Side." Tatar, *Hard Facts* 85–105. Rpt. of "Born Yesterday: Heroes in the Grimms' Fairy Tales." Bottigheimer, *Fairy Tales and Society* 95–114. Rpt. of "Tests, Tasks, and Trials in the Grimms' Fairy Tales." *Children's Literature* 13 (1985): 30–48.

————, ed. *The Classic Fairy Tales: Texts, Criticism*. New York: Norton, 1999.

————. "From Nags to Witches: Stepmothers and Other Ogres." Tatar, *Hard Facts* 137–55. Rpt. of "From Nags to Witches: Stepmothers in the Grimms' Fairy Tales." *Opening Texts: Psychoanalysis and the Culture of the Child*. Ed. Joseph H. Smith and William Kerrigan. Baltimore: Johns Hopkins UP, 1985. 28–41.

————. *The Hard Facts of the Grimms' Fairy Tales*. Princeton, NJ: Princeton UP, 1987.

————. "Invocations of Fairy Tales." Blinderman and Porges 22–33.

————. *Off with Their Heads! Fairy Tales and the Culture of Childhood*. Princeton, NJ: Princeton UP, 1992.

Theodosiadou, Georgia A. "The Use of Myth in Five of Eudora Welty's Novels." Diss. Arizona State U, 1988.

Thirard, Marie-Agnès. "Les contes de fées de Madame d'Aulnoy: Une écriture de la subversion." Diss. U de Lille III, 1994.

Thomas, Hayley S. "Undermining a Grimm Tale: A Feminist Reading of 'The Worn-Out Dancing Shoes' (KHM 133)." *Marvels & Tales* 13 (1999): 170–97.

Thomas, Susanne Sara. "'Cinderella' and the Phallic Foot: The Symbolic Significance of the Tale's Slipper Motif." *Southern Folklore* 52 (1995): 19–31.

Thompson, Stith. *Motif-Index of Folk-Literature: A Classification of Narrative Elements in Folktales, Ballads, Myths, Fables, Mediaeval Romances, Exempla, Fabliaux, Jest-Books, and Local Legends*. Rev. and enl. ed. 6 vols. Bloomington: Indiana UP, 1955–1958.

Thum, Maureen. "Feminist or Anti-Feminist? Gender-Coded Role Models in the Tales Contributed by Dorothea Viehmann to the Grimm Brothers [*sic*] *Kinder- und Hausmärchen*." *Germanic Review* 68 (1993): 11–21.

Toauillon, Christine. *Der deutsche Frauenroman des 18. Jahrhunderts*. 1919. Bern: Lang, 1979.

Todorov, Tzvetan. *Mikhail Bakhtin: The Dialogic Principle*. Minneapolis: U of Minnesota P, 1984.

Torres Fierro, Danubio. "Entrevista a Victoria Ocampo." *Plural* (1975): 18–25.

Townsend, David. "Sex and the Single Amazon in Twelfth-Century Latin Epic." *The Tongue of the Fathers: Gender and Ideology in Twelfth-Century Latin.* Ed. David Townsend and Andrew Taylor. Philadelphia: U of Pennsylvania P, 1998. 136–55.

Travers, P. L. "Grimm's Women." *New York Times Book Review* Fall 1975: 59

Tremblay, Victor-Laurent. "Who Bewitched the Witch?" *Canadian Children's Literature* 72 (1993): 38–48.

Trexler, Richard. *Sex and Conquest: Gendered Violence, Political Order, and the European Conquest of the Americas.* Ithaca, NY: Cornell UP, 1995.

Trites, Roberta Seelinger. *Waking Sleeping Beauty: Feminist Voices in Children's Novels.* Iowa City: U of Iowa P, 1997.

Trost, Caroline T. "'Belle-belle, ou le Chevalier Fortuné': A Liberated Women in a Tale by Mme d'Aulnoy." *Merveilles et contes* 5 (1991): 57–67.

Tucker, Holly. *Pregnant Fictions: Childbirth and the Fairy Tale in Early-Modern France.* Detroit: Wayne State UP, 2003.

Ude-Koeller, Susanne. "Das Frauenbild der Brüder Grimm und der Wandel weiblicher Figuren in den Ausgaben der Kinder- und Hausmärchen." MA thesis. U Göttingen, 1985.

Ulanov, Ann Belford, and Barry Ulanov. *Cinderella and Her Sisters: The Envied and the Envying.* Exp. ed. Einsiedeln, Switzerland: Daimon, 1998.

Ulla, Noemí. *Encuentros con Silvina Ocampo.* Buenos Aires: Belgrano, 1982.

Uther, Hans-Jörg. "The Encyclopedia of the Folktale." Bottigheimer, *Fairy Tales and Society* 186–93.

Valenzuela, Luisa. *Otrariana.* México: CIDCLI, Consejo Nacional para la Cultura y las Artes, 1995.

———. *Simetrías.* Buenos Aires: Sudamericana, 1993.

———. *Symmetries.* Trans. Margaret Jull Costa. London: Serpent's Tail, 1998. Trans. of *Simetrías.*

van de Walle, Etienne. "'Marvelous Secrets': Birth Control in European Short Fiction, 1150–1650." *Population Studies* 54 (2000): 321–30.

Vanita, Ruth. "No Small Achievement." Rev. of *The God of Small Things,* by Arundati Roy. *Manushi* 103 (1998). Available at http://free.freespeech.org/manushi/103/review.html (accessed 24 Feb. 2004).

Velay-Vallantin, Catherine. "Les *Contes* de Perrault entre ethnologie et histoire: Relire Arnold Van Gennep et Marc Soriano." Perrot 17–38.

———. *La fille en garçon.* Carcassonne: GARAE/Hésiode, 1992.

Verdier, Gabrielle. "Approaches to the Literary Fairy Tale: Questions of Gender and Genre." Hilgar 141–46.

———. "Comment l'auteur des 'Fées à la mode' devint 'Mother Bunch': Métamorphoses de la Comtesse d'Aulnoy en Angleterre." *Merveilles et contes* 10 (1996): 285–309.

———. "Figures de la conteuse dans les contes de fées féminins." *XVIIe siècle* 180.3 (1993): 481–99.

Verdier, Yvonne. "Grand-mères, si vous saviez . . . : Le petit chaperon rouge dans la traditon orale." *Cahiers de littérature orale* 4 (1977): 17–55.

———. "Little Red Riding Hood in Oral Tradition." Trans. Joseph Gaughan. *Marvels & Tales* 11 (1997): 101–23. Trans. of "Le petit chaperon rouge dans la traditon orale." *Le débat* 3 (July–Aug. 1980): 31–61.

Vogele, Yvonne Alice. "The Reluctant Witches in Benedikte Naubert's *Neue Volksmährchen der Deutschen* (1789–1792)." Diss. U of Washington, 1998.

Waelti-Walters, Jennifer. *Fairy Tales and the Female Imagination.* Montreal: Eden, 1982.

———. "On Princesses: Fairy Tales, Sex Roles, and Loss of Self." *International Journal of Women's Studies* 2 (1981): 180–88.

Wald, Catherine. "Ancient Traditions." *Poets and Writers* 26.5 (1 Sept. 1998): 54–55.

Walker, Nancy A. *The Disobedient Writer: Women and Narrative Tradition.* Austin: U of Texas P, 1995.

Walkerdine, Valerie. "Some Day My Prince Will Come: Young Girls and the Preparation for Adolescent Sexuality." *Gender and Generation.* Ed. Angela McRobbie and Mica Nava. London: MacMillan, 1984. 162–84.

Wardetzky, Kristin. *Märchen—Lesarten von Kindern: Eine empirische Studie.* Berlin: Lang, 1992.

———. "The Structure and Interpretation of Fairy Tales Composed by Children." Trans. Ruth B. Bottigheimer. *Journal of American Folklore* 103 (1990): 157–76.

Warner, Marina. *From the Beast to the Blonde: On Fairy Tales and Their Tellers.* 1994. New York: Farrar, 1995.

———. Introd. Carter, *Strange Things* ix–xvi.

———. "Mother Goose Tales: Female Fiction, Female Fact?" *Folklore* 101 (1990): 3–25.

———. *Six Myths of Our Time: Little Angels, Little Monsters, Beautiful Beasts, and More.* 1994. New York: Vintage, 1995.

———, ed. *Wonder Tales: Six French Stories of Enchantment.* Trans. Gilbert Adair et al. New York: Farrar, 1994.

Wehrli-Johns, Martina. "Das mittelalterliche Beginentum—religiöse Frauenbewegung oder Sozialidee der Scholastik?" *"Zahlreich wie die Sterne des Himmels": Beginen am Niederrhein zwischen Mythos und Wirklichkeit.* Bergisch Gladbach: Thomas-Morus-Akademie Bensberg, 1992. 9–39.

Wehse, Rainer. "Frau in Männerkleidung." *Enzyklopädie des Märchens* 5: 167–86.

Weigle, Marta. *Spiders and Spinsters: Women and Mythology.* 4th ed. Albuquerque: U of New Mexico P, 1992.

Welch, Marcelle Maistre. "Le devenir de la jeune fille dans les contes de fées de Madame d'Aulnoy." *Cahiers du dix-septième* 1 (Spring 1987): 53–61.

———. "L'Eros féminin dans les contes de fées de Mlle de la Force." Hilgar 217–23.

———. "La femme, le mariage et l'amour dans les contes de fées mondains du XVIIe siècle français." *Papers on French Seventeenth-Century Literature* 10.18 (1983): 47–58.

———. "Les jeux de l'écriture dans les contes de fées de Mme d'Aulnoy." *Romanische Forschungen* 101.1 (1989): 75–80.

———. "Manipulation du discours féerique dans les Contes de fées de Mme de Murat." *Cahiers du dix-septième* 5 (Spring 1991): 21–29.

———. "Rébellion et résignation dans les contes de fées de Mme d'Aulnoy et Mme de Murat." *Cahiers du dix-septième* 3 (Fall 1989): 131–42.

———. "La satire du rococo dans les contes de fées de Madame d'Aulnoy. *Revue romane* 28.1 (1993): 75–85.

West, Candace, and Sarah Fenstermacher. "Power, Inequality, and the Accomplishment of Gender: An Ethnomethodological View." *Theory on Gender/Feminism on Theory.* Ed. Paula England. New York: Aldine de Gruyter, 1993. 151–74, 298–99.

Whelan, P. T. "Women's Domestic Quest: Minimal Journeys and Their Frames in the *Thousand and One Nights,* 'The Mark on the Wall' and 'The Man with the Buttons.'" *The Comparatist* 18 (1994): 150–63.

Wiesner, Merry. "Nuns, Wives, and Mothers: Women and the Reformation in Germany." Marshall 8–28.

———. *Working Women in Renaissance Germany.* New Brunswick, NJ: Rutgers UP, 1986.

Williams, Raymond. *Marxism and Literature.* Oxford: Oxford UP, 1977.

Wilson, Kalpana. "Arundhati Roy and Patriarchy—a Rejoinder." *Liberation* Jan. 1998. Rpt. at *INQILAB* 5.1 (Spring 1998). Available at http://www.angelfire.com/in/SASG/aroy.html (accessed 24 Feb. 2004).

Wilson, Sharon Rose. "Bluebeard's Forbidden Room: Gender Images in Margaret Atwood's Visual and Literary Art." *American Review of Canadian Studies* 16 (1986): 385–97.

———. *Margaret Atwood's Fairy-Tale Sexual Politics.* Jackson: UP of Mississippi, 1993.

Windling, Terri. "Ashes, Blood, and the Slipper of Glass." *The Endicott Studio Forum.* 1997. Available at http://www.endicott-studio.com/forashs.html (accessed 24 Feb. 2004).

———. "Women and Fairy Tales." *The Endicott Studio Forum.* 1995. Available at http://www.endicott-studio.com/forwmnft.html (accessed 24 Feb. 2004).

Winterson, Jeanette. *Sexing the Cherry.* 1989. New York: Vintage International, 1991.

Wolf, Emma. "One-Eye, Two-Eye, Three Eye." *American Jewess* 2.6 (Mar. 1896): 279–90.

Wolf, Christa. *Kindheitsmuster: Roman.* 1976. Munich: Deutscher Taschenbuch Verlag, 1994.

———. *Patterns of Childhood.* Trans. Ursule Molinaro and Hedwig Rappolt. New York: Noonday, 1990. Rpt. of *A Model Childhood.* 1980. Trans. of *Kindheitsmuster: Roman.*

Wöller, Hildegunde. *Aschenputtel: Energie der Liebe.* Zürich: Kreuz, 1984.

Woodman, Marion, et al. *Leaving My Father's House: A Journey to Conscious Femininity.* Boston: Shambhala, 1992.

Yashinsky, Dan, ed. *At the Edge: A Book of Risky Stories.* Charlottetown, Prince Edward Island: Ragweed, 1998.

Yolen, Jane. "America's Cinderella." *Children's Literature in Education* 8 (1977): 21–29. Rpt. in *Cinderella: A Casebook.* Ed. Alan Dundes. New York: Wildman, 1982. 294–306.

———. "The Brothers Grimm and Sister Jane." Haase, *Reception of Grimms' Fairy Tales* 283–89.

———. *The Girl Who Cried Flowers and Other Tales.* New York: Harper Collins Children's Books, 1974.

———. *The Hundredth Dove and Other Tales.* New York: Crowell, 1977.

———. *The Moon Ribbon and Other Tales.* New York: Crowell, 1976.

———. *Not One Damsel in Distress: World Folktales for Strong Girls.* San Diego: Harcourt, 2000.

———. "This Book Is for You." *Fairy Tale Liberation* 152–55.

Young, Pauline. "Selling the Emperor's New Clothes: Fay Weldon as Contemporary Folklorist." *Folklore in Use* 2 (1994): 103–13.

Zipes, Jack, ed. and trans. *Beauties, Beasts, and Enchantment: Classic French Fairy Tales.* New York: New American Library, 1989.

———. "Breaking the Disney Spell." Bell, Haas, and Sells 21–42. Rpt. in Zipes, *Fairy Tale as Myth* 72–95, 169–71.

———. *Breaking the Magic Spell: Radical Theories of Folk and Fairy Tales.* Rev. and exp. ed. Lexington: UP of Kentucky, 2002.

———. *The Brothers Grimm: From Enchanted Forests to the Modern World.* New York: Routledge, 1988.

———. *The Brothers Grimm: From Enchanted Forests to the Modern World.* 2nd ed. New York: Palgrave Macmillan, 2002.

———, ed. *Don't Bet on the Prince: Contemporary Feminist Fairy Tales in North America and England.* New York: Methuen, 1986.

———. "Epilogue: Reviewing and Re-Framing Little Red Riding Hood." Zipes, *Trials and Tribulations* (1993) 343–83. Rev. rpt. of "A Second Gaze at Little Red Riding Hood's Trials and Tribulations." *Lion and the Unicorn* 7–8 (1983–84): 78–109. Rpt. in Zipes, *Don't Bet on the Prince* 227–60.

———. *Fairy Tale as Myth/Myth as Fairy Tale.* Lexington: UP of Kentucky, 1994.

———. *Fairy Tales and the Art of Subversion: The Classical Genre for Children and the Process of Civilization.* New York: Wildman, 1983.

———. "Filer avec le destin: *Rumpenstünzchen* et le déclin de la productivité des femmes." Trans. Nelly Stéphane. *Europe: Revue littéraire mensuelle* 787–88 (1994): 106–18. Trans. of "Rumpelstiltksin and the Decline of Female Productivity."

———. *Happily Ever After: Fairy Tales, Children, and the Culture Industry.* New York: Routledge, 1997.

———. "Of Cats and Men: Framing the Civilizing Discourse of the Fairy Tale." Canepa 176–93.

———, ed. *The Outspoken Princess and the Gentle Knight: A Treasury of Modern Fairy Tales.* New York: Bantam, 1994.

———, ed. *The Oxford Companion to Fairy Tales.* Oxford: Oxford UP, 2000.

———. "Rumpelstiltskin and the Decline of Female Productivity." Zipes, *Fairy Tale as Myth* 49–71, 165–69. Rpt. of "Spinning with Fate: Rumpelstiltskin and the Decline of Female Productivity." Bacchilega and Jones 43–60.

———. "Spreading Myths about Iron John." Zipes, *Fairy Tale as Myth* 97–118, 171–73. Rpt. of "Spreading Myths about Fairy Tales: A Critical Commentary on Robert Bly's *Iron John.*" *New German Critiques* 55 (1992): 3–19.

———. "The Struggle for the Grimms' Throne: The Legacy of the Grimms' Tales in the FRG and GDR since 1945." Haase, *Reception of Grimms' Fairy Tales* 167–206.

———, ed. *The Trials and Tribulations of Little Red Riding Hood.* 2nd ed. New York: Routledge, 1993.

———. *The Trials and Tribulations of Little Red Riding Hood: Versions of the Tale in Sociocultural Context.* South Hadley, MA: Bergin, 1983.

———, ed. *Victorian Fairy Tales: The Revolt of the Fairies and Elves.* New York: Methuen, 1987.

———. "Who's Afraid of the Brothers Grimm? Socialization and Politi[ci]zation through Fairy Tales." *Lion and the Unicorn* 3.2 (1979–80): 4–56. Rpt. in Zipes, *Fairy Tales and the Art of Subversion* 45–70.

Zuerner, Adrienne E. "Reflections on the Monarchy in d'Aulnoy's *Belle-Belle ou le chevalier Fortuné.*" Canepa 194–217.

Contributors

CRISTINA BACCHILEGA, professor in the English department at the University of Hawai'i at Mānoa, is interested in contemporary fiction, feminist theory, the fairy tale, and folklore and literature. She has authored *Postmodern Fairy Tales: Gender and Narrative Strategies* (1997) and coedited *Angela Carter and the Literary Fairy Tale* (with Danielle M. Roemer in 2001).

JEANNINE BLACKWELL is professor of German and women's studies at the University of Kentucky and director of the Kentucky Foreign Language Conference. Her research centers on German women's literary culture from 1600 to 1900, stressing autobiography, religious confessions, and fantasy literature. With Shawn C. Jarvis she is coeditor and cotranslator of the anthology *The Queen's Mirror: Fairy Tales by German Women, 1780–1900* (2001). She also coedited *Bitter Healing: German Women Writers 1700–1840* (1990).

RUTH B. BOTTIGHEIMER is the author of *Fairy Godfather: Straparola, Venice, and the Fairy Tale Tradition* (2002). She has also published *Fairy Tales: Illusion, Allusion, and Paradigm* (1986), *Grimms' Bad Girls and Bold Boys* (1987), *The Bible for Children from the Age of Gutenberg to the Present* (1996), and, with Lalita Handoo, *Folklore and Gender* (1999). She is an adjunct professor in the Department of Comparative Literature at the State University of New York, Stony Brook.

DONALD HAASE is chair of the Department of German and Slavic Studies at Wayne State University. He has published numerous articles and essays on the fairy tale in European and Anglo-American contexts. He edited *The Reception of Grimms' Fairy Tales: Responses, Reactions, Revisions* (1993) and *English Fairy Tales and More English Fairy Tales* (2002), an edition of two collections by the Victorian folklorist Joseph Jacobs. He is the editor of *Marvels & Tales: Journal of Fairy-Tale Studies.*

LEE HARING is professor emeritus of English at Brooklyn College of the City University of New York and adjunct lecturer in the Graduate Program in Folklore and Folklife at the University of Pennsylvania. His research in East Africa, Madagascar, and Mauritius has resulted in the books *Malagasy Tale Index, Verbal Arts in Madagascar,* and *Collecting Folklore in Mauritius* and numerous journal articles.

ELIZABETH WANNING HARRIES teaches English and comparative literature at Smith College. Her publications include *Twice upon a Time: Women Writers and the History of the Fairy Tale* (2001), *The Unfinished Manner: Essays on the Fragment in the Later Eighteenth Century* (1994), and essays on the *conteuses* who wrote fairy tales in France in the 1690s.

FIONA MACKINTOSH is a lecturer in the Department of Hispanic Studies at the University of Edinburgh. Her area of research is twentieth-century and contemporary Spanish American literature, in particular that of Argentine writers, following her PhD dissertation on "Childhood in the Works of Silvina Ocampo and Alejandra Pizarnik" (University of Warwick, England, 2000). She is also an active literary translator. Recent publications include a translation of Luisa Valenzuela's "El otro libro" in *Bomb.*

PATRICIA ANNE ODBER DE BAUBETA is senior lecturer and director of Portuguese Studies in the University of Birmingham, England, where she has taught since 1981. She began her academic career as a medievalist and has published books and articles on medieval Portuguese literature and ecclesiastical history but is now exploring the ways fairy tales have been appropriated by advertisers and women writers in the Spanish- and Portuguese-speaking worlds. Among her most recent publications are two edited volumes of essays, *Alice in Translation: A Homage to Lewis Carroll* (1999) and *Advertising and Identity in Europe: The I of the Beholder* (coedited in 2000 with Jackie Cannon and Robin Warner).

CATHY LYNN PRESTON is a senior instructor in the English department at the University of Colorado, Boulder, where she teaches a range of courses in folklore and literature. Her research focuses on the performance of gender, class, and sexuality in folk narrative, particularly in jokes and legends. She is editor of *Folklore, Literature, and Cultural Theory: Collected Essays* (1995), *The Other Print Tradition: Essays on Chapbooks, Broadsides, and Related Ephemera* (1995), and *Border Crossings: Legend, Literature, Mass Media, and Cultural Ephemera* (2000).

LEWIS C. SEIFERT is associate professor of French studies at Brown University, where he is a specialist of fairy tales and of seventeenth-century French literature. He is the author of *Fairy Tales, Sexuality, and Gender in France, 1690–1715: Nostalgic Utopias* (1996). Currently, he is working on two projects, one concerning masculinity and civility in early modern France and the other regarding literary appropriations of oral traditions throughout the Francophone world.

KAY STONE is professor of English at the University of Winnipeg, where she has taught courses in her specialties—folklore and storytelling—since 1971. She is also a professional storyteller who has given performances, workshops, and academic addresses in both the United States and Canada. She has written numerous articles on women and folktales and on professional storytelling. Her book, *Burning Brightly: New Light on Old Tales Told Today,* was published in 1998.

Index